BOER WAR LETTERS

War Letters to T.H.W.

from

South Africa

1899–1902

E.H.W.

Copyright © E.H.W.

First published in 1999 by Clemency Holt-Wilson

All rights reserved

ISBN 0 9537812 0 8

Typeset by Academic and Technical, Bristol
Printed and bound by Redwood Books, Trowbridge, Wiltshire

FOREWORD BY JASPER HUMPHREYS

All the hoo-ha over the Millenium celebrations make quite a contrast to the events at the turn of the last century.

The Boer War had begun in October 1899 and was expected to be all over by Christmas and in time for the centenary celebrations. Just another colonial adventure, albeit on a grand scale.

However as the new century dawned, Britain was in no mood for celebrations as the Boers had inflicted a series of reverses on the Imperial forces. Battle names like Magersfontein, Modder River, Spion Kop, and the sieges of Mafeking, Ladysmith and Kimberley still to this day have a haunting ring about them.

Gradually a combination of manpower, equipment and improved tactics ground the Boers down, but the war continued for several more years as an increasingly bitter conflict with the Boers resorting to 'hit and run', which resulted in the introduction of concentration camps by the Imperial Forces to cut off Boer commandos from support.

From a historical perspective, the Boer War started off as an 'old-fashioned' war with hidebound tactics and formations, but soon turned into a 'modern' war, for instance, the artillery barrage rained down on encircled Boer forces at Paardeburg was greater than any battle anywhere between the Crimean War and the First World War. The importance of tactical thinking on the move became paramount and all sorts of logistical innovations evolved.

What is fascinating in these letters is that the writer was witness to many of the great confrontations with the Boers, and not only that, he had the wit and intelligence to be aware of what was going on. In my opinion it is not stretching a point too far by comparing these writings with the Boer War 'classic', 'Kommando' by Denys Reisz, recording his hair-raising experiences as a young Boer fighter.

Reitz wrote his book some time after the war had ended, whereas these letters have the whiff of real-time. Though much of the detail of battles and tactics are not included because the writer was under strict censorship, nevertheless you sense his thoughts and feelings.

Furthermore the references to places back home and chance meetings in the veldt with either old friends or friends of friends give the letters a touching quality allied to his very clear sense of being English. This meant a clear sense of honour, decency and generosity of spirit, all qualities that never deserted him. As the months rolled by, you sense the odd clouds of doubt and dilemma which for someone so young showed a remarkable intelligence. Given the author's subsequent illustrious career, in these letters we watch the honing of a boy into a man against a historical backdrop that had far-reaching implications.

ACKNOWLEDGMENTS

It would be impossible for me to attempt to name everyone who has helped in the preparation of these letters, but I must name a few who have helped me especially:

Andy Petty and Catherine in the ORBIT centre at Trowbridge College who sorted me out whenever I got in a muddle with the computer
David Hancock who showed me some short cuts when I was learning to use the computer which made my job a whole lot easier
Diane Newman at Melksham Skills Centre for teaching me to use the computer at the start
Duncan Horsley of What The Dickens Bookshop for his unflagging support
Felicity Lodge at Clouds for the artwork on the cover
Helena Hirst who proof read accurately and listened as fast as I spoke
Hugh Welch, the writer's grandson, who helped me buy and install my computer
Isis Hreczuk-Hirst for the beautiful line drawings and maps
J.W. and R.W. who kept me sane
Jasper Humphreys for encouraging the project and writing the Foreword
Mark Bawtree for the photocopying and helping me sort out the pictures
Mr Crookston at Trowbridge Reference Library for locating the maps
The late W.J.West for his enthusiasm about the whole subject.

and a huge thank you to everyone else involved.

LIST OF ILLUSTRATIONS

Cover	The Author on Fusilier
Page xii	18 R.E. 2nd Lieutenants, commissioned August 1895
Page 17	Curragh Camp, Co. Kildare, Ireland
Page 38	Original Letter from Modder River, January 12th 1900
Page 74	Rev Thomas Holt-Wilson Rector of Redgrave
Page 91	Redgrave, Suffolk. Village Green
Page 93	Broom Hills, Botesdale, Diss, Norfolk
Page 96	Sketch of Bridge Repair between Malelane and Hector Spruit Stations
Page 130	18 R.E. 2nd Lieutenants, commissioned August 1895
Page 156	Springfontein
Page 177	The Author
Page 188	Rough sketch showing relative heights on Railway between the Orange River and the Vaal River
Page 194	Frank Wilson
Page 198	Boring for water with the Diamond Rock Drill (steam) (Taken by A Anderson)
Page 220	Remount Camp at De Aar (Gordon McKenzie in charge) (Taken by EHW)
Page 231	Pontoon Bridge at Norvals Pont (Taken by EHW)
Page 254	Memorials from The Corps of Royal Engineers to their comrades who lost their lives in the South Africa War 1899–1902 (East Side)
Page 255	R.E. South Africa Memorial (West Side)

BIOGRAPHICAL NOTES ABOUT THE WRITER

Eric Edward Boketon Holt-Wilson was born on 26th August 1875, in Norwich, Norfolk, the second eldest of three children born to Helen Emily Greene and Rev Thomas Holt Wilson Rector of Redgrave in Suffolk. His father originally told Eric that he thought Boketon was a family name, and although he disliked it, Eric kept and proudly used the name until his father, much later in life, told his son that there had been a mistake, it was not a family name after all. Eric was quite annoyed at this, but continued to use the name even so.

He went on from a successful time at prep. school, where he excelled in all sports, to Bosworth Smith's House at Harrow, known to all old boys as The Shop. Here he was a contemporary of Winston Churchill, whom he was to meet again on the battlefields of the Boer War, which Churchill was to visit as a War Correspondent.

After leaving Harrow, E.H.W. went to Woolwich Military Academy, where few anecdotes of his time there survive, but two which do are that E.H.W. achieved 100% in his final Maths exam, but was only allowed 99% on the grounds that "they never gave 100% on principle." E.H.W. bemoaned this 'robbery' all his life though in reality he was never a bitter man about anything. The other legend was that he and a fellow soldier raced two horse drawn fire engines down Woolwich High Street for a wager, though no more is known about the incident.

In 1895 as a 20 year old, E.H.W was commissioned as a 2nd Lieutenant and posted to the Curragh in Southern Ireland. From here he sailed for South Africa via Dublin, Holyhead and Southampton to Cape Town on the troopship R.M.S. Braemar in 1899 with the 7th Field Regiment Royal Engineers. The Regiment travelled complete with horses, E.H.W's favourite being Fusilier (because there were few sillier horses), although Fusilier proved himself far from silly, carrying E.H.W. well during several of his 22 engagements, including Modder river and Paardeburg, where E.H.W. won his D.S.O.

Another War Correspondent E.H.W. met was A. Conan Doyle who he escorted round, and to whom he later wrote to say that some of the details Conan Doyle had included in his reports were grievously wrong. E.H.W. said that the publication they appeared in was actually called the Wide World Series, but he thought it should be renamed the Wild Word Series because of these and many other inaccuracies.

E.H.W. also tells of his meetings with Lords Kitchener, Methuen, Baden Powell and Roberts, recounting many incidents first hand. The descriptions of the changing landscapes and conditions in which he found himself are remarkably fine and calm considering many of them were entries in his notebook when under fire.

After his return to England at the conclusion of the war, he went on to serve another 13 years with the 7th Field Company R.E. before being posted to Singapore, where he was engaged in remodelling its defences 1907-1909.

From there he became a Cadet Company Commander and Military Engineering Instructor at Woolwich R.M.A., General Staff Officer, Imperial General Staff 1914-1924, Joint Secretary Lord Chancellor's Committee on War and Emergency Legislation (Committee of Imperial Defence), 1923, Deputy Commandant War Department Constabulary since 1927, member of Council, Institution of Royal Engineers, 1915, Chief of Civil Police Commission, British Occupied Rhineland, 1919, British Delegate for Navy, Army and Air Force, International Convention on Treatment of Prisoners of War, Geneva, 1929.

In the Boer War, 1899-1902, he received a D.S.O. a mention in Despatches, two Medals, and seven Clasps. In the Great War, he was in Special Intelligence in France, Egypt and Greece, (Despatches, three Medals, Brevet-Major, Brevet.-Lieut.-Col., C.M.G., Legion of Honour, and Order of the Crown of Belgium; Jubilee Medal 1935.

He was in the Cricket and Football XIs, and was Champion Revolver Shot, R.M.A, 1893-1895. He was a member of the Free Foresters Club. Amongst his many other hobbies he skied expertly, and was later President of the Ski Club of Great Britain from 1934-1935.

On one occasion, alighting from a taxi outside his Swiss Hotel, a porter, viewing the vast array of skis, enquired, "Does the Colonel ski on all fours?" E.H.W. also successfully skied down the original Cresta Run.

W. Somerset Maugham used his own and E.H.W.'s exploits as a composite for his eponymous spy hero Ashenden.

On January 19th 1903, 5 months after his return from the Boer War, he married Susannah Mary Shaw, (whose brother Philip had married E.H.W's younger sister Helen in 1900), and had 4 children. He continued serving with the Royal Engineers until 1912 when he joined the Department of the Chief of the Imperial General Staff. In 1924 he was relegated to the Army Reserve with the rank of Lieutenant Colonel.

His first wife died in 1927, and in 1931 he married Audrey Stirling, and had two daughters.

He was knighted in 1933. Although Sir Eric served in uniform, with the honorary rank of Brigadier in 1939, leaving finally in 1940 at the age of 65, he was still with the Security Service. This involved having to leave his lovely Surrey home and move to six different houses in nine months for the safety of his family. He finally settled in Wiltshire in 1940, where he lived a full and happy life in retirement, with his growing family, hosting happy wartime "silly games parties" to keep up morale amongst his friends, in which he played an expert game of charades, taking up gardening, and poultry farming on a small scale, still keeping clean his collection of weapons brought home from the Boer War, reading the lessons in Church twice every Sunday, and making interesting 'things' to keep his hand in, until he died on March 26th 1950, aged 74.

R.M.S. "Braemar Castle" Tuesday 18th July 1899

My dearest Father,

I am writing a line to send off at Las Palmas, Grand Canary, where we stop a few hours to coal and shall possibly go ashore and have a look round. We hope also to see the latest wires from home, as of course all news on board at present dates from the 15th. We got off alright at Southampton about 4.30 p.m. on Saturday after a long and tedious journey from the Curragh – with much loading and unloading of horses wagons and baggage at Curragh, Dublin, Holyhead and Southampton. However all got safely on board in lovely weather, and we have had glorious weather so far ever since – at time of writing we are just south of Straits of Gibralter off N. Coast of Africa and getting on for Madeira, but we don't stop there.

Many thanks for your letter which I found waiting on board. Uncle Charlie came and saw me off and lunched on board in harbour with many other relatives and "girls they left behind them!" The Braemar Castle is a lovely boat, one of Donald Currie's best – we have very few first class passengers besides officers.

There are 9 R.E. Officers on board – 6 of the 7th Co., and 3 of the 8th Railway Co: 4 Officers of Army Ordnance Dept., 1 Army Medical Corps., and 1 Veterinary Officer, and 2 second lieutenants to join the West India Regiment at St. Helena, the only place we stop at after Las Palmas.

They feed us in the most princely manner, – all included in the passage provided by the government! About ten courses to every meal – the only difficulty is getting enough exercise before the next meal. The men have very good quarters and parade twice daily – the horses have stalls on lower deck, alright in weather like this – but I think they would get knocked about in rough weather as they have not provided slings for them.

Fusilier is quite happy at present and eats well – but I don't know how he will like standing up for 3 weeks on end without a sleep lying down.

Lord Roberts gave us a great address at Newbridge station before leaving. We passed Ushant on Sunday about 11 a.m. and Cape Finisterre on Monday. An artist from "Illustrated London News" has made a lot of sketches while we were embarking and I believe made one of me – or in which I figure – so you can look out for it – I believe I had my arms folded.

Letters addressed 7th Field Company R.E. Cape Town will be forwarded alright if we go up country. I will keep this open till we have to post at Las

Palmas tomorrow (Wednesday). Another lovely day – post collected at 6pm so must close – hope to reach Las Palmas tomorrow.

Ever your loving son Eric E.B. Wilson

We crossed the much dreaded Bay of Biscay in a sea little rougher than Redgrave Lake on a still day!!

R.M.S. "Braemar Castle"   Saturday July 29th 1899

My dearest Father,

Just a line to post at St Helena, which we hope to make at about 7 am, tomorrow Sunday. I fancy the next homeward mail leaves there on Tuesday, so this ought to reach you about Aug 15th or 16th by which time we shall be well up country I expect at the Cape – We are all longing to hear any news at St Helena from the Cape – as you at home know more of the events at the Cape by 15 days than I do as I write! For all we know old Kruger may have occupied Kimberley and blown up Johannasburg – or may have climbed down to the bottom rung by now. We have had a very pleasant voyage indeed up to the present – I had better give you a brief epitome from my journal since I last wrote.

July 20th   Sighted land early – the Isleta – a small peninsula of the 'Grand Canary' – Clouds obscured distant view which we should have had of Teneriffe Mountain 60 miles off. Dropped anchor off Las Palmas 12 noon – After being passed by the harbour doctor usual crowd of boats and fruit sellers <u>swarmed</u> round ship – very picturesque in their spanish sashes – but very unkempt and dirty, small boys diving for silver – which they always brought up.

Stewart, Boileau and I go ashore in a small boat rowed by 2 Spaniards, about a mile to the landing stage in the harbour and a fair swell on too. We take a trap to the Santa Catalina Hotel about 1½ miles along the shore – (The town is about 3 miles from the harbour) – have a nice quiet lunch with lots of fruit –

after lunch Stewart and I climb a hill at the back of the Hotel grounds (about 400 feet) and get a good view of the island and the harbour and town – wonderfully bright colours and clear sky – we then all three walked on into the town – hot and evil smelling but very fascinating and quaint – visited Cathedral – fine building with some good paintings and silver chandeliers of wonderful design – buy a set of stamps at the post office after desperate efforts of combined Spanish and French! – drive back to Hotel Metropole – the only other decent Hotel – both hotels English and very fine indeed – (cater for invalids) where we have tea and rest a bit – then back to the ship by 5.30 p.m. – Coaling still going on and everything black on board – Las Palmas lovely place for fruit and flowers – palms – aloes – bananas – cactus – rubber trees – geraniums 5 or 6 feet high, in flower – and other lovely plants. Off again about 9 p.m.. Found a stowaway on board – a nice-looking lad of about 14 – who will be put off at St. Helena.

July 21st   Warm and fine – overtook a West African boat going the same way – played deck quoits etc –

July 22nd   Much warmer – have some revolver practice at bottles hung out by a string from a yard – I broke 5 out of 6 that we shot at and then shot several of the necks out of the strings, where left. Just back on board after a run round the island – of which more in my next – pressed for time to send this ashore.

July 30th   St Helena

R.M.S. "Braemar Castle"   Sunday 30th July 1899

We had several vollies at sharks – I touched one up on the fin and he promptly bobbed under again. Some beautiful schools of porpoises leaping in and out of the water most of the day and flying fish we see every day. I had no idea how far they could fly – sometimes as much as a hundred yards before dropping in again.
Practised 'fire alarm stations' also 'boat stations'.
Met homeward Union Line steamer and fired complimentary rockets and lights – to which she responded.

July 23rd   Service at 10.15 by Captain – 1st Officer reads lesson. – Very hot, after lunch sharp shower of rain which cooled the air a bit. Full Moon. Passed Cape Verde quite close – saw coast well with glasses – scrubby trees and a few red tiled houses – and two light houses (French). Saw remains of a wreck on a rock off shore.

July 24th   Very calm and warm early – cloudy and showery later on – played in a deck quoit tournament and got left in for final tomorrow.

July 25th   Played final and won quoits. Prize 7/= sweepstake – each – my partner Thomson also getting prize – the other pair led by 20 points to 11 at one stage, (game being 21) and we pulled up to 18–20 and then won! Band after mess and dancing on deck. Coolest evening since we started though only 5 degrees N of Equator.

July 26th   Nice cool breeze all day – crossed the Equator at 5 p.m. and instead of the burning heat of the tropics just passed through, we had the coolest day.
Since we left Southampton – slept with a sheet over me without any inconvenience heat in my cabin which I now have to myself as some passengers left at Las Palmas.

July 27th   Temperature only about 68 degrees – still cool and cloudy – S.W. (head) wind fair sea on towards evening – pitching a bit. In p.m. had tug-of-war for troops – six teams entered – 7th Co 3 teams, 8th Co 2 and Ordnance 1. The 3 7th Co teams won the first round and then 2 beat 3, and 1 beat 2 in the final. (2 is my section.) No 1 section team was about 14–16 lbs <u>a man</u> heavier than the other teams, by some curious chance having all the big men of the company. Officers beat rest of ship easily – <u>R.E.</u> Officers beat <u>rest of ship</u> 1st & 2nd class one

4

pull in three and succumbed twice after frightful exertions! I suppose we were more than a stone a man lighter than the other team which included an Ordnance Officer of 17st 10lbs or so; our heaviest being 12st 2lbs!! and lightest 9st 10lbs. Saw a fine waterspout about a mile off – passed away to Northwards. Band and dancing in evening.

July 28th Head wind – still cool and cloudy and sea fairly choppy. 2 p.m., boxing competition for the men – only 2 heavyweights – won by Lance Corp. Hackett of my Company. Middleweight (6 entries) won by Sapper Davies, also 7th Company R.E. A good exhibition spar between two of the ships engineers – after tea a gymkhana for officers and 1st class – usual neck-breaking events – and races. At 7.45 p.m. engines stopped and we came to a standstill in mid ocean for half an hour while they mended a burst steam pipe in the engine room. Off again at 8.15 p.m. – lost 5 knots or so. A concert in the 2nd salon to which most of us went – not very exciting. Hope to go ashore at St Helena tomorrow and see Napoleon's Tomb etc. Much love to all. Send this on to Moonie as I am too lazy to write it all out again.

With heaps of love – ever your loving son Eric E.B. Wilson

Wynberg   Monday July 31st 1899

A Corporal of Artillery in charge of the fort pointed us out all the features of interest and lent us a strong telescope. We saw Longwood where Napoleon died – across the next valley but one – time would not let us reach it, but we saw it quite clearly through the glass – almost a mile off. We also saw the camp of the 3rd West India Regiment – near Longwood – the Governor's House and all the chief objects of interest. We then fled down the hillside – back to the Barracks – and on down the vast and abysmal ladder – which looked an absolutely sickening length down from the top! Once more below we visited the post office where I bought all sorts of stamps etc for my collection – then back on board.

Of animals – we saw donkeys, a few hardy-looking cobs, pigs, fowls and tame blue and white pigeons, and some very beautiful butterflies – one I recognised as the marble white I think a black and white spotted one – there are abundance of trees – firs etc – in thick groves all over inland, and rich green grass – bananas – oranges etc.

We did not weigh anchor till 3 p.m. however – after dropping the two subalterns for the West India Regiment and taking on board a St Helena parson who came on to Cape Town. I could not discover his name or denomination.

July 31st   Bright and sunny – usual ship routine – band played after mess – dancing –

August 1st   Colder and rather rolly sea – sports on deck in p.m. – won various preliminary heats in potato race – etc – met a 3-masted sailing barque – Norwegian – bound for Azores – after tea shown round the engine room by the chief engineer. Most interesting, but very hot – 100 degrees!! And only 60 degrees on deck – sea pitchy in evening.

August 2nd   Heavy swell all day – our ?roughest day out – but quite bearable even by the poorest sailor at this stage of the voyage. In p.m. had the finals of sports – won long-jump <u>standing</u> – open to ship – with 8 ft 9 in (on wood) – also long jump standing, backwards, (by about a foot) – also 2nd in potato race. Had the fiddleys on table at mess to keep the crockery on – for first and only time.

August 3rd   Four years service today. Calmer but cold and fine – tropics a fraud at this time of year – at sea at any rate! Amateur photographer took 'groups' etc – Band played.

August 4th Quiet day on board preparing kit etc for arrival. Black mare Medusa very weak from sickness and chilled liver. Concert on the poop in evening.

August 5th Dropped anchor in Table Bay 6 a.m. – dawn gradually appearing over the mountains – magnificent effects.

Harbour boat came off to pass us free of sickness – and brought news that "no war yet but still arguing". Table Mountain – Devils Peak – Lions Head and the bay and Town – the most magnificent panorama at sunrise I have ever seen. Day breaks blazing cloudless and brilliantly fine and warm at 6.30 a.m. R.M.S. Norman leaves harbour for Algoa Bay and East Coast. U.S. Cruiser Olympia in docks. Towed into dockside – black mare died an hour before we landed – our only casualty since leaving Curragh.

After landing, I was sent on ahead with a party of seven to find out and take over our quarters at Wynburgh – which we reached by rail about 12 o'clock and were met by an R.E. Sergeant-Major who showed us the way up – about a mile or so from the station up on a hillside above the town of Wynberg. At present we are busy shaking down – we had heavy rain last night and fear the effect on the horses – who it seems from accounts are liable to manifold sicknesses and ills on first arrival in the country – in fact the Cape ponies which are very hardy animals are the only animals which do at all well. I hope we shall have some fun for our money now we are here – the expense of living here is something terrible I believe, as all food and drink is expensive and we only get a colonial allowance of 1/6d a day extra which goes no distance.

At present I suppose the move, outfit, arms, extra saddlery, trunks, uniforms etc has cost us about £90 apiece, then we are sure to want ponies later if we go up country as one English horse cannot do much work in this country till it is acclimatised. Luckily ponies are cheap even now with the rise of price on account of war scare and government purchases. You can get a very useful animal for £25.

Tomorrow I expect to go into Cape Town with my section of the Company to unload baggage off the ship, as none of our heavy baggage or stores have been got out as yet. I fancy the mail goes on Tuesday so I must close this letter today. I don't know where we shall be by the time you get this and write –

but "Wynberg" would find us or be forwarded alright. As soon as I have had a look round Cape Town itself and the country I will write again. Please send this on to Moonie.

Love to all. Ever your loving son Eric E.B. Wilson

Wynberg, Coghill's Hotel, Capetown　　　　　　　Monday 6th August 1899

My dearest Father,

Here we are at last – safe and sound.
On arrival at Cape Town yesterday we were told off to go into camp at Wynberg, a suburb of Cape Town – about 8½ miles off – at the back (S) of Table Mountain, and the residence of all the wealthy merchants of Cape Town, and here we shall remain till we get further instructions, or are required up country. We found no fresh development of the situation on arrival but it seems they are still arguing and bickering – while we are concentrating troops up in Natal near the frontier. If we are sent up it will probably be on the Kimberley side (West). You will see by the map that the Transvaal is approached by skirting the Orange Free State either East via Natal or West via Kimberley district – and the 23rd Field Co R.E. are already up Natal way. All our men and horses arrived safely in camp by 4.30 p.m. yesterday – the latter marched from the docks (9 miles), the former by rail. We found they had, in anticipation of our arrival, run up five tin huts for us. The remainder of the camp is wood and tin huts – not unlike the Curragh in style – which is much better than being under canvas.
There is, however, no provision for officers as yet so we are living at the hotel of Wynbergh at present – and will probably be put on "lodging allowance" instead of being provided with quarters. Possibly we shall unite and take a small house near the camp and form a mess there later on.
Now that we are comfortably quartered I better hark back to our voyage where I last wrote – just before arrival at St Helena, which we reached on the 30th, and dropped anchor at Jamestown the capital at 7.18 a.m..

The island stands a great height out of the sea – averages some 600 feet or more I should say and is divided up by six or seven large vallies or clefts running down to the sea – but in only one of these on the N. side can you land viz: at the mouth of the valley in which Jamestown lies.

After breakfast on board Fuller (R.E.) and I went ashore in a boat – and found it hot enough on shore though cool and almost cold on board – we crossed the ditch and rampart which blocks the mouth of the valley and landing place – and found ourselves in the square or market place – with the main road running inland up the valley – to our immediate right, however was the Ladder Hill on which all the barracks etc are – 600 ft above the hill, sheer, the nearest foot approach being up a steep ladder with handrails, rising dead straight 600 ft with six hundred and ninety nine steps!! Up we went with pauses every hundred steps to admire the view!! On arrival (at last) at the top we foud a stone slab which said "This ladder was reconstructed by the 7th Company R.E. in 1873" – imagine my surprise – we then went to the R.A and R.E. Mess – (5 R.A. and 2 R.E. Officers I think) where we had a well-earned lemon squash and arm chair, and met Faber R.E. having his breakfast – had a chat – told our news etc., and the proceeded to explore (we had to be back on board by 12 so were rather pressed.) After another gradual climb of 1300 feet up a winding road through cactus and aloe and little bungalows on the hillsides, and very English-looking domestic fowls of a breed that I should say would beat Redgrave birds for "many crosses", we arrived at "Knoll Hill Fort" a strong fort on the summit of one of the peaks of the island – height 1916 ft from where we got a magnificent view of the island, all round- it is only 10 miles by 6 so we saw it well.

Wynberg Camp, Cape Town S.A.   **Tuesday 22nd August 1899**

My dearest Father,

I hope you are all well at Redgrave – I am keeping this open in the hope of hearing from someone by the mail which should arrive tomorrow – the third mail in since my arrival – and as yet I have not received a line from anyone in Great Britain.

We are still in Wynberg awaiting developments – the feeling grows more intense every day, and Kruger's delay in answering the proposal for an enquiry has not bettered his chances of a profitable settlement from his point of view. I hear the Boers on the Natal border are getting very busy just now – of course the whole of the Transvaal and Imperial troops have been buying up every horse pony and mule for ages past – and the expense incurred to the Imperial Government by Kruger's delay in answering will no doubt be reimbursed somehow.

It would amuse you to read the local papers – Cape Times etc – columns of details of every movement of men and stores by either side.

I have got a very nice quarter in camp now – and am messing with the Yorkshire Light Infantry who have ½ a Battalion here.

We are very busy every day – putting up new accommodation of all kinds. Yesterday I had to ride over and inspect a huge disused match factory – with a view to making a forage store of it. It has been taken over by the government now and I have a lot of men clearing it out and doing repairs – making approaches etc.

The pressure on the Army Service Corps and Veterinary Officers is exceedingly heavy, buying and storing forage and the Vet: travelling hundreds of miles buying up horses and mules. A mule here costs about £45, an average horse £25 to £35 and a good pony about £18. In time of peace of course they are much cheaper – but the mule is far the most useful of the lot.

I am very anxious to hear some news from home soon.

We have had the rainiest wet season known for years here – rain 5 days a week and all day, but one fine day of blazing sun dries all up very quickly.

Some of us went to a great charity concert etc in the Opera House at Cape Town last night and enjoyed it.

Incoming mail not arrived yet so must close.

Much love to all – ever your loving son Eric E.B. Wilson.

Tuesday 29th August 1899

My dearest Father,

Very many thanks for your letter dated August 4th received last mail. I am glad Mother is going on alright. I rather like the name Rachel. I have had a birthday since I last wrote* and a very wet day it was – we have had a very great deal of rain up to date – but the weather promises better now.

We have been very busy this week – still preparing for the coming struggle. The general situation is considered more critical now – and local feeling on both sides is very strained, the papers of course as usual full of little else than details of preparations – the standstill of business up country – the departure of families from the North and all the latest rumours as to where the hostilities will commence. It seems really very hard to imagine how things can be settled peacefully after all the enormous preparations and tension of race feeling being fostered from day to day by all means and parties.

It seems that unless Kruger admits the undisputed suzerainty of the British, that no offer of additional franchise or other concessions will be considered at all by our people now. There has been great feeling displayed in the Cape Parliament lately over a question of allowing ammunition etc to pass through the colony for the use of the Orange Free State and the Transvaal and as the present ministry here is 'Bond' or in other words more than suspected of Dutch sympathies – the state of affairs is only embittered by their indifferent loyalty to the English flag. Last night I dined with Colonel Morris, our C.R.E. at the Castle in Cape Town, we had a pleasant evening with music etc.

The new general should arrive shortly to replace Sir William Butler who returned home rather under a cloud – having expressed opinions of undoubted Dutch sympathy – and so found himself quite out of touch with leading the British forces in a campaign against them.

I am gradually making the acquaintance of some nice people round about. I went to call on three families on Sunday.

We are thinking of beginning the cricket season now, it seems very funny after leaving home in the middle of our own cricket season.

Love to all – I am very anxious to hear some news of our invalid.

Ever your loving son Eric E. B. Wilson.

* He was then 24 years old, born 26 August 1875.

Wednesday 6th September 1899

My dearest Father,

Many thanks for yours dated Aug 11th. This is the first letter I am sending under the new tariff – 1d instead of 2½d.

The new General Forestier Walker arrives today by the mail and guards of honour etc are awaiting him at the Docks and Government House. He possibly has some letters for me on the same boat – which I shall get this evening – after the outgoing mail has left.

We are all very well and busy as usual – preparations going on apace, and the crisis still un-passed. During the week I have been to Cape Town once or twice and to Muizenburg about 8 miles south to make the annual inspection of Government land there – check the boundaries and see that the tenants haven't sublet their houses – a favourite and paying game they often indulge in. Saturday I think some of us are going to see the Mikado at the Opera House in Cape Town – and Tuesday I have been asked to a dance given by some wealthy colonials called Struben.

I hope your visit to Norwich was successful.

Many thanks for the magazine.

I met Major Heath of ours this week – he has been up country obtaining information etc and has just returned to Cape Town.

There is a subaltern in the Yorkshire Light Infantry, that I am living with, of the name of R M.D. Fox – was in Marshall's at Harrow with me – You know that W.F.H. Kincaid my Colonel was an old Harrow man?

Best love to all. Ever your loving son Eric E. B. Wilson.

R.A. and R.E. Joint Mess,   Wednesday 13th September 1899
The Castle, Cape Town

My dearest Father,

I was afraid I should miss this mail today as I deferred writing till the arrival of the incoming mail which got in yesterday – and today I found myself detailed as a member of a Court Martial in Cape Town – which sometimes takes all day – but luckily we finished up by 11.30 a.m. so I have had till 1 p.m. to catch the mail.
Many thanks for yours dated 25th August, arrived yesterday – for once the mails overlapped the right way.
We are very busy now – tomorrow the new general inspects all the troops at Wynberg in Field Service order – everything packed up etc as though ready to move.
The situation today has reached its penultimate stage – on the publication here of the despatch of the Cabinet meeting last week – which only leaves Kruger the option of fight or surrender.
Last night I went to a very nice dance at some people called Struben, the father of the Struben who ran 2nd in the international athletics recently – I think in the ½ mile.
Last Saturday several of us dined with an A Service Corps Officer in Cape Town and went to see the Mikado afterwards. I got a short note from Moonie by mail this week – which with your weekly despatch is the sum total of my mails since arrival – even the bills haven't penetrated here thank goodness! She seems well and happy.
Frith R.E. head of my batch at Chatham has arrived for duty with the 8th Railway Company R.E.
We were to have played hockey this p.m. but rain and pressure of work will stop it as far as I am concerned, I think.

Best love to all from your ever loving son Eric E. B. Wilson.

Wynberg Camp   Sunday 17th September 1899

My dearest Father,

I will keep this open till the mail comes in – due on Tuesday.

We have had a very busy week indeed with work and play combined. The Royal Munster Fusiliers arrived in camp yesterday to replace the Liverpool Regiment who have gone up to Natal.

A large vessel ran ashore in Table Bay during the week – the Thermopylae – quite unaccountable – a bright night and all the harbour lights visible – yet she was run straight on to the rocks. All passengers landed safely but the ship (from Australia, about 3,500 tons) has broken up beyond hope of salvage. The valuable race horses on board were cut loose and managed to reach shore alive by themselves – jumped into the water and scrambled on to the rocks – rather knocked about but not seriously injured.

On Friday at 12.26 p.m. we had a slight earthquake – a considerable undulation of the ground was felt for a long way round – no damage done that I have heard of – beyond bottles being broken etc. I believe they are unusual here – so considerable interest was evolved.

On Thursday we had an inspection of all troops in camp, by the new General, Forestier Walker – in field service order – everything packed up even to the food and forage ready if necessary to march off parade then and there.

I served on a Courtmartial on Wednesday at the Castle, a fact which I think I recorded in my last letter. On Tuesday and Thursday, I attended two very pleasant dances – so that you see we are burning the candle at both ends well, before the general advance into the arid veldt on the road to Pretoria.

The situation today is more than serious:– after interminable shilly-shallying on Kruger's part, as you will have gathered from accounts – news has reached us of the intended rejection of Mr. Chamberlain's final overtures for an amicable settlement – which leaves no doubt whatever here that war is now a question of hours – unless – the actual despatch of the inevitable ultimatum – has the effect of turning Pharoah Kruger's heart at the last minute – a very doubtful contingency.

The exodus from the Rand and Transvaal generally continues to increase. Distress is becoming more acute and funds are in full swing to afford relief to the refugees as they arrive down country. Moreover the paralysis of trade is beginning to react seriously on the loyalty of the merchant community here, whose faith in the wisdom of the policy pursued by our Colonial Government is beginning to be tinged with irritation at the indifference as to the 'time' which may safely be wasted in futile and pointless negotiations.

I will add to this on Wednesday. Tuesday 10 a.m. – just received orders to move up country – destination unknown. Expect to start this p.m. You must expect next letter when it arrives.

Best love to all and God Bless you all, ever your loving son Eric E. B. Wilson.

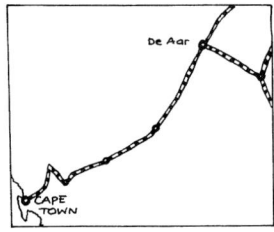

De Aar Cape Colony about   **Sunday 1st October 1899**
6,500 miles from Curragh Camp

My dearest Father,

You will probably have been a little anxious at not receiving my usual last mail, so this will be the more welcome.
In the stress of our departure from Wynberg I was unable to manage a letter. Just received yours of September 8th forwarded from Wynberg – which place we left on September 25th with one hour's notice to pack, and travelled up with men horses and stores of ½ Battalion Yorkshire Light Infantry, my section 7th Field Company and Wolff R.E. with 25 men of the 29th Company R.E., from Cape Town to De Aar, about 500 miles up country – within a day's ride of the Orange Free State border, and the most important junction in the Colony, being the junction for Bloemfontein and Pretoria as you will see by any good map.
Here we are under active service conditions in camp – busily engaged in forming defences for the railway here. De Aar consists of one long railway station and depôt about mile long with one row of houses on either side occupied entirely by railway employees and natives, about 600 in all. The leading man of the place is a Mr Heatley – railway boss Inspector or something – who was at Peterhouse in '81 and stroked their boat 3 years I believe.
Well here we are at last – sleeping on Mother Earth – I mean Mother Rock! with a blanket or two and tents to keep off sun and rain at present – our next move will probably leave the tents behind – and here am I, at I suppose one of the summits of the R.E. subaltern's ambition – designing and constructing real fieldworks and defences to keep out real bullets and knowing that every stone placed in its right place may save a life – with large working parties of infantry and my own men wielding the pick and shovel – axe and crowbar, at my word, never knowing how many hours may elapse before the very works in hand may be stormed by determined men!
The general disposition of our small army at present in the colony is along various points of the frontier – pioneering for (we hope) the vast army to follow – and doing our best to strengthen and hold the most vulnerable points of ford and rail against large numbers until the others arrive for the general advance.

7th Field Co. R.E. mobilized for departure to South Africa - July 1899. Curragh Camp, Co. Kildare, Ireland.

Col Kincaid, Boileau, Musgrave and Johnson of my Company are at Orange River Bridge with 2 section 7th Field Co doing ditto there. McClintock and No 1 section are at Kimberley and I with No 2 at De Aar. The chief interest after working hours (6.15 a.m. to 5 p.m. in a mid African sun is to see the trainloads, trucks – vans – anything full of refugees coming down from the Transvaal – whence all are clearing at full speed.

A hundred rumours a day reach us of the movements of the enemy's troops – now they are here – now there – now just preparing to blow up the line and now preparing to ride over the border and make a dash for this place or that – none of them I suppose ever true.

The country round here – desolate rocky red veldt for miles – with rocky knolls or kopjes – is sparsely inhabited by very hostile Dutch farmers – who however do not appear much near the camp. Water is plentiful however and our supply department working splendidly.

I dare not write you detailed accounts of the defences and works in hand here as there is a strong feeling that at places the Post Office is a bit 'leaky'.

War is now regarded as practically existent – I mean Englishmen are being hustled out of Pretoria etc and all business stopped and shops barricaded – of course we shall be on the defensive until the army arrives – an event that is prayed for hourly!

Some of the scenery coming up was superb. The Hex River Pass especially so. Fusilier is with me and very fit. I also have a Basuto pony named Bill Sykes who is a very useful little chap about 14.1 and cost me £25. I have to keep two horses on service and we are now under service conditions now – only a couple of shirts and a sock besides what we wear etc.

Personally I have never been fitter, happier, or more pleased with things in general. This dry climate seems to brace up every string, and moreover we are just about to put the soldier's hand to the soldier's trade – an event which cannot happen often in his career like the more peaceful occupations and professions.

We had a sharp thunderstorm on Thursday – the day after we arrived – it blew up from N. and poured for about half an hour – then the wind veered clean round to S. and brought it all back again within and hour! Otherwise it is hot and dusty but not at all unbearable, about 85° to 95° at midday.

I hope all are well at home – as soon as I can find time I must try and write some more letters, at present my weekly one to you is about my limit.

Best love to all from your ever loving son Eric E.B. Wilson

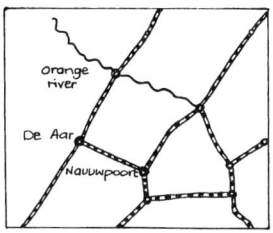

De Aar, Cape Colony   **Monday 9th October 1899**

My dearest Father,

Received yours of Sept 15th this mail. I am glad to hear such good account of Helen. We have had a very busy week and a very dusty one. We are still at De Aar and likely to remain for some time.

The defences are going on well. I have completed a redoubt on the N.E. front of the town and I think it will do very well. We have named it "Prince Edward's Redoubt" as he is the young man probably for whose benefit we are trying to keep the old empire together, though I should not like to predict what sort of a South African empire he will find by the time he comes to the throne – I hope a larger and more consolidated one than at present.

On Thursday I went with two of my men up to Orange River Bridge, 70 miles up the line and on the Free State Border, where the headquarters of my company are. I went partly to escort some explosives (which we sat and smoked over in the guard's van! and partly to see the Colonel on various matters connected with our routine etc.

We also escorted an armoured engine and two armour plated trucks en route for Kimberley. We reached Orange River at 2.30 a.m. Slept in the waiting room – on the floor – unusual luxury after the rocky floor of my tent) till 6 a.m. when I met the Colonel – rode round their camp – had a look at the bridge – about 1 ½ miles from the Camp – over the Orange River – about 1200 feet long – and generally took in their environments and defences. Had breakfast with the Colonel, Boileau, Musgrave and Johnson, who were all flourishing, and returned to De Aar at 10.50 by goods trains – arriving at 4.30 p.m. – nearly six hours for 70 miles – about 12 miles an hour!

The scenery on the Orange River is grand and bold and I think they have entrenched themselves pretty securely. Attack has repeatedly been threatened there, as by destroying the bridge, our communications to Kimberley and north would be cut. So you may imagine they are on the qui vive there.

All through the week crowds and crowds of refugees have been passing through from the Transvaal, each lot with more bitter execrations on the Boers for breaking up their homes and livelihood and driving them homeless and destitute down country with no chance of employment and doubtful even of their food.

I believe Cape Town is simply crammed with them by now. One gets quite used to seeing crowds of women and children in open topped trucks travelling over a thousand miles on end over the blazing veldt with no means of relieving their distress as our work is cut out to keep supplies going here to start with. They all beseech us with tears in their eyes to give the Boers a real good dressing down when we get there.

On Saturday while at work on my redoubt, I was surprised to see several distinguished looking 'civilians' approaching – and being shown round by Major Hunt – commanding the station – after their departure I heard that it was no other than General Forestier Walker and staff – commanding the whole of the forces in the Colony – who was travelling round the various frontier posts to see how the defences were progressing.

I overheard him say that he thought my redoubt was "splendid" and "most excellently constructed" and that he wondered at the amount of work done in the few days we had been here. So we haven't worked in vain so far at any rate! Later in the day he asked me various questions on the defences proposed etc., also for information about Orange River Bridge where I had just returned from – and finally walked all round the camp with me examining and discussing various points and features of our proposed scheme of defence.

In the afternoon on Saturday we gave the men a half-holiday as they had been very hard worked all the week – and we played a cricket match – Garrison v De Aar on their cricket ground – excellent hard smooth pitch – no grass of course – but green coconut matting on the wicket.

They batted first and we outed them for 49. I took five wickets bowling for about 20 runs – caught one and ran one out at my bowling end – so helped 7 to leave altogether.

We then batted and made 107 I think, of which I made 4 only, bowled by a fast left-hander.

The strange pitch and ball the same colour as the ground (sandy yellow) rather baulk the eye of a man straight from England – but I think we shall have some fun out of it when we can find time to play more. The King's Own Yorkshire Light Infantry have just had a valuable young officer join – Luther – late of the Rugby and Sandhurst XI's. He played very nicely indeed, and bowled two wickets, I think.

I called on Heatley the Railway Inspector, on Sunday, also Rev Lott, the English Minister – a nice man trying to live out a consumptive tendency in this wonderful air – 400 odd feet we are here, it freezes often at night but goes up to 80° or 90° by day – rather trying when sleeping on the ground.

This afternoon, I rode out with Wolff to a farm about six miles out – to have a look round the country. The old farmer who lives there is bitterly anti

Imperial and we thought he might possibly let his gun off at us – but he contented himself with a surly stare. Tomorrow we are sending an escort up to Kimberley to get money to pay the men. Major Heath R.E. was round here last week arranging camps for more troops when they arrive etc and doing general staff work. I showed him round. We want a little rain of course badly – dust storms blow at uncertain intervals and simply bury everything in one's tent inches deep.

Much love to all at home – Ever your loving son Eric E.B. Wilson.

On reading this over I see I have not said a word about the situation – but you probably have gathered it from the papers.
The Boers have massed all their troops on their borders and we have done the same – now we sit snarling and waiting for our reinforcements – as yet no overt act of hostility has taken place – but I can promise you that fight or no fight out troops <u>are going to Pretoria now</u> and moreover Kruger will have to pay the bill for expenses to date – if no further.

De Aar　　　　　　　　　　　　　　　　　　Tuesday 17th October 1899

My dearest Father

Just able to snatch a moment to write you a line in the Station Master's office at De Aar – My news will all be very old to you by the time it arrives – War was declared on Wednesday October 11th at 5 p.m. and we knew here privately that such would be the case at 7 p.m. the day before. It is needless to remark how busy we all are, that you can faintly imagine for yourself.

The Boers' first overt act of hostility was wrecking an armoured engine at Kraiipa some way up the line – which was piloting a train of women and children – and this before war had been declared – it is known that 15 men were killed or captured. I believe an assault on Mafeking was repulsed with heavy loss to the Boers – about 200 English to 1500 Boers – killed and wounded – our news is scrappy as the wires are cut in several places and the rails pulled up. Other engagements are reported but you will have had full details ere this reaches you.

The 5th Fusiliers arrived here Friday and left to reinforce Orange Bridge on Monday. Captain and Brevet Major George Ray from whom I bought Fusilier in September '96 was here and was intensely surprised to see the old horse fat and flourishing.

Festing also of the 5th Fusiliers I met – he kept wicket for (Winchester and) Sandhurst when I played against them in '94. Also Crispin – the Methlods' cousin (?), who said he met you there early in the year.

The other half battalion Yorkshire Light Infantry have arrived from Mauritius and are now here – also some of the 9th Lancers and other troops.

De Aar is going to be a large base – about 8,000 men – and what with laying on water for them and building forts my time is quickly passed.

My first redoubt which I named Price Edward's Redoubt – has been re-named by the Officer Commanding the troops "Fort Wilson", as he was very pleased with it. I am too busy to detail minor events this week but you will see all accounts of the fighting – which I knew all along was coming – it is a great bit of luck for me and I am extremely hard and well although a bit black in the face.

Best love to you all – I haven't received any English mail since I last wrote but no doubt shall get it in time.

Ever your loving son Eric E B Wilson.

De Aar   Monday 23rd October 1899

My dearest Father

A line to say all well at De Aar. We have been joined today by the Border Regiment – under our old friend Colonel Hinde whom I have not seen since they were at Woolwich. He was much surprised to see me and has grown stouter and greyer. He asked after you all.

I expect one of the two battalions here will now move on. We hear news of several glorious victories round Natal side – at great loss I fear to us – but greater to the enemy.

A wire tonight says that at Elandslaagte, out of one "Commando" of Boers 800 strong, only 250 escaped. We have been threatened often here but not yet attacked – though we hear that a few hundred Boers have been seen some 15 miles off.

My chief work this week has been improvising a field carriage for a 6 pounder Hotchkiss quick-firing gun – which arrived here on route for Kimberley after the line had been cut and so could not go forward and join its carriage there. As they sent about 200 rounds of shell with it; I considered it would be more useful on a carriage than in its box; so gathering six smiths around me we fitted it up on a field carriage – axle – wheels elevating gear – and all complete in 47 working hours, of which the first 18 – viz 2 p.m. Tuesday through the night to 8 a.m. Wednesday were done in one stretch. It took us 14 hours to forge the axle by hand. I then fitted it up to another cart to act as an ammunition limber and we have a field gun with four horses complete. Next I cut a road up a very steep hill commanding the camp and environs, about 200 feet high, hauled the gun up with sixty men and made a strong stone redoubt on the apex and there the gun reposes, with seventeen conspicuous objects all around accurately measured and ranged for exact distance. I am not boasting I hope when I say that it was considered a useful piece of work.

We also fired four trial shots to test the strength and stability of the carriage at ranges of 1150, 1550, 2100 and 2300 yards – with considerable accuracy.

Many thanks for your last letter – I have not it on me to quote date but it was the one about September 30th – after missing a mail. I also heard from Moonie.

We expect the troops will soon be coming now – in fact a few driblets are arriving by degrees now – that is perhaps the only and indeed a very serious mistake made by the armchair people at home – not reinforcing the Cape Colony <u>the moment</u> a row was inevitable. As it is Natal has been seriously invaded – and though it is grand to think that the handful of men there have repulsed twice and thrice their numbers – there is still a lot of ground to regain before the advance on Bloemfontein and Pretoria begins.

Kimberley and Mafeking our side are holding out well and the Bridge at Orange River is strongly held by our troops now.

I see that C. N. Perreau was wounded – I fancy he was in Bushells or a small house – while I was at Harrow.

Landon of the Times is here – he seems a very nice man.

No more news at present – love to all – Ever your loving son Eric E. B. Wilson.

De Aar   Sunday 29th October 1899

My dearest Father,

Your letter dated October 6th received this mail – probably the last I shall get from you before you discover that the war began on the 11th inst:– the 3 weeks difference makes a curious gap in the information which we send each other – though of course in reality your information on current events only differs by a few hours from mine – possibly some of the news reaches London by wire before it does De Aar. I am surprised at the accuracy with which you have guessed my whereabouts in your letter of Oct 6th! I shall have been here 5 weeks on Tuesday. I haven't any very special news for you this week – as regards the fighting and our victories in Natal we probably both read the same descriptions from the same sources over the wire. As regards De Aar we still only have the one battalion here – the Yorkshires, others have come and gone to various places as occasion arose – but we have nearly completed our preparations for the 8,000 men that we have been preparing for – and have built numbers of large store houses – sheds – workshops – platforms – laid down numbers of extra sidings – water pipes, tanks etc., and built ovens etc., etc., – all ready for a very large depot here.

We have not been seriously threatened with attack lately – but I have no hesitation in saying that if we had not blown down the main bridge on the road over the Orange River at Hopetown (of course we are strenuously protecting the railway bridge there), we should probably have had a large commando of Free State Boers down this way – if they only knew how weak De Aar has been the last five weeks and the large amounts of food and stores we have been accumulating I am sure they would have been down here. Now it will be too late and it is we who shall do the advancing.

Landon of the 'Times' who is here knows the Montgomeries well and another man Earle of the Coldstream Guards who is on the staff here knows George M. very well.

I see that a lot of our Egyptian Railway Officers – Girouard and Co – are arriving – Ozzy du Port's Field Battery has been in the thick of the fighting and I am glad to see he is alright at present. McClintock, commanding no 1 section of my company at Kimberley (I have no 2 here) was slightly wounded last week in a sortie from Kimberley – but I think not seriously. I believe General Forestier Walker is coming here tomorrow to take up his quarters here, he is commanding the lines of communication. We have fixed him up a tin kitchen, bathroom etc., etc.

My Hotchkiss gun is in position now on a hill commanding the country all around and I have measured the ranges of likely objects all round and am longing to have a chance of using it before real artillery arrive here! Next week I have to lay out about two miles of road and make three bridges – as well as completing my new redoubt and some other defences.

I have not yet received magazines etc., you refer to in your letter, but perhaps they will filter up presently. I am anxious to hear news of Moonie and know whether I am an uncle or an aunt!!

We had a grateful shower of rain last week and today the heat is intense. I hope the railway scheme comes off, it would be a fine thing for the Redgrave Estate. I am glad you are giving up the Felixstowe house – as you will be able to choose your place as you wish now without the cares of a fixed house.

My animals Fusilier and Bill Sykes are doing splendidly. The pony is a great treasure. I drop the reins on his neck and he stands for hours where I leave him. My boots are wearing out a bit now. I shall have to fall back on Tommies' ammunition boots. Shoemakers are unknown here as far as I can find out – though we have several at headquarters of my co: at Orange River.

Best love to all Ever you loving son Eric E. B. Wilson.

De Aar, Cape Colony   Sunday 5th November 1899

MARTIAL LAW DECLARED AT DE AAR

My dearest Father

Very many thanks for your letter dated Cotton Oct 13th. I also heard from Moonie by the same mail. All my letters go another 60 miles up the line, to my headquarters at Orange River Bridge (near Hopetown), before they reach me! We are fairly busy now, to put it in the mildest terms – that is to say we have to work on Sundays from 5.45 a.m. till 5 p.m. or dark, as well as other days of the week. During this week all the troops from Naauwport have come in here as we are concentrating a bit, as De Aar is such an important place and has such important supplies and stores collected that they do not want to run any risk.

We now have at De Aar: approx rifles

2nd Battalion K.O. Light Infantry	850
½ Battalion Berkshire Regiment	400
Yorkshire mounted Infantry	100
Rimingtons Horse	200
1½ Batteries Field Artillery	9 guns
2 nine pounders	2 guns
(my) 1 Hotchkiss Q.F. sixpr	1 gun
R. E. Detachments of 7th, 8th & 29th companies	120
and Army Service Corps etc	50
	1750

with four or five maxim guns.

A lot of extra Staff Officers etc have arrived – General Wood R. E. arrived today and is very pleased with our efforts so far, in attempting to defend a perimeter of about four miles and commanded by hills on West and East like being at the bottom of a horse trough.

He has appointed me Field Engineer here although there are now many other senior R.E. Officers – but of course it would be only natural after I had done five weeks pioneering here, and knew the value of every ant-heap.

Today we did one of our best pieces of work – we cleared a road up the side of a hill about 150 ft high, intensely steep and covered with boulders about six feet square – hauled a nine pounder field gun and limber up with about 12 mules and about 50 Kafirs, and cleared a platform for it on the top and left it in situ commanding the country all round, in two and a half hours.

I think some of our quiet rural labourers would be rather 'hustled' if they had to work at the pressure we are at now and find the difference between 'daily toil' and 'sweating blood by the second.' There is a strong rumour that the Free States intend to make a desperate effort to capture De Aar before the troops come out – it would paralyse our advance for a month or so – but if we can hold on for another week I think we shall be alright.

In Natal people are holding out splendidly – it was most unfortunate those 1200 men running out of ammunition and being surrounded, but every war has its little checks and crosses even though successful in the end.

Martial law means that all civilian population must obey military orders – and have to be in their houses at certain times etc., and bars shut by order etc., etc. Contravening some of these orders means being shot on short shrift! The last two days I have been working 11 hours each day on some hills 1½ miles away and 4500 ft above the sea making defences.

I shall keep this letter open till tomorrow when the mail goes – I was very glad to get Helen's letter – she seems much better – also magazines.

Monday night – mail just off – Have just heard of glorious victory near Ladysmith. Boers played treachery again with the white flag – reported 800 killed and 2000 prisoners. All well here.

Much love to all – Ever your loving son Eric E. B. Wilson.

Have just met Pigott, was in Cruikshanks, and cousin of Upchers etc – is now Capt in A.S.C.

De Aar   **Sunday 12th November 1899**

Too busy for more than "All's Well"

Tomorrow Monday 13th November 1899

My section of 7th Field Company and ½ Battalion King's Own Yorkshire Light Infantry march to Orange River – 70 miles – and shall take 4 – 5 days over it at least. I join my company again after 7 weeks hard work at De Aar – which will bear the impress of my hand for many a year in the way of roads up the hills – bridges – forts etc., etc., or as the papers say "De Aar is now strongly fortified."

While we are on the road – many troops will probably pass up by rail – and arrive before us. It is now 6.30 p.m. on Sunday and I have not yet got my orders for the march in detail – though I hear we start at 6 a.m.

Between now and then we have to strike our Camp and pack several tons of stores and equipment – so we shall be busy tonight.

They had fighting near Orange River on Friday – 3 officers killed 1 wounded – 3 men wounded – among the officers killed was H.C. Hall of Stogden's who failed for Woolwich when I got in – and afterwards went through Sandhurst to the 5th Fusiliers – a great Harrow friend of mine.

Best love to all – Have not got this week's mail yet but expect it at Orange River.

Ever your loving son Eric E. B. Wilson

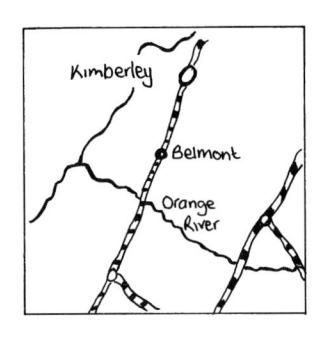

Orange River Camp   Friday 17th November 1899

My dearest Father,

Time being at a premium, am just snatching a moment to write you before we go on.
As my last note will have told you we left De Aar on Monday to march by road to Orange River – and arrived safely after five days marching of about 16 miles a day – and very hot indeed – no casualties in men or animals. The total march by ?road? (imaginary of course!) being about 80 miles – and we had to wind about a good bit to avoid the hills. On arrival at Orange River the band of the Northumberland Fusiliers played us into camp – where we rejoined the 7th company once more – minus one section still shut up in Kimberley with McClintock.
On arrival I found your letter of Oct 20 waiting for me and two hours later got yours of Oct 27 – both very welcome and interesting. No – I had no hand in Hope Town Bridge, though it was done by my company here by Boileau – who by the way was the R.E. Officer attached to Uncle Teddy's regiment for some time in the Chitral Expedition in India – Boileau swears by Uncle T. as one of the very best!
The situation here is briefly thus:– The 1st Division 1st Army Corps under Lord Methuen is collecting here and some or all of it (if all, about 10,000 men) including the 7th Field Company Royal Engineers and so – yours truly – are to start early next week – we believe Monday, to march to the relief of Kimberley – so we are in for hard fighting and no mistake.
We know there are two to three thousand Free State Boers waiting for us about 15 miles from here – at Belmont – where the skirmish was the other day – so there will be "wigs on the green" there to start with.
While we are marching, the Railway R.E. will be trailing along the line mending it at the many points at which the Boers have cut it and so bring our supplies and ammunition to us. This camp is very different to when I was up here five weeks ago – when it was a peaceful little station with half a battalion of Infantry and the 7th Company – now it is a seething buzz of

all arms – rough riders – guides – volunteers – war correspondents and the bulk of the 1st Division of the 1st Army Corps.

I made enquiries and found that Herbert Payne is not with the 11th Co: now so I do not know his whereabouts.

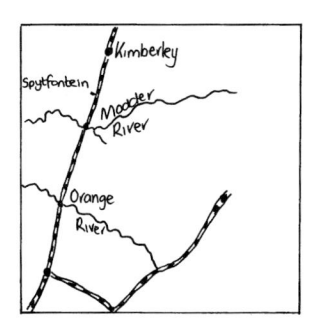

Modder River   Wednesday 29th November 1899

All well – Have taken the position at Modder River after a very terrible fight lasting all day yesterday – Fear our casualties must be heavy – Lord Methuen wounded in thigh – 7th Co R.E. lost three wounded (Sappers).

We had to sleep round the position last night after trying to assault all day – at 5.45 a.m. today I was sent along the line to see how things were and rode on and on and on expecting to be shot and found the village deserted – Love to all.

They consider it such a serious matter the knack these farmers have of picking off the officers, like poor Keith Falconer-Hall – and Wood last week – that all officers on this Column now starting have to wear accoutrements etc just like the men – even carrying a rifle and no sword. Mounted officers – like us – are wearing kit just like the mounted infantry, viz: bandolier and carbine – no sword or brown belts etc.

I forgot to tell you that it is a great bit of luck my company going up – as the 11th Field Company just out from England were on the paper to accompany the 1st Division – but Lord Methuen has since decided to take the 7th – and I think we deserve it really, as we have been pioneering here like niggers for two months and more or less know the ways and means of the country better than newcomers from England. Between you and me I hear he is extremely pleased with the work done by the company which may be another item in favour of our selection. The 11th are very good about it and not grumbling at all, as they see the force of our prior claims, and only one Field Company is told off to a division.

We are taking no tents and very light baggage – a waterproof sheet and two blankets – a pair of spare boots and a shirt being about the sum total of an officers kit – so if we have rain which means flood here – we shall have a roughish time.

I cannot say when I shall next catch a mail – perhaps Kimberley, perhaps Bloemfontein.

Love to all – ever your loving son Eric E. B. Wilson.

Modder River   Friday 8th December 1899

My dearest Father

Many thanks for your letter dated November 11th. I was very glad to get the good news of Moonie – I heard from her and also from Bertie by the same mail, I am so glad the nephew is a boy!

Am writing this sitting on the bank of the river where my men, having an hour 'easy,' are busy washing themselves and their garments and otherwise desporting themselves in the water.

The railway is across now after very hard work. We had to cut down about 20 feet solid, cutting down each bank to get a possible gradient to the water, over which the line is carried on crib piers of sleepers and 20 inches by 20 inches baulks of wood. We expect to advance now almost at once. We had to send a party down the line to Enselin siding yesterday as the Free State Boers made a dash and cut the line behind us there – but a few of our cavalry soon cleared them off and the railway men are now patching the line again.

We shall have a big fight at Spytfontein (pronounced Spatefontein) as soon as we advance. That will take us half way to Kimberley which is about 22 miles from here. We have been talking by signal with them over the Boers heads ever since our arrival. Their searchlight is very plain at night and we have one fitted up on a truck here.

Lord Methuen is alright again now after his wound. Captain Sidney Earle, Coldstream Guards who was on staff duty at De Aar and with whom I had much work in common was shot clean through the head at 1700 yards. The effective range of the rifles in use is enormous now. Our company were under fire for upwards of 13 hours, but we had a slight ridge covering us and only had 3 men hit and not seriously. Fox of the Yorkshires who was in Marshalls had his left arm shattered. Major Earle who marched our convoy up from De Aar shot through chest.

I think we leave the Northamptons and ½ Battalion North Lancs to hold Modder River while we are up at Kimberley. The 1st Division will have had its share of the fighting if we also go up through the Free State after this – as we expect about 4 clasps or so for this show alone by the time we reach Kimberley – as they always give one for each general engagement.

They had a Maxim Nordenfelt 1 pounder firing very rapidly at the fight here – it made the most awful row I have ever heard – the men call it pom-pom. I have one of the shells (unfired) left behind by them, also a fine Dutch family Bible which I am trying to bring along.

We had heavy rain last night so the dust is not so vicious as usual. Best love and New Year wishes to you all at Redgrave.

Ever your loving son Eric E.B. Wilson

Modder River   Friday 22nd December 1899

Many thanks for yours of 24th Nov: fear I missed last mail – not knowing when it left, and very busy. On the 11th we started with 5 days provisions to try and reach Kimberley – advanced about 4 miles and attacked enemy in great numbers and enormously strong position. After fighting all day found we could not penetrate – so returned to Modder 12 noon next day and have been here ever since.
Have thrown up entrenchments towards enemy, and mounted guns and bombard their works at intervals every day but Methuen does not seem inclined to advance further till reinforced.
All well and flourishing but very hard worked – 15 hours a day on the trenches.
We get native runners through to Kimberley every day or two – expect English mail today. First opportunity will write you fuller.

Love to all – Eric.

Modder River Camp   Friday 29th December 1899

My dearest Father,

The last time I shall put '99 on a letter, probably. Got yours of Dec. 1st in which you still believe me to be at De Aar, whereas I had safely passed through 3 general and victorious engagements.

I cannot say what tone the papers report the Magersfontein affair in – yet – but the facts are as follows: After repairing the railway and resting till 11th Dec, Lord Methuen decided to make his dash for Kimberley – we set out in 3 columns with 5 days provisions and marched about 4 miles north in the most howling rainstorm and pitchy blackness at dead of night. In the early dawn the Highland Brigade having marched further than they reckoned – blundered in 'close formation' right into the enemies' trenches. The shock and intensity of the enemies fire caused the leading companies to recoil on to the human column, and the loss of so many hundred men and most of the officers shot like cattle in a pen resulted in the loss of that critical rush forward when weight of numbers would have carried all before it, and they gradually waved back to about five or six hundred yards' distance. The other columns reached about the same line by degrees, but all the heart was gone out of the attack – the Boers were discovered to be in immense numbers – powerfully entrenched behind earthworks and after bombarding their trenches and raking their lines that day and night with artillery and rifle fire till noon the following day – the force was ordered back to Modder River – and gradually withdrew to camp. The Boers never stirred a yard from their trenches and had there been any water near us we were to have entrenched ourselves and remained 'in situ.' Since then, however, using Modder River as our base we have pushed forward earthworks nearly up to the same position and our heavy guns bombard them on and off every day, all along their trenches and laagers, which I should think must keep them very uneasy.

As regards the next advance in force – I fancy Methuen has been told to wait until some of the other columns are a little "forrarder", so we are fairly fixed here for some time. Rail and wire open, supplies and papers etc, etc, every day and regular service from Cape Town, and yet about 12,000 Boers only 5 miles off!!

I had a warm time at the end of the attack on Magersfontein as I was up with our firing line with tools etc., for entrenching (or burying) – and when the order to return to camp came up and our guns withdrew we fairly had hell let loose from their guns etc., shells bursting all round and over us.

On Boxing Day I went out with some cavalry and 2 guns to destroy a farm. About 4 miles up the Modder I blew down a farm and two houses successfully (Van McKerk's farm), and we returned to camp. They fired at us pretty continuously all the time, but I think they were a little sleepy with Xmas cheer as they only hit a few horses in about 2 hours firing, and we were right on top of them.

Our defences are nearly finished thank goodness – we have had very long hours lately.

Xmas Day was storms of dust, rain, flies and wind and not very cheerful. Troops all well and fit and longing to be at 'em again. They have drawn off Kimberley a bit to check us – so K is having quiet just now. Native runners easily get in and out of Kimberley to here, with dispatches.

Much love – your loving son Eric.

Modder River Camp   Thursday 4th January 1900

My dearest Father,

Unwonted luxury – a scratchy pen and some watery ink – just got yours of Dec 8th – mail unaccountably delayed this week. No exciting news this week – I have nearly finished entrenchments here and can now sit down and smoke in security.
We have closed in a bit round the Magersfontein ridge and Boer position – and hammer them at odd intervals of day and night with our heavy guns and Lyddite shell – as a rule we drop a heavy shell in their chief laager at about 2 or 3 a.m. just to give them something to wake up for!
Their guns reply most days but cannot reach our camp and never hit anything on the ridge our guns fire from – the 1st Jan however being an exception as one shell wounded two guardsmen working on an advanced redoubt we are making.
I hear Billy Darell is with the guards here – I must have met him and had his men working with me in the trenches a score of times but I haven't made his acquaintance since I heard of his being here.
Poor George Ray of the 5th Fusiliers was shot dead at Magersfontein – the officer I gave £60 to for old Fusilier in '96 and one of the very best men. He saw the old horse about 2 days before he (G.R.) was killed and wondered at his wonderful condition and stamina after the work he has done.
I dined with my old friends the King's Own Yorkshire Light Infantry last night, in my opinion the finest fighting battalion in South Africa – coupled with the 5th Fusiliers but they are hard men with fighting experience in the Indian Hills. Major Earle who marched us up from De Aar and was badly wounded has been invalided home, and Jim Fox of Marshall's (R.M.D. Fox) who had his left arm shattered is doing fairly well I hear.
A good lot of tobacco and pipes for the troops came this week – from various donors at home.
I have got a Dutch family bible here abandoned in their flight from Modder River which I shall try and bring back.
We have just got English papers with glowing accounts of our 3 victories – the varnish – padding – exaggeration and guessing between the lines are in some cases so funny that one wonders if one was there or not!
<u>Not one</u> Boer body was recovered from the river – though plenty were found lying on the bank – which was their line of defence. No-one here heard anything of a "truce for Xmas"! it sounded like the luncheon interval at cricket!! It so happened that we did not attack them that day.

I am sorry to hear Piers is not well – I am taking my turn with the Redgrave pheasants this year and being shot at – without a licence!!

Please remember me to Uncle R. and Aunt Amy next time you see them and thank Uncle R. for his dividend.

The heat is very great – flies very small but very numerous – dust smaller still but even more ubiquitous!

I should be glad of any English papers or magazines – serious or comic – as literature for spare moments is at a premium.

Tell Uncle George I think of him whenever I see a new animal – a bird with new habits, sound or flight and wish I had time to describe them all to him.

Tell him that while I was lying flat on my face on the billiard table-like plain facing Modder River listening to the ceaseless whiz and whirr of bullets flying over and striking all round, I saw what I thought was a few sticks and bits of dried grass crawling along – I picked it up and it turned out to be some species of insect or grub, with a coating of natural glue or viscous fluid with which it carefully dressed itself up to "match" the ground it was traversing. As I have since seen the same grub in different costumes – I know this is a common phenomenon in the insect world, but this was an interesting case. Please don't print this episode however. I wished at the time that we had similar powers and also the same stature as the caterpillar!!

Many of the Highlanders had the backs of their knees so blistered from lying all day in the blazing sun that they could not walk for days afterwards.

We are all anxiously waiting to hear of further progress by Buller and Gatacre – as it is no good our pushing on till they have made some more headway.

Please convey my best wishes to Edward and Mary Bloomfield, also to Chris' if he is still with you. I am glad Helen is going on so well – give her my best love when next you write.

We are gradually repairing the big girder bridge over the river – destroyed by the Boers on Oct 14 and the first thing that isolated Kimberley.

We are collecting large stores of food and ammunition – this place will probably be our advanced depot for operations further north in due time.

Much love to all at home – Ever your loving son Eric E.B. Wilson.

Modder River
Jan 12th 1900

All quiet and well here — no particular news to record this week — extremely busy all day looking after my section of the defences — about 3 miles — and strengthening all weak points — as they seem determined we shall be secure from attack while we stay here — the lie of the ground roughly may interest you.

Modder River   **Friday 12th January 1900**

All quiet and well here – no particular news to read this week – extremely busy all day looking after my section of the defences – about 3 miles – and strengthening all weak points, as they seem determined we shall be secure from attack while we stay here – the lie of the ground roughly may interest you.

Modder River   **Friday 19th January 1900**

My dearest Father

Many thanks for yours of December 22nd.
We still remain quietly here – in general ignorance of the plans and schemes of our forces elsewhere.
No news from Natal for five days except a wire today saying Buller has crossed the Tugela.
We made 'demonstrations' in force towards Kimberley on Tuesday and Wednesday and heavily shelled the enemies' trenches and strongholds in the Magersfontein hills, but did not attack.
Still very hard work for the R.E. here, no rest from one month to another – making roads and bridges and adding to fortifications etc. We have several more heavy guns up now and bombard the enemy at all hours. Constant rumours that they are short of food etc., and sick of it – but I don't expect they will leave till our forces elsewhere 'poultice' them back to their own lands – or we are reinforced sufficiently to turn them out.
Heavy rain today – the river rising rapidly and threatening to wash away our temporary railway bridge.
I have been very busy rigging up a horse ferry this week – it is now working. At present I am working in the big gun pits making magazines etc., and watching the shelling.

Love to all – Your loving son Eric

Modder River Camp   Friday 26th January 1900

My dearest Father,

Just realised in rush of work that today is mail day – for once the incoming mail has beaten the outgoing and I have just received letters from you Dec 29 – Moonie Jan 4 – Helen Dec 16 and Aunt Julia – Chamonix Dec 31st. I did not receive any letters last mail, I fancy you wrote in between the mails somehow and one has missed.

I have spent all this week 5 a.m. to 10 a.m. and 2 p.m. to 7 p.m. with 2½ miles each way = 10 miles putting up barbed wire obstacles in front of one of our big guns on the outpost ridge, the guns meanwhile banging away merrily at uncertain intervals just over our heads. Most terrifying but quite safe – only two Boer shells came over our way and they went a couple of hundred yards over – but sounded close enough.

I am also clearing out a well in front of our outposts to supply them with water – it is about 90 feet deep through rock and has got rather choked up with silt etc. I was lowered by rope to inspect it and found about 9 feet of water – very hot and bad smelling – while I was being 'bumped' up – a Boer shell came over – and I'm glad to say the men did not let go of the rope! which they might well have done.

We have had splendid views of the Boers and their trenches with glasses and through the big naval telescope – and have been dropping Lyddite shells into any groups of them that look worth scattering.

Anxiously waiting news of advance Natal side – they seem to be getting on alright so far.

You will be sorry to hear that Fusilier is very ill indeed with pneumonia and laminitis – fever in the feet from hot sand etc – I fear I shall lose him – and he has been so fit up to date and a wonderful soldier's hunter and charger to me – still I couldn't expect him to go last for ever and he has been through four general engagements where many good horses have been lost.

We had a terrific storm yesterday – sheets of corrugated iron flying through the air – one made straight for our horses – I tried to intercept it – luckily missed – it and it swept full; into the middle of the troop horses – most providentially injuring none though causing great stampede.

We have just received our Queen's chocolate – a most acceptable present. Intensely hot and flysome.

I have just got some photos taken by me at De Aar and printed in Cape Town. Very successful some of them.

Send me any odd papers when you think of it – nothing is so prized as the English papers or magazines.

Two of our De Aar staff in the early days of the war are gone – Sidney Earle of the Coldstreams and Mackenzie of the R.H.A – (buying horses) – one shot at Modder – the other enteric, and such nice men.

Best love to all at Redgrave – Ever your loving son Eric E.B. Wilson

Modder River   Friday 2nd February 1900

My dearest Father,

Just got yours of Jan 12 from Montgreenan – you must have enjoyed your visit.

We have great moves impending here – more troops are arriving daily and the Essexs, Buffs, Cheshires, Oxford Light Infantry and Yorks Regiments are already here. We expect the bulk of the 7th Division, and also expect Lord Roberts to be here shortly – and though nothing is known it points to this place being made a base for operations possibly Eastward – at present it only means enormously increased work for the R.E. here preparing additional water supply, bakeries etc., etc.

The heat and flies are very much in evidence at present. We hear that Buller has chosen a stiffish road to Ladysmith, and only drew back to try another just in time before things got too hot for the column.

I am meeting many old Curragh friends in the Oxford Light Infantry, cricketers etc. Our men are in very good health considering the terribly hard work they have been through every day since early September. I now have only 3 N.C.O's (in my section of 50) out of 7 – other 4 down South sick – I am very fit myself and scaled 11st 8lbs the other day with practically nothing on. It is very lucky I didn't get the exchange to 23rd Co. I applied for as I should now be in Ladysmith or possibly in the shoes of poor Digby Jones or Denniss, two of the 23rd Subalterns!

Just off to work again – Best love – Ever your loving son Eric E.B. Wilson.

Modder River   Friday 9th February 1900

My dearest Father,

Just found your letter of Jan 19 awaiting my return to camp – also one from Aunt Minnie, please send her a line from me and thank her as I cannot tell when I may be able to write to her personally.

I do not expect to be able to catch this mail as we have only just come in from an expedition, I will describe it presently, after marching all night and day and well nigh done up – you must excuse me if I am a little incoherent, hard work and little sleep is the cause.

Well the even tenor of our regular if severe work at this camp was broken on Sat last ?Feb 3rd by the 7th Field Co being turned out at 11 p.m. and told to pack up ready to start marching at 5 a.m. – and as during our long stay here and various jobs had tended to 'spread' our equipment, tools etc., it was no easy work loading everything up in the dark at short notice.

We left our baggage and tents and a few sick and weakly behind and marched off and then found that we were to join MacDonald of the Highland Brigade for some little job <u>down</u> the river at Koodoesberg Drift about 20 miles West – on the Riet.

We camped 7 miles out at the first drift or ford West of here that day – Fraser's Drift and the following day marched the other 13 miles and a terribly hot and trying one too – we were with the advanced guard and had to cover more ground than the main body – the Highlanders in front of us fell down like flies after about ten miles of it – sun, fatigue and previous hard work etc and I was very proud of our men who stuck to it splendidly – hardly any unable to keep up and none left right behind – two highlanders died and I think over 100 had to be sent for with ambulances in the evening.

Well, we got to Koodoesberg at about 11.30 a.m. I think and rested that day. I then heard that we were to build a fort there to prevent the Boers using the ford and leave 200 men – then return to Modder – 4 days in all.

However the next day we had just begun digging when news came of "Boers about", so the infantry were sent out scouting ahead, and the R.E. were sent up the Koodoes-Berg – a hill about 500 feet high by a mile long and shaped like a dumbbell bent into a horseshoe, with the hollow towards the river, to hastily put up a few walls of rocks and stone to hold the highest end of the Berg. Berg – Kop – Kopjie is the dutch sequence of 'sizes' for hills.

We worked from 8 a.m. to 4 p.m. through the heat of the day on a biscuit and very little water. We were just collecting our tools to return to camp when we saw a swarm of Boers about 600 strong galloping over the plain from the

North chasing half-a-dozen of our cavalry scouts in front of them about 4,000 yards off.

We signalled into camp to get the troops out and proceeded to man our half-finished trenches on the hill-side – and were joined by a company of Highland Light Infantry soon afterwards who proceeded to make a wall at right angles to ours and so isolate our end of the hill.

Soon after the 9th Lancers turned out on our right and rode out to meet the Boers and assist their scouts in. The Boers then dismounted and fired at them as they saw they couldn't catch the scouts – they killed one lancer and checked the main body who then opened fire with their Maxim on the Boers who mounted and swept on round to the south west end of the hill.

Nothing took place then for nearly an hour – when suddenly ping-ping-zip-zip came a shower of bullets at us from the other end of the hill.

They had scaled the western end and were going to try and occupy the hill <u>still</u> completely unaware that <u>any</u> troops were on the <u>top</u>!

The H.L.I. were holding the trench facing the fire and replied with interest. We were flanked by it and below the top of the hill so could not fire at them – this went on till dark and luckily with no casualty to our men. All night we were very much on the qui vive but though prevented from resting, all was quiet.

Next day a few stray shots only and a few down west towards the river and at 4 p.m. we were relieved by the Seaforths and returned weary and done up to camp on the river.

Next morning the attack was renewed by the Boers and to our surprise, at 9.30 a.m. a gun opened fire from the top of the hill at their end! Shelling our men with shrapnel at 1400 yards range only! That was what they had been so quiet over the day before – dragging their gun up.

However out came our guns from camp and four of them kept it quiet and what had been treated as a game of bagatelle on the hill top between our pickets and a few Boers became something of more importance and men began to get killed and wounded – three companies of Seaforths held the hill that day and the rest of the brigade started to work round the hill to cut the Boers off from the river at their end and then clear the hill for the cavalry to catch 'em on the run on the North side. The Boers had not wasted time, however, and were holding Sandheuvel Drift by now firmly nor were they dislodged that night.

In the evening some cavalry and guns came in to join the fun from Modder by wire but the 'Heavies' who charged the Boers still hanging about the N.W. of the hill charged a wire fence instead and had 6 men shot slightly – so came the dark.

Next day, in fact I must have come to yesterday, at 3.30 a.m. a strong party including us went for them down at Sandheuvel drift but the bird had flown on scenting our strength. The Highlanders at last decided to sweep the Berg from end to end finding only a good few Boer dead.

The cavalry and guns were just in time to dust them up as they fled to the North back to their hills in the purlieus of Kimberley and we returned to camp to go on with our much interrupted fort and have a good bathe in the river and rest – but war is a hard master – a wire came from Modder – "Back you come – fort or no fort – wanted here" etc., (this in metaphor) and at 6 p.m. off we started for Modder again – cool and half moon luckily. Fraser's Drift 11.30 p.m., rest till 8 a.m., back at Modder 11 a.m. and what a change!! As our tired grimy little week old column came in to join the guards and 9th brigade as usual, what did we see? Acres and acres of new tents – new horses – new white-faced Englishmen, new guns – in fact the Seventh Division had arrived – Lords Roberts and Kitchener were here and all was hum and buzz. Evidently something is going to happen – please God our tired men get a few hours' rest first. I feel as if we came here in the early sixties!!

By the way, our week at Koodoesberg cost us I think 3 officers and about 6 men killed and about 30 wounded – Boers about 15 or 20 killed and ? wounded. Probably about 100 in all chiefly from our guns – F.G. Tait the golf player was killed and buried there – I needn't add that we (R.E.) had a warmish time that first day on the hill and were lucky to have no-one hit. Bullets were cheap that day had they been intended for a billet in one of us. Have just had time to glance at an English paper or two. They seem absurdly feverish at home, and talk the most awful rubbish about 'gravity' of the situation etc. It is very annoying to the troops here, as all are confident and contented with ultimate success as if it were only a game of opening tins with a knife which kept breaking or bending. As soon as the knife is strong enough open will come the tin, and we shall laugh at the way we cut our fingers at first. A box of socks etc has just arrived addressed to Boileau and the men are wild with delight, other goods, tobacco etc, are invoiced – I think this must be the consignment you refer to as having a share in ?

Best love to all – I think you have my week's news –

Ever your loving son Eric E.B. Wilson

By the way Fusilier has recovered wonderfully and though far from well, is not so ill as he was – and stands up, walks to water etc, now.

Paardeberg Drift, Orange Free State   **Thursday 22nd February 1900**

9th Division Camp – on the Modder River

<u>All Well</u>

Sending this back by sick convoy. The pursuit of Cronje's disorganised rabble is now almost over – we hope they will surrender tonight.

Best love – your loving son Eric E.B. Wilson

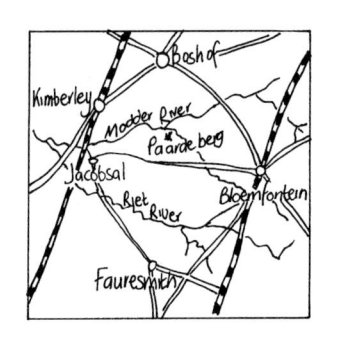

Paarde Berg Camp on the **Wednesday 28th February 1900**
Modder River Orange Free State

My dearest Father

I wonder if you ever got a scrap of paper I sent off after the fight here on Sunday week, in an official envelope?
Hitherto great stress of work and marching every night has prevented me writing, and only the hand of Providence protecting me on the morning of the 27th enables me to now write you of my doings since we left our long-pitched camp at Modder. I have received no mail or news of the outer world since about Feb 9th or so – I will trace my movements for you since then.
On our return from our little expedition with the Highland Brigade 20 miles west to the Koodoes Berg Drift – a very hard week too – we found Modder Camp filled up with acres of new tents and troops – which proved to be the 6th and 7th Division – Lords Roberts and Kitchener were also there.
They then formed a 9th Division, composed of the Highland Brigade under General MacDonald consisting of the:

> Highland Light Infantry
> Seaforth Highlanders
> Argyll & Sutherland Highlanders and
> Black Watch

and the 19th Brigade: Duke of Cornwall's Light Infantry
> 1st Royal Canadians (volunteers)
> Shropshires
> Gordon Highlanders

under General Smith-Dorrien (Brigadier), the Division being commanded by General Sir Henry Colvile – other odd troops with us were the city volunteers, Kitchener's Horse etc.
Well, to this scratch Division the veteran 7th Field Company R.E. were posted as Divisional Engineers – you will remember we were usurpers with Methuen's (1st) Division, as we supplanted the 11th Co. at Orange River on

their first arrival, by Lord Methuen's request; so we have now left them with the 1st Division at Modder; and come in for all the work and worry and marching (and I hope the honours) of a practically fresh campaign.

After due concentration, the 6th, 7th, and 9th Divisions with extras – and French's independent Cavalry Division – took the field on Feb 12th by marching South to Enslin (2 stations down) and striking over the border East into the Orange Free State.

Feb 13th Marched to Ramdam 9 miles and bivouacked – for the first time in the (?)Free State.

Feb 14th Struck N.E. to the Riet River at Waterval Drift after pushing back a few prowling Boers.

Feb 15th Along the Riet west, to 4 miles short of Jacobsdal – 16th Entered Jacobsdal at last and camped. Fine market square, post office etc., for a small veldt townlet. Here I bought a fine pair of chickens for the mess from a Boeress who was unable or too frightened to name a price – so I think I dealt well with her under the circumstances by paying 5/= for the pair!

The whole town was given up to Boer hospitals and doctors – as all the Modder and Magersfontein wounded had been sent here. I could not buy any bread or flour which we badly wanted – biscuit of course to carry with us (and hatchets to cut it with) nor butter, eggs or milk – these I have not tasted for some while.

We heard that General French was through to Kimberley with his cavalry and that the Boers from there and Magersfontein had fled hastily East towards Bloemfontein and North over the Vaal – in great haste.

Feb 17th. On to Klip Drift on the Modder where the 6th Division had just caught the tail of Cronje's column of Boers trekking East and were harrying them.

Feb 18th. One hour's sleep and on to Paarde Berg Drift by 5 a.m. where we found the Boers had laagered their wagons and entrenched themselves on the River banks – terrific fight all day ended in our heading them off from the East and closing them in on the other sides and causing them to quit their entrenchments and entrench anew about two miles move to the East, where they made themselves secure in hundreds of holes and gorges and nullaks amongst and around their wagons.

After bombarding them on and off for a week or so while we closed the net around them by trenching every night a little nearer, we finally established a long trench about 500 yards from their main defences and waited a while. Finally on the night of the 26th it was arranged that 480 Canadians with the 7th Field Company, 42 men and 4 officers, should steal forward at 2 a.m. in the chill morning and try and establish a lodgement or trench as close as possible to their trenches, ready to hold them or even rush them as soon as light came. Well all night work is chancy stuff and this was no exception – the Canadians advanced as arranged and we followed ten paces behind carrying a pick and shovel per man. The orders were " When fired on all will lie down at once and entrench if possible on the spot and hold on."

I forgot to say that half the Canadians were supposed to have brought (and <u>had</u> been issued with) shovels for entrenching, but by some blunder most of them left them behind – however we stealthily pushed on and on through the bushes and trees and dark brambles – passed over some fairly open ground to a slight rise in the ground – to say it was jumpy work <u>knowing</u> that we only left cover <u>400 yards</u> from the Boers! would be a mild description – I don't think my heart beat once that night! Reached as I said a slight rise in the now quite open hard flat ground, not a bush or shrub in sight – when BANG – CRASH – BANG – BANG – BANG – CRASH – BANG – CRASH came from a perfect hell of rifles seemingly right in our very faces.

Down went every mother's son as flat and as hard onto his dear mother earth as any pancake. The man next to me charged me flying into a nice little rut about a few inches – blessed inches – deep, spraining my little finger and digging my rifle into the ground muzzle first. There we lay till the fury of the first firing expended itself – for a while we heard our own rifles answering back word for word – remember <u>we</u> could not fire as we knew we had Canadians ten yards ahead also lying down firing – and when after what seemed ages and all eternity the fire dropped for a moment, the silence was only broken by the low agonised groans of the wounded and the click of the rifles being loaded and opened.

Well how we spent the next few hours I shall never quite remember – sufficient to say that in the hundred and one intervals between the ringing vollies which shrieked over our heads into the night and the fit-fit of bullets throwing up showers of earth in our mouths we dug – yes stolidly dug, a trench about 3 feet wide and 3 feet deep with a very respectable bank of earth in front of it and lay there wondering how the light would break, and where were the Canadians? Should we be rushed and surrounded or should we be reinforced by masses of our own troops.

Well, by daylight we had about 40 Canadians and all our men in this trench about 50 yards long – and over the river bank – and realised that the Canadians – small blame to them – had broken and fled under the blast of the storm, and instead of lying flat and quiet like our veterans, had – madness – got up and run back to the old trenches – a quarter of a mile through the woods – where some of them actually jumped over onto the bayonets of the astonished outposts (Gordons) <u>excepting,</u> (to be fair), the forty odd, who retiring over our commencing trench, had joined in and worked with us till daylight.

<u>Their</u> casualties by hearsay I believe were about 9 killed and 30 or more wounded – R.E. casualties NOT-ONE-SCRATCH!!! I have wandered with you to daylight now – when our little force looked over the parapet to see the Boer trench facing us 95 short puny yards off!! We banged into them with a will and in a quarter of an hour out came a man with a white flag to say that Cronje surrendered unconditionally that we could take them all over to our camp and do what we would with their arms and belongings.

<u>TOTAL BAG</u>	General Cronje	1
	Transvaalers	2,592
	Orange Free State	1,327
	Wounded of sorts	161
		4,081

including Albrecht their gunner chief and engineer in chief. God forbid that I should accredit any of this to one or other unit or battalion, as three Divisions had been hammering them and <u>dribbling the ball up the field,</u> but I think I may claim that the 1st Royal Canadians and the 7th Field Company R.E.

KICKED THE GOAL!!

That afternoon, after our visit to their deserted laager – miles of wagons burnt and gutted – piles of rifles – many thousands more than the men captured – millions of cartridges – saddles – clothes – and every article in vanity fair – trenches and rifle pits in all directions, Lord Roberts addressed the Canadians and our company on parade and told us that we had done well. To us he said that he remembered addressing us at Newbridge Station on leaving the Curragh and hoping that we should uphold the honour of the Corps, and he was proud to say we had not only done so but added to its good records.

Truly this was a glorious <u>Anniversary of Majumba</u> – February 27th – four thousand misguided but brave men laying down their arms to a handful of Englishmen. I fear I may have painted our share too vividly but we are only human and God knows I do not want to boast – and there is much hard work still before us should He still spare us to carry it out for Him.

We have had heavy rains the last few days making our work hard and our wet beds in wet clothes not pleasant on sodden ground. We (the men not the officers) have also been a little short of food as a heavy convoy was attacked and lost down country somewhere owing to lack of proper escort and it has taken time to replace the stores and wagons and oxen lost – valued at about £100,000 – who is to blame I do not know. Horses have been put on 6lb of corn only – ponies nil – mules nil. Supposed to "graze", a pretty sarcasm on sand and scrubby bushes – The stink from thousands of dead animals killed in the fighting is almost intolerable – hundreds drifted down the river from the Boers before we took them.

McClintock should join us from Kimberley with 50 men of the Company today – he will tell us about the siege. I met a Kimberley officer, Clifford of the North Lancs – who was shot through the scalp – grooving his skull, a very close "shave" for which he is none the worse. I told him chaffingly (thinking of Mrs Squeers at Dotheboys Hall) that another "couple of inches"(!) lower and it might have entered his brain! Did she not have a backcomb driven into her head by someone?

What is the meaning of Sir T. Tacon? Is it party funds or Mayoral remuneration?

Best love to all at home – please send on to Moonie as I haven't time to duplicate.

Ever your loving son Eric E.B. Wilson

P.S. I am in excellent health and spirits – clothes and boots a bit ragged but otherwise twice the man in all round health, thank God!

The officers R.E. in the night assault were

Col Kincaid
Capt Boileau
Lieut Wilson
Lieut Musgrave
} and 42 N.C.O s and men 7th Co I believe.

Did I tell you that Major Sir W. K. Jenner Bart. has a son and heir – I am so glad for both their sakes, as they were very good friends to me at the Curragh and one hardly expected the event, all things considered.

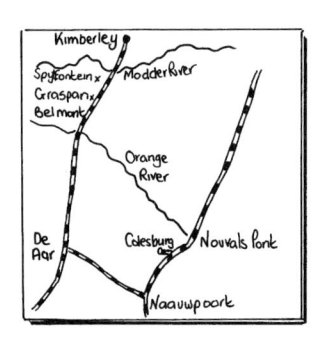

Kimberley Club, Kimberley, South Africa Saturday 24th March 1900

My dearest Father

A line to say I got yours of Feb 2 and 9 also some magazines – very acceptable indeed – at Bloemfontein on the 20th.

On the 21st I was despatched by rail to pick up our heavy baggage – tents etc, left at Modder (Feb 11th).

I had a most interesting journey round 400 odd miles – via Norvals Pont, (blown down, ferry over river), Naauwpoort, Colesberg and all the 'Gatacre' country to my old haunt De Aar! where I spent some hours between trains, saw old friends and scenes etc, which I enjoyed intensely – on that night (22nd) to Modder over the old Orange River – Belmont – Graspan – country to Modder – about 8 a.m. 23rd where I found all our baggage, sick men, etc, had been moved on for storage at Kimberley.

I wasn't sorry for the excuse either, and on I came – arrived Kimberley through the Magersfontein Spytfontein positions – very interesting if only one had forty eyes! – at about 6 p.m. last night.

Found our stuff in camp about a mile off – but cannot get railway transport south for a day or two owing to block of traffic so am fixed right up here! Meals at the famous Club – diggings in town – met McInnes R.E. who did pilot – shall probably get back B'Fontein middle next week – all well.

Plenty to see here – great luck my being the one sent – others I know dying to see Kimberley etc.

Saw Musgrave in hospital, you remember he was sent back from Paardeberg with enteric – he is making good recovery and seems very cheerful.

I slept in a BED last night for the first time since I left Wynberg in September!!! I have slept in many places since but always on the ground sometimes under a wagon, sometimes in a swamp. Can you imagine the comfort.

Kimberley though of large acreage is nearly all one storey and tin – better shops etc., but not so fine or picturesque a town as Bloemfontein – no scenery, dead flat ground and mine shafts etc, all round – more like our Black Country districts – breathes nothing but mining and diamonds etc.

Bloemfontein more the Haslemere type – allowing always of course for the surrounding veldt, thousands of miles more desolate than Rushford Heath!

This town does not seem much the worse for bombardment – few holes in walls – and shops full of shells, bullets and curios etc, connected with the siege.

I saw the big gun made by De Beers workshops – a marvellous production from a military point of view – they made and loaded own shells etc, each shell had "Comp^{ts}..C.J.R." on them, a pretty sarcasm of Rhodes!!

I believe a few had some of Kruger's favourite texts! – one being "Thousands shall flee at the rebuke of one!", rather clever!

Much love, ever your loving son Eric E.B. Wilson.

Kimberley Club, Kimberley   Sunday 1st April 1900

My dearest Father,

Still at Kimberley! The line to the south has been so blocked all the week with traffic for all parts that they have been unable to despatch my load of luggage and stores of the 7th Co: which were left at Modder when we marched and which I was sent round to collect.

Well the nett result has been ten days complete and idle holiday for me and three good meals a day at the Club!! Expensive holiday but very acceptable after roughing it for the past six months. There are several more officers in the same situation, sent round from Bloemfontein and unable to return!

My letter therefore this week is essentially a peaceful one! My war news is read and not witnessed for the present.

I have met a lot of old acquaintances passing through Kimberley – amongst others a certain Whittaker of the Suffolk Yeomanry with whom I have played mud cricket at Drinkstone and who is a great friend of Raymond's. I hear R is somewhere up this side but has not appeared in Kimberley yet.

I have just got a letter from Mother dated Mar 9 as the 7th Co: mails again found their way to Kimberley. Please thank her very much for it – I am very sorry to hear of Charlie R.G.'s sad death – Mother reports that Rowland has a son and heir! I am glad – I hope the boy will flourish.

All this week I have passed in leisure – visiting diamond mines – the defences of the siege – and Herbert Musgrave in the town hospital. He is recovering well from his fever and is getting light food, and has cheered up wonderfully since my daily visits. No doubt Modder water saturated with dead oxen etc, was the cause.
My capability of being able to do with little to drink has stood me in wonderful stead during the campaign – and though at times I have had to drink water that required scraping out of a mug to convey it to your mouth, as a rule I have subsisted on tea and cocoa made with boiled mud – no spirits except on rare occasions a nip of neat whisky or brandy – such as when we had to ford the Modder chest high in pouring rain at night and sleep all night as we were , in six inches of chilly mire! at Paardeburg.
The Kimberley mosquito is a most determined animal and dines freely off one at night to the detriment of one's rest.
Probably as soon as I return to Bloemfontein we shall advance again to the north where we shall have some very severe fighting when the republicans get their backs against the wall.
On Tuesday Helen will I believe be 23 – I am so glad she is keeping so well – give her and all my best love if with you.
I think Mother will probably have done so – but it would be as well to give any clothing sent home in my cases an occasional shake!
In spite of the optimism of the papers and others – I have grave doubts as to the ultimate fate of Mafeking – they are so far north from here and Plumer has but a small force to relieve with, and though the military loss of the garrison would be insignificant – they have made such a magnificent defence that it would be very hard for them to await the end of the war in Pretoria.
I am sorry to see the death of Sir Donald Stewart – poor Lady Jenner has a very sad time now, with the loss of the heir to the title, so unexpected and so welcome, followed by the death of her father – such a magnificent old warrior. The present generation hardly realise with their military idols of the moment that he belonged to a generation that educated our present generals – and actually ordered Roberts on his famous march to Candahar.
I fear the leniency with which we appear to be treating the cape rebels will have a serious reaction on the loyal colonists if strong measures are not taken – they feel deeply that their loyalty has not been acknowledged – when their next door farmer joins the rebels with a gun and after robbing him of his cattle and corn – gets captured – is sent home and is told not to do it again – and keeps his ill-gotten plunder, while the loyal farmer is

insulted and ruined. They ought to publicly shoot half a dozen on market day in the chief towns of the tainted districts, fine the others heavily – disenfranchise and disable from civil rights for a period. That would put the fear of God into the rest.

I have just met an officer I met in the 17th Lancers who was beseiged in Ladysmith. He says it was a nearer thing than people thought – 2 days would have absolutely exhausted meal and corn foods – and disease from meat alone would soon have crippled the rest. It is difficult to realise the intense value of elementary food and water in bountiful England.

We are all very anxious to see the final chapter now – and hope that ultimate success may be speedy.

I have no sympathy with those who talk of the 'sport' and 'fun' of a campaign, you don't hear much of it after two or three real blood-letting fights.

Much love to all at home, ever your loving son, Eric E.B. Wilson

Naauwpoort Junction, Cape Colony   Sunday 8th April 1900

My dearest Father,

I succeeded in getting away from Kimberley with my truck load of baggage last Tuesday but my triumph was short-lived! We sailed gaily enough through De Aar and round to Naauwpoort and then got brought up short with a bang – and run into a siding where we have been ever since – the truck – my house – the station restaurant my home!

This was because word was sent down from Bloemfontein that nothing but troops and grub were to go up for the present and all baggage was to be off-loaded at Naauwpoort. We are getting quite a colony of derelict officers and acres of baggage in stacks. So that my holiday is getting rather prolonged now!

I have wired of course many times to the 7th Co to report progress (!) but have had no response.

Two events occurred since I landed at N'poort – first I found that my dear old Fusilier whom I had left sick at Modder when we marched for Bloemfontein had been sent to the N'poort remount depôt and by them had been sent on to the 7th Co at Bloemfontein – fit – so he should be awaiting me there all well, secondly, the second day here, I was strolling round the camp wondering who the various militia etc., encamped here were, when I heard an unmistakeable shout of 'Eric'. I looked round and saw Raymond.

The Suffolk yeomanry have since moved up to Colesberg. I dined with them the night before they left. Raymond was very well and had been with Kitchener to Prieska just before. By the way the last homeward mail was partly if not almost entirely lost on the Mexican. So I am in doubt which letter if any may fail to reach you – my last two were both from Kimberley, one saying I had been sent round from Bloemfontein for baggage – the other to say I was still at Kimberley – so you can trace the missing one if any. The Boers still seem, to be giving trouble east and north east of Bloemfontein. I see my division (Colvilles') has been out north and back since I left – without doing much apparently.

I am writing this on the top of my truck under some difficulties!

I was glad to see Cambridge won the Boat Race so easily.

It will be very annoying if the mail is lost, as being idle in Kimberley I wrote off a good many arrears of correspondence.

They have an enormous hospital camp here – 600 beds. I have met several invalids I knew. Enteric simply raging but very few fatal cases luckily.

A detachment of volunteer R.E. and one officer have just gone through here to join the 7th Co. I however am a part of and inseparable from my baggage! I expect a good accumulation of mail at Bloemfontein viz. Feb 16 and 23 from home, (I have Mar 2 and 9) and Mar 16th possibly.

Best love to all at home Ever your loving son Eric E.B. Wilson.

Bloemfontein Wednesday 18th April 1900

My dearest Father

By chance and good luck I managed to get my truck load of stores and baggage put on a train going North from Naauwpoort on Good Friday – so I once more found myself in Bloemfontein after some 3 weeks absence. To my surprise the 7th Co were still camped on the same piece of ground to west of town – though they had been out twice for short expeditions. Since my return the weather has been miserable – the cold season would be on now anyhow but the rains should be over – but we are having it very cold and wet every day at present, just like an English November. It is very trying for the horses and men, especially the latter who have to sleep in the mire. I found the company very busy superintending the defences of the town which are being carried out to enable a small force to hold it when we advance. This means work for the officers nearly as arduous as Modder River – 6 a.m. to 6 p.m. daily – (dark at 5.30 p.m.) So under ordinary circumstances one has no time even for letter writing. Today it is so wet that work has been abandoned for the morning and I hasten to seize the opportunity. You will be sorry to hear that Denis Murch has been shot through both lungs from side to side – but they say he will recover with luck, he has been sent south – here he would have got pneumonia at once I fear. I went to the Cathedral Easter afternoon and heard a good organ for a treat. On my return I found awaiting me 4 letters from you dated Feb 16 and 23 and Mar 16 and 23 which I opened in due sequence. You remember I got two mails at Kimberley by a lucky mistake, also a Diss Express, 2 papers from Uncle Rowland and 2 splendid parcels of things from Aunt

Minnie with things for self and men, which they appreciate immensely. Boileau also has received consignments which he tells me include goods from my people.

I have heard nothing of Ozzy Du Pont since we were at Cape Town – where I got a letter from him. Capt. Ottley of the Yorkshire Light Infantry, a great friend of mine who showed me round when I lived with them at Wynberg, has broken his collarbone and been taken prisoner, as the result of a fall from his horse. Raymond left Naauwpoort long before I did, I fancy they went to Colesberg.

It was very interesting coming up through all the Arundel – Reisberg – Colesberg country. I saw Suffolk Hill where the Suffolks came to grief. The Boers had destroyed every bridge and culvert up the line, but they have all been repaired now except Norval's Pont where we have a low level bridge in working order and are building the big iron bridge by degrees.

We have no news as to when we are likely to advance from here, probably not until the districts to East and South have been well cleared.

Boileau has been taken away to form a new unit to work with Mounted Infantry – a small body of mounted Sappers. We have been reinforced by 1 officer and 25 men from the Middlesex Volunteer Engineers – who are very keen and well-nourished at present. I never saw such a sight as our men were when I returned with their kits and clothings. They had marched and fought and worked in one suit of thin khaki for months – some had no clothes on to speak of – mere fragments – and other were mended with bits of corn sacks etc., still, they are very hard now. There is a lot of enteric about now we are halted – several deaths a day – but troops are pouring up the line almost as fast as we can get food for them.

The shops in the town are cleared out and they of course are unable to procure stores as the single rail barely serves the military requirements.

I have not yet found Fusilier – at Naauwpoort they said he had been sent there – but he seems not to have arrived yet. I doubt if I shall ever see him now. He has probably been issued as a remount.

I have heard from Muriel recently – also from her friend K.B.N. of Baltimore.

Much love to all at home – ever you loving son Eric E.B. Wilson.

P.S. Many thanks for March magazine.

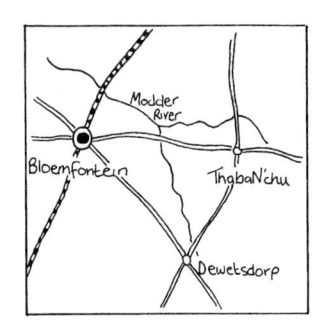

Detached Post at Israel's Poort,   Sunday 29th April 1900
35 miles East of Bloemfontein,
5 miles West of ThabaNchu.

My dearest Father,

I write to you from a good many different addresses nowadays – my last was on my return from my wanderings after baggage to Bloemfontein – now I am writing from an isolated mountain pass overlooking the town of ThabaNchu, where I have been left with my section, a Company of Gordon Highlanders and a Company of Norfolk Mounted Infantry, about 200 rifles all told under Captain Meyricke of the Gordons – to hold this pass or 'poort' behind the column which has gone on to ThabaNchu to join hands with French, and Rundle with the 8th Division.

On Monday 23rd the 7th Company got orders late at night to march at daybreak with the Highland Brigade towards Bushman's Hoek and the Waterworks – 22 miles distant to support the advance of our other brigade of the 9th Division (19th Brigade under Smith-Dorrien) who had started a few days before and now were reported to have recaptured the waterworks and to be pushing on towards ThabaNchu.

Well, we marched off in a great hurry at short notice and no time or transport to take half our mess stores and food etc., and camped at a spot just beyond Sannah's Post where Broadwood lost the guns some time back, and on the 25th we marched on 3 miles to the Waterworks where the 7th Co. and Highland Brigade halted, and I, to my surprise, was sent on with my section to try and catch up with the 19th Brigade and report to General Smith-Dorrien who had no Sappers with him. I caught them up halted about 3 miles on, and marched on with them towards ThabaNchu – at 11.30 a.m. we got in touch with the enemy who were strongly holding the line of hills I am now writing on – our Mounted Infantry and guns got at them on the right and the 19th Brigade on the left. We cleared them out by 4.30 with slight loss – I don't know our total loss at all.

My section was under fire for some while but at long range – the first bullet I heard struck the ground in front of my horse's feet, he shied and nearly had me off – a hint however which I was not long in taking, and saw the rest of it on foot. We camped at the foot of these hills after a hard day.

Next morning the Mounted Infantry and 19th Brigade went on to ThabaNchu which they occupied about 10.00 o'clock leaving the force I mentioned above at this pass with my Sappers to help in making a few defences – which took us most of that day – that evening I took a few of my men round a big hill to bury a dead boer we found there – a fine young chap of about 25 shot through side of head above the right ear. An unpleasant job but we made him as good a grave as any soldier could wish for.

<u>Fri 27th</u> Quiet night and very lone. In the morning rode out with Whitecross to a Boer farm and rounded up his sheep to the tune of about 2000! We brought them back about two miles to camp and had fine fresh chops for lunch and dinner! French reported into ThabaNchu from South and Boers plying North.

As I write Sunday heavy shelling can be heard some miles away and we see the shells bursting on a distant kopje.

<u>Late Fri evening:</u> De Lisle of the Durhams (who stayed a few days once with Uncle George) arrived with about 600 Mounted Infantry and camped at foot of our hills and is still here, patrolling the road to keep it open for convoys.

On Sat: rounded up more sheep as others had strayed – tapped a passing convoy for three days' grub – biscuits, tea and sugar – and in p.m. rode out with Meyrick to another farm where we found an aged boer and his wife – here we bought fresh butter 2/6 a pound – half a dozen eggs 2d each – about a stone of potatoes 2/6 – 2 fowls 1/= each! some bread 1/= a loaf and some dried peaches – and on the road back picked up several bundles of oat hay – a good foraging trip.

One learns the meaning of the words "Give us this day our daily bread" when you are alone on the veldt with your own wits to feed on and an occasional convoy with biscuits and oats on it.

Today we are having a rest – a lovely still sunny afternoon lying on the hillside looking over miles and miles of hill-strewn veldt dotted with grazing mules and sheep with the dull boom of guns to the North East betokening some phase in the great drama of blood which is being enacted at such cost to the players.

Have just heard that a return convoy is in and taking mails to Bloemfontein so this I hope will go by it. Thank God I am in splendid health still and feel as if I had lived in the open and slept under the stars all my life!

I believe the 7th Company are still at the waterworks. De Lisle who is a local Lieut. Col. wishes to be remembered to Uncle George. A subaltern named Allen of the Gordon Highlanders who failed for Woolwich the exam I got in, knew Uncle Teddy at RawalPindi and seems to be a friend of Barbara and Cicely's! We are hoping to see a convoy through the pass tonight as our grub expires today – though we can get heaps of fresh meat we cannot feed the men on mutton alone!

I wish you could see the beautiful scene before me now – the quiet camp at the foot of the hill and the green veldt dying away into the waves of blue and brown hills – certainly only man is vile.

Love to all at home from your ever loving son Eric E.B. Wilson.

10 miles North of Winberg O.F.S.   **Monday 7th May 1900**

My dearest Father

I got a letter from you dated April 6th at Winberg yesterday, also one from M[oonie] and one from H[elen].

I last wrote to you on April 29th from Israel's Poort where I was on detached post with a company of Gordons and Mounted Infantry, since then we have had a good bit of hard fighting and marching.

On Monday 30th April we were called up to join the main column at ThabaNchu and were relieved by a party of XIV Hussars under Hill-Whitson whom I knew at Harrow and Newbridge (Curragh) – we caught the column up on the move after bearing off some miles north of ThabaNchu, just as they got in touch with DeWets force of Boers who were holding a strong position at a place called Houtnek and Thaba Kop.

Shells were falling freely into our transport column when we came up – however they took ground behind the slope of a hill and out of range while the attack developed, the fight lasted all that day and all the next (1st May) till 2.30 p.m. when we carried the position and the Boers fled North with their guns, leaving a good few prisoners wounded and whole in our hands.

We marched over the Nek and camped in the valley beyond. Here I met E.M.Birch R.A. of my term at the shop, who made runs for us the time we won the term challenge cup and a great friend of mine.

Wednesday 2nd May we rested after our two days fight and prepared for the great march on Winberg.

On the 3rd we marched 16 miles to Isabellafontein – the cavalry had a few brushes but no serious fighting. On the 4th we marched off at 6.30 a.m. and came in contact with enemy strongly posted in another chain of hills, about 8.30 a.m., after a sharp fight lasting till 3 p.m. We cleared the hills and they fled very hurriedly towards Winberg. I hear since they suffered heavily from our shelling and left several wounded in our hands.

We camped at the Vet River that night, a very raviney place which they meant to have fallen back on and held strongly but had such a dusting that they fled through.

Boileau of ours did a fine thing that night. Winberg as you will see is on a branch line – he was sent out with a couple of Scouts and rode 20 miles at night and 20 back and blew up the line between Winberg and Smaldeel Junction in case the Boers wanted to get any stores out of Winberg by rail, as a matter of fact I believe they had done so already – but it was a fine exploit and right through the enemy lines.

On the 5th we marched on Winberg expecting a great fight, but were met by a white flag to say the town surrendered and the boers had fled further north still, so we occupied the town and camped on the hills outside – town very pretty and fine new church building (Dutch Reformed?), market square, shops etc.

I was luckily early in and secured a few things at the store before all was sold out – oatmeal – cocoa – matches – cigars – jam – tinned herrings – etc. So I am well set up for some days in food.

Sunday 6th May we rested till 4 p.m. – meanwhile the Highland Brigade came up behind us and the 7th Co. from whom I got some letters etc., and who were very envious of my section being on ahead and seeing all the fighting with the XIXth and XXIst Brigades. We marched off again at 4 p.m. – leaving Highland Brigade at Winberg and camped here – about ten miles north – last night.

Today we were to have gone on at 7 a.m. but orders came from Lord Roberts to say we were getting along too fast and must wait a bit for supplies etc., to catch up, so we have a days' rest here – good alike for man and beast after our recent hard marching – I am not sure where we are making for now – whether Kroonstadt via Senekal or Ventersberg, anyhow we are sure of terrific fighting before we get to Kroonstadt as all the republican forces are concentrating there for a great stand.

I have no idea what the other columns are doing or where and what they are – facts of which you are daily informed by wire! These last fights bring No 2 section 7th Co up to 11 general engagements – probably as many as any

unit in the Field Force – Belmont – Graspan – Modder River – Magersfontein – Koodesberg – Paardeburg – Poplar Grove – Dorefontein – Israel's Poort – Hout Nek – and Vet River or some other name perhaps officially. I wonder how many clasps they will give the survivors of that lot!
Poor Lady Jenner lost the son and heir and then her father – I hear she is broken-hearted over it all and she was such a bright and charming woman. Moonie appears to be in good health and spirits now, also the poor child, who seems very flourishing which is very satisfactory.
Send me out a flint and steel – if possible the sort with a buzzing emery wheel, you can get specially handy ones with yellow slow match stuff to light – I rather fancy myself at taking a light with them and am often out of matches, tho' in the daytime I use the end of a field glass and take a light from the sun – thus do we return to simple and primitive habits!
Also many thanks for magazines – The Weekly Daily Graphic (six no's in a cover, would be very acceptable. I believe one can order them anywhere. Mails being collected in a hurry so must close now.

With best love to you all ever your loving son Eric E.B. Wilson

P.S. I have enough warm things – cardigan – wool cap etc., and have (I think) learnt to take care of myself to a certain extent! Nights are very cold now in the open – though midday is roasting hot.

Kroonstad   Monday 14th May 1900

My dearest Father

I fancy I last wrote to you from or near Winberg – since then we have marched on and on over weary miles of country, with some fighting and are now camped near Kroonstad, which town fell into our hands on the 12th after some resistance, and the flight of Mr Steyn to other climes to name some other one horse hamlet the capital of the Free State – <u>no doubt</u> – as for the burghers – judging by their recent performances they <u>must</u> be very heartily sick of it, and I wish they would make up their minds to chuck up and go home for good – that is the Free Staters – the Transvaal Boers are a factor to be dealt with hereafter – and I fancy will produce a considerable amount of trouble yet.

When we left the camp just North of Winberg we heard that the Boers were entrenching along the Sand River and would make their next stand there – and so it proved. On May 9th we marched to a farm called Bloemplaats – some 3 miles short of the Sand River and could plainly see Boers on the hills beyond.

That night the Derby Regiment pushed on and seized the drift over the river unopposed curiously enough – I spent most of the night with them – entrenching them to hold on, and improving the approaches to the drift by the light of the moon – testing the depth of the water at the crossing etc., ready for next day.

During the day a fine herd of buck galloped bang through the camp and I regret to say there was some pretty indiscriminate firing at them – luckily without mishap but nonetheless foolish, the result being about half a dozen fell to the cooking pots!

Well I got in to camp about 2.30 a.m. from the drift and snatched a few hours sleep – before one of our heavy guns opened the ball at 5.50 a.m. with a shot at long range. The attack and general advance lasted till well on into the afternoon when the position was ours at slight cost I believe. We marched on about 7 miles that day to a camp near Ventersberg.

I met Winston Churchill during the day, much subdued and less blatant than in his earlier days.

On May 11th we pushed on many miles without incident and camped. On May 12th we marched on here – the advanced force of cavalry etc., sufficing to clear the boers from the hills round the town – but I believe the Greys and Iniskillings lost heavily.

As a matter of fact I have not had time to explore the town but can only see it below us in the valley, as I have been unable to leave my men being the only R.E. officer here.

We hoped this was to be a slight haven of rest but I hear that our particular force (XIX and XXI brigades – Mounted Infantry etc., under Ian Hamilton) are to push on Eastwards – this time to Lindley – some 45 miles – where Steyn is reported to be hiding – starting tomorrow early. I am out early with my men to bridge some bad bit of road before the Column marches.

This is about all my news – no mails or papers received for ages – in fact one is quite out of touch with everything now except the daily tough beef and hard biscuit.

Much love to all Ever your loving son Eric E.B. Wilson.

P.S. I am very sorry to hear that Denis Murch died after all. By the way I enclose a very rough sketch I made of Reggie Bell's grave at De Aar – Mr Bell might like it?

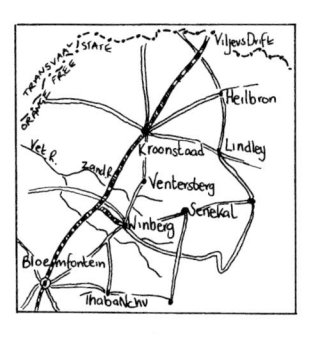

15 miles North of Johannesberg   Monday June 4 1900
T.H.W. 57   20 miles South of Pretoria

My dearest Father,

I fear it is ages since you had a few lines from me, and indeed I hardly know when this will find its way South. I last wrote, I think, from Kroonstad, and since then we have been marching, marching, marching all day and every day till we simply feel as if all our lives had been spent marching. Over the veldt – up steep craggy kopjes, over deep sandy drifts, over the endless green grass on towards Pretoria.

Long before this reaches you I hope we shall be there for good and all. My great good luck has still stood by me and not only am I still at the extreme front as I have been since the first shot was fired, but thank goodness I am still as fit and well as possible.

Hamilton's Force as we are known now (XIX & XXI Brigades – Mounted Infantry etc.,) has I may honestly say, been doing all the work and all the fighting. A glance at the map will show you our route – first mentioning that the Main Column under Lord Roberts has solidly loafed up the main line from Bloemfontein to Johannesberg with scarcely any fighting, while we have scoured the country right and left as follows :–Bloemfontein – fight at Israel's Poort; ThabaNchu, fight at Houtiek 10 m north of T. fight at Vet River 14 miles south of Winberg, capture of Winberg, fight at Zand River 20 miles further N.; capture of Ventersberg, capture of Kroonstad where we touched rail for a moment, wide sweep out East to Lindley, capture of Lindley and heavy skirmishing all way to Heilbron, captured.

Striking due west, cross railway slightly N of latitude of Heilbron, sweep out West and North making the Vaal at Boschbank 12 miles west of Viljeus Drift, crossed Vaal and marched N.W. over the Witwatersrand hills, swept round Boers right flank and great fight at Doornkop, close to actual spot of Jameson's surrender – made the J'berg – Krugers railway at Florida 10 miles due west of Johannesberg – and all amongst the goldmines – moved close into Johannesberg and camped two nights at Braanfontein on outskirts.

Spent all June 2nd in the town buying cocoa and candles etc., looking over the Fort etc., etc., etc.. All <u>most</u> engrossing – then on 3rd June on here – en route for Pretoria! where we naturally expect very severe fighting – possibly a siege.

The Gordons did well at Doorn Kop and charged a position at point of bayonet, a rare feat these days – when it isn't safe to stand up on open ground at 2000 yards.

My little party which left De Aar 50 strong now number 1 officer and 26 men at the front. A true survival of the fittest as none have been killed though one died of enteric at Modder, simply broken under the strain of hard work and short food.

At times we have really been a bit short of grub, horses have been 4 days without corn etc., at a stretch – men on ½ lb of crushed maize and 1½ lbs meat.

(just <u>dark</u>)

Continued at Pretoria   Wednesday June 6th 1900

Since writing on the 4th things have moved apace – we marched from Johannesberg on the 2nd and reached a spot 6 miles south of Pretoria on the evening of the 4th where we had some hardish fighting – shelled the forts etc., and camped – next day we heard that the Boers had fled – we marched on the town through terrific mountain passes which they ought easily to have held.

Camped on the western outskirts and in the afternoon had a tremendous march past Lord Roberts in the main market square – the most imposing spectacle and the proudest moment I suppose of all our lives – certainly a great historic event to have taken part in.

Today we camp here – tomorrow I believe we start marching back to Johannesberg – the 19th Brigade has been dispersed and the Hamiltons force is scattered – anew.

I understand Gen Smith Dorrien commanding 19th Brigade is to be Military Governor and Commandant of Johannesberg and my little crowd go with him possibly en route to rejoin the 7th Company eventually – so you may hear from me next from Johannesberg.

As I write great cheering denotes the arrival of another batch of our released prisoners – who were nearly all liberated today – as a cavalry force went out to Watersvaal and the Boers fled leaving us to bring our prisoners in by rail and walk. We have got back Matty and Oldcorn the two telegraphists who were captured on Nov 1st at Colesberg while we were still at De Aar. They are weak and pulled down but will soon pick up again.

I had a walk round Pretoria this afternoon – visited Kruger's house – the Parliament etc. I stole into the Raadzaal (House of Lords) a splendid chamber and sat in President Kruger's chair! where I dated a piece of Transvaal official paper with his pen and ink – passed a law putting him on half rations for life – declared the session over – pocketed the lid of his ink stand as a souvenir and strolled out! But of this, silence, as Lord Roberts would not approve of such conduct. Coming out I met in one of the corridors a Major of the Guards walking off with a ballot box!! I also got some leaves from his private garden.

The town is very pretty and much more residential and less commercial than its enormous neighbour Johannesberg, which is more like Woolwich compared with say Blackheath.

I will now give you a copy of an address of congratulation sent round to us last night:

By General Smith Dorrien –

> "The 19th Brigade has achieved a record of which any troops might be proud. Since the date it was formed – 12th February 1900 – it has marched 620 miles, often on half rations and seldom on full. It has taken part in the capture of 10 towns, fought in ten general actions and on 27 other days. In one period of 30 days it fought on 21 of them and marched 327 miles. Casualties between 400 and 500."

So far so good – <u>now</u> take no 2 section 7th Co. R.E. which has been <u>with 19th Brigade</u> ever since 12 Feb. and <u>add</u> 200 miles – De Aar – Modder – Koodesberg to Graspan – before starting in the Free State – 5 more general actions and fighting on at least say 30 other days (shell fire at Modder – Magersfontein position and Koodesberg) and you get 820 miles marched, say 15 general actions and fighting on 57 other days – though of course except on one or two occasions our share in the fighting has been infinitely less dangerous than that of the Infantry.

Still it only takes one bullet to kill a man if it is meant to be so!

I expect there will be plenty of hard marching and fighting yet before it is all over but the backbone of it is broken now we have occupied Pretoria and Bloemfontein. Thank God I have lived to march into Pretoria with the very first and fighting line. I think that barring Staff Officers we were <u>the</u> first attachment of marching Royal Engineers to march in.

I hear the Free State has been proclaimed a British Colony though I fancy it will take some settling down!

No mails received of course since I left the Company and goodness knows when I shall rejoin it. My horse 'Happy' and the Boer pony 'Dick' are both still flourishing but very weary I fear – the pony was given me by poor Meyrick of the Gordons who commanded our little force at Israel's Poort and who was shot at Doorn Kop through the top button of his coat, throat and chest – he died almost at once. Three of the four Gordon Officers of that party were hit at Doorn Kop.

I wonder how all the County Cricket etc., is going on.

I should have liked a day or two more here to go over the forts etc., but I may revisit it in later days.

Fingers cold now writing on the grass at night by the light of a captured carriage lamp!

Much love to all the family, Ever your loving son Eric E.B. Wilson

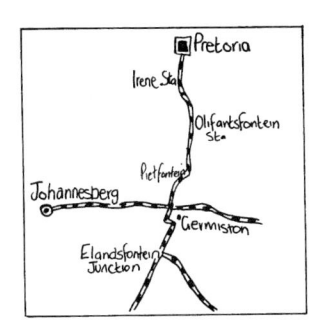

Elandsfontein Junction nr Johannesburg   Monday 18th June 1900

My dearest Father

I last wrote to you just before leaving Pretoria – in which I said that we should probably be near Johannesburg when next I wrote. I hope the letter reached you safely, as the line has been somewhat insecure further south until recently, in fact I hear that 3 weeks accumulated mails fell into the hands of a marauding body of Boers who attacked the line further South and captured some militia – at least so we hear – so my chances of getting my back mails are slight – I think April 7th was the date on the last I have got.

We left Pretoria on June 7th with the Gordons, Cornwalls, Canadians and Suffolk regiment, ten guns and some mounted infantry to take up the defence of the railway line between Pretoria and Kroonstad – this force under Gen Smith Dorrien has been distributed at points all along the line with headquarters here, at the junction practically of all the railways in the Transvaal, some 8 miles west of Johannesburg. Here we have the Gordons and 2 guns, 74 Battalion R.A., ourselves, and some odds and ends – and the general and staff – and we live in readiness to fly by train to any point required. Well, on June 7 we marched some 10 miles South and camped near Irene Station. On the 8th we began leaving our force in small bodies down the line and camped 3 miles north of Olifantsfontein station. On the 9th we marched about 19 miles South to Pietfontein mine and camped. On the 10th we marched here and have remained here since. That night we had a great sing-song round a big camp fire with the Canadians, who gave good backwoods choruses and quaint old French-Canadian songs. On the 11th I proved the resources of the town – called Germiston, which adjoins the railway – and has several useful and fairly well-stocked shops still open. I bought some canvas to make a tent with as we have been having bitterly cold weather lately – frost and sharp winds with rain – very trying in the open – even as hardened as we are now.

On the 12th most of the Canadians went out East along the rail to Springs and Boeksburg – and my men had a bit of a holiday, for mending their clothes I was going to say but patching their rags would be better – you see the system is that clothes can only be got through your company and they get it from the Ordnance depots and so on , so when one is on detachment like this and miles from any of these sources of supply, nothing but a few old sacks are procurable.

On the 13th we spent most of the day packing up camp and loading trains to proceed on some trip or other – but as the movement was counter-ordered the afternoon was spent unloading the same and marching to camp again – a very unprofitable amusement!

On the 14th we did nothing much – men employed as usual on roads, water supply – defences etc. On the 15th I went with a certain 2nd Lieutenant Ballingall R.A. by 7 a.m. train to Pretoria to get some money from the paymaster to pay my men – we got there about 11 a.m, 35 miles in 4 hours, and spent a pleasant day, after our business with the paymaster – looking round the Staats Artillerie Barracks etc., etc., had a good lunch at the Grand Hotel – met numbers of friends and heard all the latest yarns – saw Riley and Ottley, King's Own Yorkshire Light Infantry, two old Wynberg friends and the latter a released prisoner.

Saw strings of burghers handing in arms at the Government Buildings and getting passes signed, to go back to their farms and be good.

I met among others a certain Ingham R.H.A who was at the shop with me and remembered me because I once struck him on the head with a cricket ball at the nets. He appears to have known Uncle Teddy in India and inquired after them all and wished to be remembered.

So many of the Gordons too have asked after uncle Ted and the family. I think they were at Pindi when he was commanding.

We had a bitter cold return journey from Pretoria on a chance troop train – open coal truck – got to camp at 11 p.m!

On the 16th, Moonie 27, we were working on local defences and had some rain (quite out of season) in the evening. On the 17th – Sunday, bitter wind and rain. Church at 11 a.m. at Germiston English church – to seat about 120 – and crowded with about 200 – conducted by Rev. Chaplain Southwell attached Gen. Dorrien Smith's Staff – a charming and very clever man – that night we had much rain.

Today we worked on defences – and saw several trains through – on one I met my old friend Major R.C.B. Hoking who was Commandant at De Aar in prehistoric days and was delighted to see me and have a talk. He is much pulled down from the man he used to be – by fever etc. Well here I suppose we shall be for a bit – rather lonely but handy for getting into Johannesburg and supplies etc.

I am reading Bleak House which chance threw in the way of my boy Scrimshaw (groom and equerry in chief) and which he produced for my inspection – and I am most interested in it – by the light of my solitary candle in a picked-up carriage lamp (near side!)

We long for the war to end its dreary existence, and I don't think it will be far off now. It is very trying about the lost mails but there is just a chance of mine not having been there.

I have heard nothing of or from the company since we left Winberg – and I hope ere this reaches you that Harrow will have performed the annual chastisement on those who aspire to cricket at Eton.

Much love to all and each from your ever loving son Eric E.B. Wilson
8 p.m.
18.6.00

Elandsfontein Junction Monday 25th June 1900

My dearest Father

Very little news for you since last week, when I wrote from same place. We have been quietly camped here – and the men kept busy making trenches and defences etc., more to keep away the inevitable enteric, which always follows in the track of rest after severe exertion, than the Boers – I have in fact been so busy myself that I have not even run into Johannesburg since we came here, which is the usual occupation of those with leisure for a day. De Wet, we hear, has been busy down South making raids on the railway – but I fancy there are lots of people on his track now.

Still no mails received, or any chance of any till I get in touch with my company again, who I believe are at Heilbron or thereabouts. There seems no doubt also that 4 weeks mails were destroyed by the Boers when they attacked the Derby militia. The Gordons, with whom I am messing now, have English papers – of May 14th and Cape Papers of June 4th. I see therefrom great accounts of the fêting of the Naval Brigade in town.

I expect by now everyone looks on the war as over – but though 'broken', things will be long in emerging from the status quo – and much hard work remains and many lives will yet be lost – in the scouring and sweeping up of the odds and ends of commandos who still prowl about in an irresponsible manner and attack here and there, and then run for it like detected thieves.

Rev Southwell Smith conducts two services in the Germiston (tin) parish church – a very clever speaker and pleasant man. We had a hymn for peace yesterday – I think ?378 – to tune 'When I survey'. A colonial volunteer officer plays harmonium very well – if you remember, Corporal Sherborne in 7th Co: It is very curious to see the versatility of some of our men.

We are making a redoubt near the camp here which will be quite a model I think when finished – on a small scale – one of Maj. Phillips' R.A. 6 inch guns arrived here this week and is a great stand by to the defences.

We see trains and trains of supplies and horses going through North and East every day – but not much news reaches us by them.

I wonder if the C.E. Rose Capt. R.H. Guards was the one at Everards with me, the face in a paper seems like him – he had a pony kept for him if I remember and had much money –

Longing to hear from someone at home!

Ever your loving son Eric E.B. Wilson.

Elandsfontein Junction   Tuesday 3rd July 1900

My dearest Father

Still here and quietly busy. Hitherto we have been occupied in the defences which are now fairly complete as far as one can cater for a garrison of changing numbers. I have also been occupied on a survey of the locality and various other small jobs – platforms and railway work.
The Gordons and the 2 guns of 76th Battery that live here went out for a trip to Springs about 20 miles East during the week to cope with an impending attack on the coal-mines there and reinforce the Canadians posted there – but nothing came of it and they returned next day.
Today they are off again to Boksburg – between here and Springs which is supposed to be threatened – but nothing more is known at present.
I met Col. Barker R.E. – our C.R.E in the old 9th Division – who gave me news of the company – said they were (still) at Heilbron – and that McClintock and Musgrave had gone out on some move of MacDonalds – and otherwise all were fit.
The 7th Fusiliers – the battalion formerly at the Curragh, passed through this week en route to Pretoria – for garrison duty I expect. I met many old friends, J.C. Hartley-Carey (cousin of Billy Darell), Phillips – (wicket keep), Clark (racquet partner) and many others that were my daily companions at the Curragh – they had marched from Kimberley via Potchefstroom – and had earlier been in the relief of Ladysmith.
I have not yet received any mails, but shall apply to 7th Co. for them now I have heard of them – however, I have seen English papers of June 1st which have reached the Gordons – but none between April 7th and May 7th – as they were bagged by De Wet.
We have a Field Post Office at the Station now, which is a convenience.
Rain today and very cold every night – about October weather at home – never very warm even at noon.
I am still very fit and well – with much love to all at home –

Ever your loving son Eric E.B. Wilson

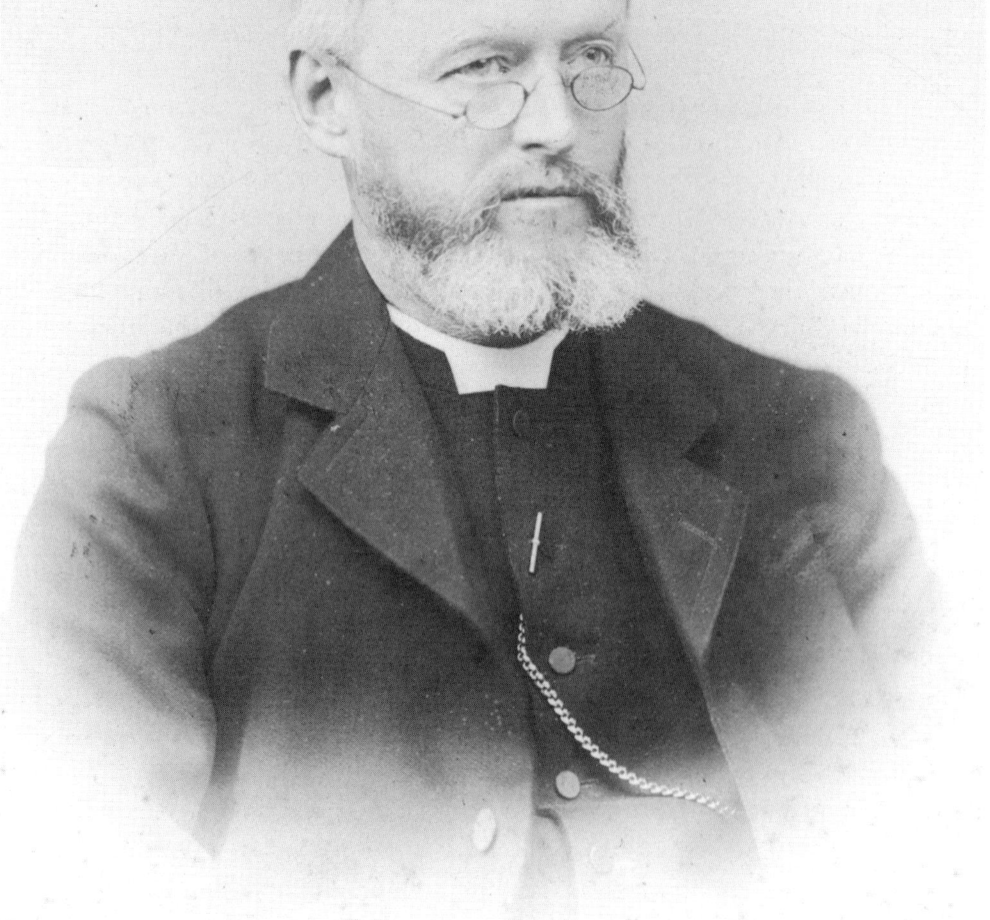

FROM T.H.W. TO E.E.B.W.

> Redgrave Rectory, Diss, England,
> Diss.
> England.
> Parcels – Mellis
> Tel – Botesdale
> Friday July 6th '00

RECOVERED FROM MAILS
LOOTED BY THE ENEMY

My dearest Boy,

It will be a month <u>tomorrow</u> since we last heard from you – but as we read of the disappearance of Mail Bags etc it may be that your letter or letters may <u>not</u> arrive. I omitted to write to you last Friday – by some mistake – but otherwise have sent a weekly letter with only one or two interruptions all the time.

Moonie came here last Wednesday week and brought 'Bobs' with her – she only stayed the week and went away last Wednesday to stay with the Gwilts nr Bury St Edmunds – until Monday – when she goes on to London. She has left nurse and Bobs here – he is a dear little boy and always bright and pleasant looking: – much stronger than his Aunt Rachel. During her stay we did not see much of Moonie – she was on the move most of the time – the bulk of her attention being given to Hinderclay Hall, she and Gwendoline seeming to hit it off very well.

Mrs Turner was here too during the time – and Uncle Charlie swooped down on us for two days. We were so full that he had to sleep at Cousin Annie's.

Now we are quiet again and have resumed our normal life. On Sunday and Monday we had an <u>excellent</u> letter from Helen – describing how busy she was getting her house at Blair straight – and saying that she had received all her goods and chattels from her own room here <u>safely</u> and unbroken.

Mr <u>David</u> Shaw, the eldest brother, has been married some 8 years – and has an only child – a girl. He and his wife have money and keep up somewhat of an establishment.

Moonie says that Helen and Mrs David have made great friends. At present they are the only two <u>son's</u> wives – as Patrick and James Shaw – the other two brothers – are as yet <u>Bachelors</u>!!

Tomorrow Mother goes to Cotton for the Sunday – and to help her father to decide what he will keep and what he will sell – as of course he will not want all his present furniture for his new house here in October.

It will be 10 years on Sunday since I married at Cotton!! And I was married to your mother just the six weeks over the 10 years!!! to the day – 13 September 1870 to 25 February 1880. Hoping that another of your valuable letters may arrive between this and Tuesday – I am as ever, your loving Father.

Grand Hotel Pretoria   Monday 9th July 1900

My dearest Father

A change of scene again since I wrote from Elandsfontein. On Thursday last we suddenly got orders for the 19th Brigade to concentrate again and proceed up the line to Irene – about 9 miles South of Pretoria. This was completed by yesterday night and we are all now at Irene awaiting the next move – which is supposed to be to the East – to roll up Louis Botha once for all. We (R.E.) marched up from E'f'n' to Irene, 27 miles in 3 easy stages, 5–11–11 miles. The day we were ordered to move, I was about to go into Johannesburg to get two new horses from the Remount Depôt – one for the tool cart and one to replace my 2nd animal recently destroyed as incurable by the Vet. As we did not move till 2 p.m., I just had time and rode in the 9½ miles to Johannesberg, got an excellent strong draught horse and a short-backed cobby countrybred for myself, and rode back to camp just in time to march, so that with the 5 miles march my old horse 'Happy' put in 24 miles that day. Today I came in from Irene by rail to try and get clothes and boots for my men from the Ordnance Depôt – the former they had none of – up yet, the latter only 10's and 5's in sizes!! And as all normal people want 7, 8, 9, they were not much good – however I am taking some down on the chance the men may manage with some big ones – better than walking in bare feet. I also got some horse shoes and nails – badly wanted.

I have discovered, I think I told you, that the company is at Heilbron – but I fancy most have gone out now on trek with General Hunter – however I have agitated for mails to be sent forward – and faintly hope they may reach Irene before we start on the next and I hope final chapter of the Campaign. Whitecross, my man left sick at Winberg, has refound me – and brought verbal news of the Company – but by some idiotic mistake allowed the mails to be forwarded seperately by train from Heilbron – instead of keeping his hand on the bag since it left Heilbron where it was put on the train with him. I met Boileau at this Hotel today – he is coming with us (Ian Hamilton's column) as D.A.A.G.(A) as promotion to Staff duty for him, and he has certainly earned it – I fancy I may take over his mounted sappers possibly – Buller was up here yesterday to see the C. in C. and may be still here for all I know.

I see Uncle Walter has been made a Baronet! I haven't seen the future Sir Raymond again since Naauwpoort. I met several Suffolk officers who knew mutual acquaintances – a Capt. Prest – formerly adjutant and others. The Suffolks have joined the 19th Brigade instead of the Canadians who were terribly weak – 400 out of 1150 from Quebec! I hear from Whitecross that the 7th Co have only lost two mails by Christian De Wets capture – so I hope I shall see several weeks soon.

We complete a year of foreign service in S. Africa on the 15th of this month – I hear the 23rd Co. R.E. which came out in June and were Ladysmithed, have gone home.

This afternoon I climbed up to one of the forts round the town (Schanzkop) – a stiff pull – but I was anxious to see what the Boers had laid out £100,000 on and run away without using! This fort is a strong affair of its kind and prepared for 2 big guns 4 field guns and about 70 riflemen with strong underground casemates, kitchens etc., etc. A detachment of Norfolk Regt now occupy it.

Pretoria is very empty now – we have sent away about 3000 Hollanders whose presence was undesirable. I will keep this open and post at Irene before we march, in case I get mails there. (4 p.m.)

Irene 8 p.m. – same date – I resume my pen(cil)and continue more by the minute than by the day for never have I received five letters from you by the same mail! The last I can trace amongst my limited property here seems to be April 6th from Diss but I may have acknowledged receipt of one later? On leaving the Hotel for the station I called at the Post Office on the vague chance that there might be stray letters there by mistake – and there I found the whole mail for 7th Co dated June 15 and one from you, this I opened. Mind, there was a two-months gap in my mind – and this letter might have been Chinese cypher for all I could make of it!! I read words like "returned home," "trip," "Helen's honeymoon," (Heavens! I thought, the child must have married!) and so on. This gave me something to speculate on – and when I reached camp at Irene (6 p.m.) I found 4 more letters from you had come in as follows – May 11 Diss – May 18 St Austell

May 25 Falmouth – June 1st Irvine – and I had June 15 with me – so I fear the gap before May 11 is in De Wets hands – June 8 may turn up if existing. Well from this somewhat headless chapter of events I gathered enough to piece in the rest – I also (today) heard from Helen May 21- telling me she was going to marry – however it is a relief to be up to date again – I hope she will be happy – I think I remember Philip Shaw.

You must have enjoyed your outing – and I hope it has done Mother and you much good and refreshment, you seem to have looked in at most places!

In Johannesburg lately I was discussing routine affairs with an infantry officer whose features and appearance seemed so familiar to me that I said to him straight out – your name doesn't happen to be Carlyon does it? "Yes" he replied "it is"!! He had the Carlyon look – but I didn't trace his exact connection like you could have done – except that he was a relation of Edmund Carlyon etc., etc., and lived in Cornwall – I cannot even recall his regiment now.

No orders for a move yet. Today I hear that some late Free State officials have surrendered – I hope with good further effects. I fear you will not have got a letter after the Kroonstad one May 14 – till our entry into Pretoria June 5 or so, still you will have had several from Elandsfontein since.

I, as an individual, seem fated by decree to see the complete performance of this tragedy of nations from start to finish – may the same fates and decrees leave me a body to wear round my soul by the end of it! as really the number of powerful men and healthy who have gone under is something awful – so much so that one's debt becomes a very lasting one indeed for mercies past and hopes to come.

I hope to get a line off to Helen before we leave Irene – write and tell her how the news has failed so long – my fingers are too cold for more tonight – in the open and freezing slightly!!

Best love to all the family from your ever loving son Eric E.B. Wilson

(addressed and stamped in Pretoria)

Herbert Musgrave of my Co: had a shave of being captured by DeWet on the railway lately – servant caught – he got off in clothes he stood in! Have recently finished Bleak House – now re-reading Oliver Twist – both "captured" in Boer farm!

Daspoort Camp 3m: N.W. of Pretoria   **Wednesday 1st August 1900**

My dearest Father

I last wrote from Irene – telling you that we were just off for another trek – we have just come in off it and are resting a day or so here to refit – we had a pretty hard time this journey and not much fighting to compensate for it. I have just heard that mails are waiting in Pretoria for my section and have sent in for them – so in anticipation of answering yours I will get on with my news first.

We have just heard that General Hunter has captured Prinsloo and 5000 boers, this ought to help the waverers to quit the field I hope. I expect Musgrave and his section 7th Co. were with him – so he will have been present at both big captures.

I must now refer to my scribbles in my notebook:

Sat 14th July We marched from Irene by road to Pretoria arriving after dark and camping near the Stats Artillerie Barracks – now occupied by our troops in garrison here.

Sun 15th July We marched out of the town to the camp I am now writing from and where Hamilton's force was once more assembling – here we joined in with a section of IXth Co R.E. under Buckle (my term at Woolwich) who had also with him a civil Engineer (volunteer) named Lyell – who through up the post of chief engineer to "our" G.E.R. in order to see some campaigning – a level headed Scot of about 34 but looks much younger – he built the new Liverpool Street Station and was in charge of all the extensions round Chelmsford etc which you will recall have been going on for the past few years – and told me as a fact that the Suffolk extensions and branch which you recently quoted are by no means warmly supported by the board of the G.E.R. and he thinks will be put off 'sine die'.

Our two sections R.E. together with 100 natives carrying picks and shovels for road mending and making were then formed into a composite R.E. company under a Captain Clifford Coffin R.E. – a nice fellow – with Major Kenny as C.R.E. (formerly commanded the 11th Field Co: when I was attached to it at Chatham).

The rest of the force consisted of a cavalry brigade under Col. Hickman, Mounted Infantry under Mahon (of Mafeking) 1½ Infantry brigades under Cunningham – Argylls, Border Regt (Col Hindes battalion), Kings Own Scottish Borderers and Royal Berks – 7th Fusiliers (J.C.Hartley & Co) and Connaught Rangers – two heavy six-inch Howitzers – two 5 inch guns –

two 4.7 guns – one battery quick firing 12 pounders (Lady Meux' present) and one battery Canadian Artillery – a pretty useful force of about 6500 to 7000.

Mon 16th July Marched North to Watervaal where the prisoners had been kept – saw all the wire enclosures – tin shelters – rubbish and debris of the enormous camp.

On arrival in camp Coffin and I were sent 3 miles further up the line with a few Sappers as escort to make a cut in the line as it was believed the Boers had heavy guns on the rail and might run them down to shell the camp – we blew a hole through a girder and rail over a culvert some 3 miles out with gun cotton and got in after dark without mishap.

Tues 17th July Marched on North to Haman's Kraal Station about 28 miles N. of Pretoria – here we entered a dense bush country – very trappy and difficult to manoeuvre in – some of our advanced scouts came suddenly on a small party of boers sitting down by the roadside and before they could dismount or fire the boers shot 3 out of the saddle – I killed 2 wounded, and made good their escape. This delayed the march some while as the firing caused the column to deploy to the flanks – guns came into action etc. etc. but nothing further came of it.

Wed 18th July Finding no signs or news of boers up this way we turned down S.E. and marched to Walmansthal Mission Station and camped.

Thurs 19th July Marched N.E. again to Boekenhouts Drift where we had a lot of work damming up a streamlet to make a pond to water the animals – here we stopped in an old ruin labelled "Hotel and Store" – but the 'lift' was not working and the doors wouldn't shut – because there were none.

Fri 20th July We marched S.E. again to Wagen drift – thus forming an M on the map with about 15 mile strokes. The camp at Wagen drift had beautiful scenery round it – wooded hills and orange groves with ripe oranges on the trees – here we caught 4 or 5 boers with their wagons and families complete trying to join their friends further east.

Sat 21st July We marched off from Wagen drift at 7 a.m. with the advance guard- we had hardly got clear of the camp into the dense bush surrounding the road when the boers opened fire on the camp and transport (thinking our guns had left) with three guns – and out of the beautiful wooded hills too – whence no doubt they had been taking good stock of us However our 5 inch guns soon cooled their ardour and they temporarily evanesced leaving us the losers by some half dozen mules killed and a native driver wounded.

About four miles further on we emerged from the bush into rolling veldt again and were just about to enter another patch of bush when boom! swissss-hhhh, perlop – came another shell over the valley at us – they had marched along their same ridge parallel with us and were starting again with the same guns – this time the Canadian battery and the 5" guns had a talk to them and some very pretty shelling was exchanged – though it was hard to locate their guns in the bushy hillside – the R.E. company was following the Canadian battery in the order of march and when the battery came into "action left" the Company wheeled off with their ammunition limbers to the right – and rear – to put more distance between theirselves and the enemys guns – as it were – my curiosity however to see how the Canadians could handle a gun led me to linger by the battery a minute or so – while shells meant for the guns were falling pretty thick anywhere else than amongst them.

I had just turned my back on the battery to walk after the Company which was now halted under a fold of ground some quarter mile back when I heard a shell coming over my way, and by now one knows by the sound almost exactly where a shell is making for – to my horror I realised that it was coming straight for me – the next doubt was is it 'short' or 'over'. I decided it was just going over my head and was about to bend down in a most undignified manner to allow of the transit when 'scrash' went the ground under my feet and over I went with a regular storm of clods and stones battering me – the shell had pitched right under my heels – about a yard behind according to a witness – and burst underground – luckily in very soft ground – rock or stone and I must have been shattered! Several men ran up to carry my broken remains to the ambulance but as I hadn't a scratch on me I was compelled to smile and decline – however it was 'miss' and not 'hit' that time. We camped at Rietfontein about 8 miles N of the Delagoa Railway and 30 miles East of Pretoria.

Sun 22nd July Marched to Rustfontein further S.E. and about 5 miles from railway – en route we chased a boer gun which fired 3 shots and fled – I fear – successfully away.

Mon 23rd July Rested a day here after 10 successive days marching – here we found some dynamite which by the generals wish was expended in blowing down a huge eucalyptus tree for firewood – the tree was about 4 ft or more through and I used 6lbs dynamite in 6 auger holes to the heart – fired simultaneously by electricity and the giant fell.

Tues 24th July Marched to Bronkhorst Spruit Station – about 3 miles from the massacre of the 94th in Dec '80 which was on the old coach road – of which more anon. The fine girder bridge over the spruit had been broken down by the boers. Lord Roberts came into camp that night.

Wed 25th July A terrible day – marched from Bronkhorst Spruit to Balmoral on the railway, vile road and heavy work for us over drifts and bogs to get the big guns along – about 4 miles short of Balmoral the most indescribable storm came on – deluge – lightening – fierce hurricane blasts and awful rain – the troops got to the camping ground – but the storm effectually stopped the food and baggage and stores – so we spent the night – no food – no blankets – no shelter – utterly cold and sodden – fires a farce of smoke and smoulder.

Later in the night the doctor major whose camp adjoined ours offered his hospital tents to the men and the ambulance vans to us – as there were no sick or wounded – this some availed themselves of but sleep was out of the question in a chill, sodden, hungry body – and one simply chattered and shivered the long night through, too numb to walk around to keep the circulation up.

Thurs 26th July Rain ceased early in a.m. – a native said "unknown for 19 years at this time of year" – the transport crawled in by 10 a.m. with some hundreds of animals killed by the storm – we lost 12 in our own company, bitter rain on hot and exhausted animals – died like flies. Nearly all the 10-span teams came in 6 or 7 animals only – we had a meal then at 10.30 a.m. after 28½ hours solid fast since 6 o'clock breakfast – day before.

An officer in the Argylls – Maclaren – died during the night from cold and syncope – and 3 men were brought in half alive to hospital – needless to say we didn't march that day – and as chance would have it our presence there proved 'de trop' as we got news that French was driving all before him and was nearly in Middleburg, and Buller was around somewhere close and so on.

The upshot being that our force was ordered to march back to Pretoria as superfluous after all our trekking – I lost 24 boxes of matches in the storm – most serious loss here – had my writing case and kit sodden etc., however I took 10 grams of quinine off my own bat and am as well as ever now.

Fri 27th July Marched by the main road some three miles South of railway – back to Bronkhorst Spruit – camped near Nooitgedacht farm passed hundreds of oxen and mules victims of the storms.

Sat 28th July Foggy and cold morning – marched off at 7 a.m. R.E. in front of all the troops except mounted scouts – so as to get a start on the holes in the road – passed the graves of the 94th and the scene of the slaughter which was the declaration of open hostility in '80 – graves well kept and walled in – all spread along the roadside for a mile or more just where they fell.

The Connaughts were with us but it was the other battalion which were the 94th Foot, camped at Kaalfontein after crossing a bad pass in the hills.

Sun 29th July Marched to Christinen Hall farm (Lewis and Marks) a fine estate – we crossed the Donkerhoek pass en route where Lord Airlie was killed and fighting took place soon after we took Pretoria.

Mon 30th July Marched into Pretoria and out 3 miles to Daspoort Camp – (a long 15 miles). Lord Roberts watched the column pass through the Market Square in the same manner as the day of triumphal entry only from E. to W. this time.

Got into camp about 3 p.m. – at 4 p.m. it was reported that one of our wagons had broken a wheel some 7 miles back so I had to ride back on a tired pony with a spare wheel in an empty cart for it – some 4 miles through the town, coming back in the dark I got some sausages and eggs at a butcher's, some mealie meal (for porridge) – crushed maize in England! and heavens above, half a dozen fresh eggs!! it is true at <u>only</u> 5/= a dozen – 5d each – but <u>fresh</u> eggs!

The problem was – dead tired and stumbly pony – rocky road and ill-defined, and other parcels – how to carry eggs? Solved it by putting them in my helmet and carrying it gingerly by the chinstrap in one hand and got them safely to camp – nay rather two of them are safely put away in the writer!

Tues 31st July Resting in camp at Daspoort – uncertain where we shall be required next, must pause a moment for news.

Buckle, who has been in Pretoria all day getting stores, boots etc., has just come in and reports that our mails came here alright with a sergeant who was to join us. The Sergeant went sick to hospital – returned the mails to the Post Office and they have sent them off, heaven knows where again to the 7th Company – alas! however they have wired after them to have them sent back and after Hamilton's Force – as I expect we shall be on the move again West this time as it seems the remaining boers are messing about there somewhere.

So now au revoir till next halting place.

Best love to all at home from your ever loving son Eric E.B. Wilson

P.S. On search I find that my last remaining envelopes are all firmly 'stuck up' by the wet!! must try and borrow one.

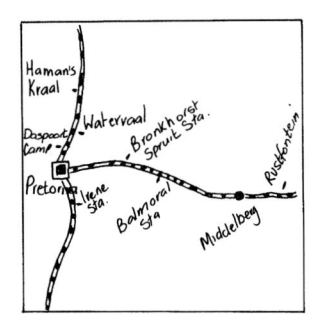

Opposite and S of Commando Poort   -Grootplaatz-
                                       18m. West of Pretoria
                                       under the Magliesberg hills
                                       Friday 10th August 1900
                                       9.45 a.m.

My dearest Father,

Have just heard that a convoy is going into Pretoria and will take mails at 10.30 so only time for a hasty line. I last wrote from Daspoort at Pretoria about Aug 1 – on which day Hamilton's force with Mahon and Hickman's mounted forces marched west between the Magaliesberg and Daspoort hills along the valley towards Rustenberg where we had heard of the presence of some 3000 boers and 10 guns menacing Baden Powell who was in Rustenberg with a few hundred men – we camped that day opposite a gap in the hills called Zilikats Nek which we found occupied by some 200 boers intent on giving trouble before they were driven out – however beyond a few shots nothing took place that night.

Next day Aug 2nd – it was decided to clear this party out before proceeding further West and Mahon's force was supposed to attack them from the North while we sent the Berkshires and Argylls from the South to make them bolt into Mahon's net. Meanwhile we turned a 5 inch gun on to the Nek and the 7th Field Battery shrapnelled it well all over as a preliminary dusting – while the infantry advanced – the infantry soon crowned the adjacent heights and also pushed straight up the Nek and after some warm firing the Boers cleared <u>but</u> Mahon was late or something the other side and they all got away except 7 prisoners who fell into our hands and a few wagons. Our loss was Berks – 4 killed 33 wounded, Argylls 1 killed 1 wounded – the Boers had several killed but got the wounded away.

On Friday Aug 3 – 5 years' service completed.

We marched on at 6.30 a.m. and crossed the Crocodile River and Magalies River and passed over to the N side of the M'berg range through Commando Poort, where we left Hickman's force, the King's Own Scottish Borderers and 2 guns to keep the road open 'agen our return like' – much as we were formerly left at Israel's Poort.

Very pretty and bold scenery round here and bush pretty dense on N side of the hills – we camped at Zandfontein farm – running stream and rocks and orange groves with ripe oranges galore!

Sat Aug 4 Marched to Elandskraal close to some hills running N and S across the road and reported to be held – but found empty.

Sun Aug 5 Marched on over these hills – very up and down going for heavy guns and wagons – to just short of Oliphant's Nek, and about 12 miles (S) from Rustenburg – that afternoon Baden Powell himself rode into camp to see General Hamilton and exchange news. It seems the Boers had trekked off N and W and were attacking a convoy coming from Mafeking with unknown results – however we rested there on the 6th and 7th got orders to start back for Pretoria – and marched back over same road having been joined by Baden Powell and Kekewich with the North Lancs. We camped on same grounds on 7th and 8th as going out – on the 9th we recrossed Commando Poort and got new orders which looked like our turning South instead of holding on E to Pretoria – anyhow we camped just South of Commando Poort on the Magalia River and are resting today – not a glimmer of what we shall do next.

It is very weary work this everlasting chasing of small bodies of Boers and trying to round up Commandos who 'trek' like foxes on the least sign of our troops unless they see a trap which will give them some great advantage over some small fragment of our force, which they will go for then.

I can see no finality in the war at all at present unless some strong man arises in the Boer rank with the courage to say 'Enough' on behalf of the rest – however we hear that Hunter is doing well in getting submission.

Best love to all from your ever loving son Eric E.B. Wilson

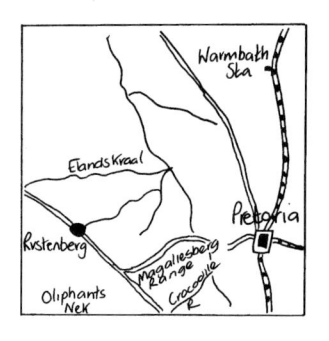

Racecourse Camp, Pretoria
E.W. 25 and 4 days

Thursday 30th August 1900
9 p.m.

My dearest Father

Just back again at Pretoria for a moment, after 19 days continuous marching without a rest!

I last wrote on August 10th from Commando Poort and since then we have made a 250 mile ring landing us in Pretoria! We hoped for a few days rest here but are off again at 4 a.m. tomorrow – by rail, for the first time, and Eastwards to join the great move on the Lydenburg stronghold – possibly we may train as far as Belfast – I have been out most of the night getting horses from the Remount Depôt to replace our sick and sorry ones, and had a great job picking them out in the dark, though they were selected by daylight – I hope I have the right ones!

No mails have found their way to us yet since June 15th though I have frequently agitated the post office and others to find them.

Our recent adventures here have been too normal to detail daily – only marching miles and miles – the general idea being to clear the country N.W. of Pretoria before drawing large bodies off to the East – we have now I think pushed them far up to the N.W. and I don't think they will give much trouble down here for a while, even if they venture South at all – perhaps 3000 men and 10 guns is the force we have been pushing away and trying to catch, should they venture to stand and fight – which they never did. We went due West from Commando Poort till 15th Aug then turned N and made for Oliphant's Nek – a rugged pass leading to Rustenburg – here we had a bit of a fight with the rearguard of the Boers, who having no guns in action waited till we got within rifle shot to begin – so that the R.E. who were with our advance guard and mending the road to the pass came under a very heavy fire for a short time – luckily without casualties – we took the pass with 3 wounded.

We passed through Rustenbury on the 18th and went on East at about 17 miles a day to try and overhaul them – but they meant running and did so – dropping ammunition, wagons, gun limbers etc., all along the road. On the night of 18th we came to a muddy stream which would not stand our heavy five-inch guns without getting them bogged and we worked the whole night through cutting away 4ft 6 of solid mud on to a rock bottom making a road 12 ft wide and about 35ft long through the swamp with pumps going all night to keep the water out. Finished at 3.15 a.m. and marched at 3.30 a.m! 17 miles! Not bad 34 miles and a nights solid work in the 36 hours without a wink of sleep. General Hamilton ordered the R.E. an extra tot of rum the next day.

On the 20th we caught them up again and fought at Roodekopjes just North of Commando Poort again – they fled early – we followed North – doing 20 miles on the 22nd right into the Bush veldt – dense spiky thorn – tears all to pieces – much cutting and chopping for R.E. – we got as far North as WarmBath station (nearly) then were ordered back to Pretoria down main road by line – leaving Baden Powell and Paget to worry them – got in here yesterday – just time to get the men some boots and clothes from Store then off again tomorrow!

Such is the life of the few thousand favoured (?) troops who are always on the move – at the front every day – what the 150,000 other troops that one never hears about except in the papers and not that since we took Pretoria – do – Heaven only knows – no one can tell where all have got to, except the Head Quarter Staff perhaps – one never hears of any except a few divisions (say 30,000 men) doing anything – where indeed are the 170,000 others?

Officers will tell you that their battalion has 1500 men in the country – and they parade (at the front 600 strong – where are the 900?) The truth is that the moving and fighting columns once they drop a man – if only with a blister on his nose or a thorn in his finger – never see him again – he drifts away into "Rest Camps" and lines of communication etc., etc., etc., and no doubt eats his food heartily.

Heavy wind blowing now – we had rain last night – I hope we have good weather out East to end up with as the country is very difficult, alas poor Sappers! – I see heavy work still before you!

I heard that Cordun, a Boer Lieut who plotted to kidnap Bobs, was tried and shot since we have been away.

Will try and write from East soon – must turn in now as rest is rather precious, also <u>Candles</u>!

Still in excellent health and spirits thank God.

Ever your loving son Eric E.B. Wilson

P.S. There is absolutely nothing to be bought in Pretoria for love or money now – we have been living on our rations – beef and biscuit now for a long while!
Normally Pretoria's shopping capacity about equals say Bury St Edmunds – but of course no stores have come in except military for some months now.

Race Course, Pretoria   Friday 31st August 1900

My dearest Father

Just time for another line, owing to a change of plans – We went to the station to entrain for the East this morning when much to our chagrin an order came to say that we were to march instead – so more weary trekking lies before us. I suppose 14 days marching will get us out as far as our troops are now.
While we were at the station we got 2 bags of mail for the section! And I received letters from you dated April 12, 20 and 27 and June 8 and 22 – so I have now had all missing links filled up to June 22!
I also heard from Cousin Nellie – and got papers from Aunt Minnie, Uncle Rowland, yourself, the girls and others, including April and June Harlismere Magazines. Please thank all for them as they are most welcome for reading on the march and in camp.
I don't suppose you or anyone has seen the official mention of 7th Co Officers in any gazette yet because I don't think the official written accounts of any fighting later than defence of Kimberley have been published – only the brief telegraphed accounts as yet – and then again it was only a 'promise' and many things may have occurred to cause such incidents to escape the official memory since then.
I did not come across Archdeacon Holbeach in Bloemfontein – as the Cathedral services were taken by our Army Chaplains.
Many thanks for accounts of Helen's wedding – John Holt's Christening – your and Michael's travels and other most interesting events recorded in last letters to hand.
I have been unlucky in meeting papers re Harrow and Eton match so far – I once saw 1st day viz Eton 290 Harrow 270 for 7 – but no result as yet.

I came across a very sad paragraph re Cousin Ben Lake recently – I hope things are not very bad for him? I should be so sorry if the children suffered – tell me what you know of the case?

I knew all about Tommy Knight's marriage – the man's name is Wilkinson(!) he was a Lieut R.A. at Sheerness when I was at Chatham – of which an allegory – There was once a maid and two men – 'one' man loved the maid, the maid loved the 'other' man – the 'other' man time removed unmoved from the maid – the 'one' man pressed his love on the maid, who at last consented and there you are – but of this tush!

We march tomorrow – along familiar road as far as Balmoral.

Best love to all at home and elsewhere – and a kiss for Algy –
From your ever loving son Eric
10.45 p.m.

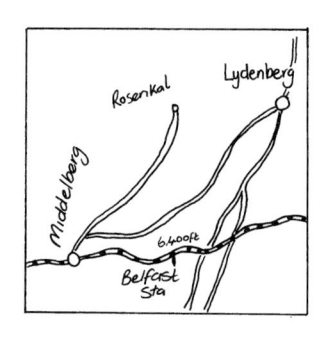

Belfast Station   **Monday 10th September 1900**
90 m: E. of Pretoria
Height 6,400 ft. the highest
Station in Transvaal –

My dearest Father

We got here safely after nine continuous marches from Pretoria – about 110 miles by road, on the 8th – and have had two days rest and quiet – tomorrow we march on to the next station, Machadodorp –about 13 miles. Lord Roberts and all the headquarter staff are here – Kitchener etc – and they are moving with us tomorrow.

Being in the same camp as theArmy Head Quarters has many advantages – chiefly the certainty of the best rations the commissariat can produce, and the quickest delivery of mails, for instance I received here yours of Aug 10 on Sept 8th!! Your last to hand being June 22, so I am about 6 weeks deficient in the gap. Many thanks for your birthday wishes – I expected about the 24th Aug to be my furthest North on the 26th but we turned South a day sooner than we expected so I was 2 marches South – at Haman's Kraal – on that day – last year I was at Wynberg – feverishly scanning the 'Cape Argus' for signs of the outbreak – it seems two centuries ago now!

I am so sorry to hear about Chris Blomfield – I was very fond of the old man indeed.

I am glad Algy does not approve of my being made a target of!

You couple Cicely's name with that of a 'Lieut Ovans'? does that imply another impending alliance of the great Wilson stock!

I cannot recall any circumstances connected with the death of a Capt. Lennox at Paardeberg – and have no reference that I can make here – he did not come under my ken during the 9 days fighting there.

My old Curragh troop horses that have drawn my 'toolcarts' so faithfully for so many hundreds of miles, are breaking down at last – another died today – sheer 'useduppedness'. I have to replace these with mules.

We had a great Race meeting here today, steeplechases etc., for Officers' animals – my brace of crocks have seen too many miles of veldt for such games – most of the races were won by well rested animals of staff officers etc – however they were great fun – the mule race for natives – bareback – 3 furlongs – was immense.

The country between here and Pretoria is very plain rolling veldt – like the Northern Free State – East of this it suddenly changes to the most broken and rugged of all the Transvaal, and there the boers are hiding – and very difficult to get at.

I hear that since I left 7th Co. Col Kincaid has got a staff job – and a Major Haggitt is to command us – lately O.C. of 38th Co. R.E. – I have not met him. Next time you write tell me the latest news of the following – and their whereabouts – Geoff & Jack – Basil – Arthur – Frank and Villiers – Tom Gilbart –(if possible) –Edward Greene – is Miss Colekin still alive? – what are Tom and George going into? Have they shot the Glebe yet? Burgate? Or Hinderclay? What happens to poor Denis Murch's Diss property?

I have been unable to trace Raymond's whereabouts once since I met him at Naauwpoort.

I am glad to see Uncle Walter is to stand for Bury.

How is the grass doing on the field you laid down behind my old revolver butt? How does the Mission room 'weather' and any other things you can think of – I like to picture Redgrave according to the seasons!

Best love to all with you from your loving son Eric E.B. Wilson.

Redgrave, Suffolk. Village Green.

Komati Poort　　　　　　　　　　　　　　　　Monday 1st October 1900
(Transvaal – Portuguese Frontier)

My dearest Father

I received today from you letters of July 27th and August 17th also August Magazine for which many thanks. The only mails of which I have no trace now are:– June 29 – July 6 – July 20 (no letter I think) and August 3 – and subsequent to August 17 which is the very latest at present. July 13 has a tragic history. A friend of mine in the R.A. – E.M.Birch – you may recall his name – sent me an open envelope – addressed by you to me – dated July 13. This was picked up on the veldt six miles from the railway south of Johannesberg after a successful raid on a train by the Boers – who destroyed a complete mail apparently and left empty envelopes after their flight. The irony of it comes in beautifully when I tell you that he also forwarded me another empty envelope – from Craig my bootmaker at Woolwich – and this one had the bill still inside!! Nice feeling on the boer's part that!

Well, I must try and describe our movements since we left Machadodorp – where I last posted to you. We have had a time full of incident and hard work since then but no fighting, and we have been traversing a country almost worse than Switzerland. To enable you to follow in detail places I mention you should write to:– Edward Stanford, 26 & 27 Cockspur Street, Charing Cross S.W. for sheets nos: 4, 5,and 6, of JEPPE'S large scale map of the Transvaal. The mere inspection of these maps gives you a very fair idea of the vastness and difficulty of the country we have been over, though there are plenty of mountains not shown on it that are only too visible in the real country!

On Tuesday September 11th we left Belfast at 6 a.m. for Machadodorp – getting into camp about 1.30 p.m. En route we passed over the scene of the big fight at Dalmanutha where I picked up some bits of lyddite shells etc.

In the p.m. walked round the station, after after fixing up water pumps etc – posted letters, and looked at our monster 9.2 inch gun which was mounted on a truck in a siding there – with a range of about from Redgrave to Eye Town Hall – and a 250 lb shell to burst when it gets there. It is hard to bear in mind

BROOMHILLS, BOTESDALE, DISS

the relative distances at which fighting is carried on now. The ordinary Field gun would take up a position at the Greyhound Inn on the cross roads and drop shell after shell into Diss – while the riflemen firing from Barley Birch would make it uncommon warm for anyone crossing Wortham Long Green! You hear of 'snipers' – well he would be the individual who lay in one of Tom Wright's stacks and kept having pot shots at Broom Hills – very unpleasant for the latter and very hard to tell where exactly the shots were coming from. The enemy at Broom Hills would probably shell Redgrave Rectory in retaliation as the nearest thing they could see! And the moral effect of the shells shrieking over the snipers head would probably remind him that it was time for his tea, which would have been boiling over a few sticks under the bank of the pond at the 'cottage' next Elijah Broome's old cottage – and made with the water from the pond, unless he had the nerve to draw from the well in the open in front of the cottage.

Well, back to Machadodorp – after a walk round I met Col. Bethel R.E. Staff Officer to Chief Engineer, an old De Aar cooperator of mine and had tea with him.

Wed Sept 12th Quiet morning in camp – but got orders to march at 4 p.m. to join Hamilton's Force once more at Helvetia – 6 miles by road N.E. over the mountains – in the Lydenburg district – got in long after dark.

Thurs Sept 13 Marched at 7 a.m. with the force now consisting of Gordons – Royal Scots – Royal Irish – 20th Field Battery – Canadian 12 pr battery and Elswick battery and two 5 inch guns to Waterval Onder, down a rugged pass with a drop of 3,000 feet in about two miles or so. Here we camped on the line again. Went over in the p.m. and had tea with the Gordons who were pleased to meet me again after an absence since July 11th when we parted at Irene.

Friday Sept 14 Marched at 6 a.m. to one mile beyond Nooitgedacht where the last of our prisoners had been kept – in a wire enclosure opening on the Elands river. Heard here that Kruger had fled the country. I also saw here some of his 'blank sovereigns' simply discs the size of a pound cut out like a counter from gold plate – they passed current for 20/= tho' there wasn't a scratch of head or tail on them!

Sat Sept 15 Marched on past Goodwan Station to Roodewal – found the Welsh Regiment there. Heard French in Barbertown – and much rolling stock caught. Here (Roodewal) the valley becomes impassable and the road takes to the hills to the S.E.

Sun Sept 16 Marched at 3.30 a.m. because of enormous hills to climb to Kaapsche Hoop a climb of 2,300 feet – a terrible time for the mules and horses. The italic '1768' at Kaapsche Hoop is the height in metres = about 5,800 ft almost exactly. (Metre = 3.28 ft). The infantry were spread all along at all the worst precipices to man haul the wagons and guns up.

Mon Sept 17 Marched to Joubertsdal almost due N. and more fearful hills. Splendid view of Barberton in distance and the De Kaap goldfields.

Tues Sept 18 Marched S.E. to a place about 12 miles from Barberton – very poor water – and while I was riding some miles from camp looking for water alone I put up a splendid 'bok' but was too late into getting my carbine to hand to get a decent shot.

Lions are reported fairly common about here still. Got the empty envelope from you from a bag of despatches in the evening. We also had a shower of rain – the harbinger of more I expect.

Wed Sep 19 Marched at 5 a.m. to North Kaap River station on the Barberton branch line over several baddish drifts. In the afternoon Gen.Smith Dorrien, Boileau and I and a few scouts went down the river to try and dynamite a few fish! The scouts walking it up first! We tried in about three places but only got some 6 or 7 fish – one of 6 lb – a barbel – others smaller, I think there were too many people about. It is a fine river – and has the remains of a huge masonry dam across it here which must have cost thousands of pounds to build and is now long in ruins.

Thurs Sept 20 Marched at 5 a.m. to Honeybird Creek via Avoca, where I met J.R.White who was there (from French at Barberton) to repair a badly broken bridge. At Arran Station were about 40 engines left by boers in sidings. Got some raisins, cornflour, candles and bottled fruit in Avoca.

<u>Fri Sept 21</u> Marched at 11 a.m. in advance of the whole force with 40 natives to clear a bad bit of road reported a mile out from camp – turned out a hoax or mistake as road was goodish for 4 or 5 miles – but bad towards end. Marched to Louws Creek through some lovely wooded valleys.

<u>Sat Sept 22</u> Marched at 4 a.m. to Kaap Muiden – the junction with main line again and where a big girder bridge is down. Heard that two leopards seen here – also puff adders. No sooner arrived at K. Muiden than ordered to hurry on <u>by train</u> (never yet used by us since we left De Aar!!!! Though thousands of troops moved daily by it) to mend a railway bridge between Malelane and Hector Spruit stations.

<u>Sun Sept 23</u> Got to bridge this a.m. after considerable delays waiting for an engine then found some mistake about order for material for repairs which did not arrive till next morning, two miles to fetch our water here – from the Crocodile River – a magnificent stream, about 200 yards wide here.

<u>Mon Sept 24</u> Started work on arrival of rails and sleepers early and worked hard all day. Kitchener turned up with an engine and three carriages and calmly sat there till the bridge should be built! Worked straight through the night – during the evening a train of guards and supplies also arrived and formed queue behind Kitchener.

About 1.30 a.m. <u>Tues Sept 25</u> a third train arrived full tilt in the dark crash into No 2, derailed four trucks and sent them flying over embankment sideways – sent No 2 train into Kitchener's – which as near as a toucher came over the broken gap down a 30 foot fall! The crash was terrific – but very few hurt. At 8 a.m. bridge was nearly finished and Kitchener insisted on crossing before the rails were spiked down or anything finished up at all! But he got over without mishap. This bridge no sooner rebuilt than we were ordered to load up our tools and stores and go on with Kitchener's train to the next broken bridge – 5m beyond Hector Spruit Station. We were all pretty tired after 24 hours continuous work at high pressure but more was to follow! Got to Hector Spruit Station about 10.15 a.m. and found Hamilton's (our) force in camp there having marched past us while we were repairing bridge, filled up with water here for drinking, and got to broken bridge 5 miles on by 11 a.m. and started clearing debris. We were badly delayed for a while by the old girder which was only down at one end and had to be cleared aside as it was too damaged to replace – besides weighing some 40 tons. We tried hauling it aside with 200 men on strong ropes – but the ropes broke over and over again – so we had to cut it in half with a charge of 180lb of guncotton!

This was quite successful and left it as per sketch:–

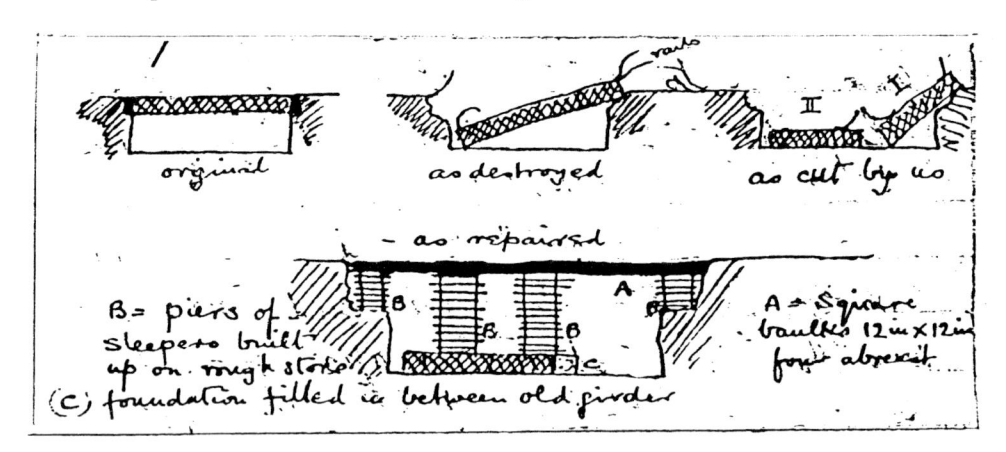

[sketch with annotations: "original", "as destroyed", "as cut by us", "as repaired"; "B = piers of sleepers built up on rough stone"; "(C) foundation filled in between old girder"; "A = Square boulders 12in × 12in four abreast"]

It only remained then to remove portion I which I accomplished with a screw jack – a very slow and tedious job as it had to be cross-jacked 11 ft before it fell, and could only be moved about ¼ inch at a time with the jack! This took me till 1 a.m. – but meanwhile they were building up the piers over the other half girder which had been built in with large stones to form a solid foundation.
<u>Wed Sept 26</u> I got a spell of rest from 1 to 6 a.m. after about 42 hours continuous!! When I took over my turn of charge of the work again I found good progress – and by dark we had all building work finished and turned in to wait for the plate layers who were to train up that night and relay the rails across.
<u>Thurs Sept 27</u> Found at daylight platelayers train had been – laid rails – and on over the bridge to Komati Poort and the line was for the first time open from end to end – Pretoria to Komati Poort. We got a wire to proceed to Komati Poort by the "first train that passed" but as we had 5 miles to send for water to Hector Spruit we thought we might as well wait there as anywhere so marched in that afternoon with as much stores as we could get on to 3 trollies, leaving the rest with a company of Gordons, who had been left to guard the bridge and who were loud in their execration of the distance they had to go for water. At Hector Spruit once more we got comfortably installed in an empty bungalow and had dinner – soon after which a train came along and we once more all packed up our stores and jumped into the least crowded cattle truck – but did not get away till 1 a.m., as the engine was thirsty and the pumping station was 2 miles away on the crocodile River, and the pump engineer had drawn his fires for the night and turned in, so it all took time before water ran out of the stand pipe in the station again. We stopped en route at our new bridge to pick up the rest of our tools and

stores – then on to Komati Poort, arriving 5 a.m. Station all burnt out and hundreds of smouldering trucks in the sidings – the boers farewell touch. Still there are some miles of good carriages and trucks up the Selati railway which joins here, and these we are sending off in numbers daily – westwards. When we arrived the Grenadier Guards were all trained up en route for HOME and since then all the Guards Brigade have gone back – and we are following back by degrees, but not, I fear "home" – for some while yet. The morning we arrived they had a parade in honour of the King of Portugal's birthday and a special train of Portuguese officials and ladies came up from Lourenço Marques to see it – unfortunately going back this train left the line and several injuries resulted – 3 saloons overturned and wrecked.

Well, we settled down into camp here and rejoined Buckle who had marched along with the column to conduct our transport mules and vehicles while we were using rail. Several stores here are still well stocked from the coast and trains of supplies running in daily from Lourenço M., so we are well fed for the moment.

However it is intensely unhealthy here from the low ground and climate – without the acres of boer garbage and dead animals etc in all directions. I noticed on arrival that the few decent houses were all built on stone "rickbottoms" off the ground – a sure sign of the place – however as our favourite joke has it now – we are warranted to kill any microbe at 40 yards, after so much roughing it, and all troops are sleeping on the ground, heat intense and humid and awful stinks after sunset.

The boers have not destroyed the fine seven span girder bridge over the Inkomati River here. A mile lower down the Crocodile R. joins in and the double river some 300 yards wide (in flood) runs through the Komati (poort) or gate in the hills and thence to the sea – magnificent river scenery, but country dry and monotonous thorn bush all round.

The Boers left tons of ammunition and stores flour etc here, also a Long Tom, which however they had blown up – I have several fragments to bring home. I forgot to mention that at Hector Spruit we found remains of pretty well all our captured guns (Colenso) etc., blown up and thrown into the Crocodile River – also several boer Krupp guns, pom-poms etc.

Sat Sept 29 Commenced a survey of the country around here for official records – tramping all day in boiling sun but got time for a bathe in the river in evening. Coffin and Lyell destroying boer shell and ammunition all day in their last laager on the frontier – about ½ mile from Ressano Garcia the Portuguese frontier station.

Sun Sept 30 No rest for the wicked – continued survey – worked along railway to Ressano, had a chat with Portuguese soldiers on guard (French our medium), and clambered all over the Lebombo Mountains – very muggy and hot.

While I was thus engaged the party burning ammunition had a bad accident, as usual cause unknown – anyway result of a premature explosion was 3 men killed (Gordons) 17 wounded (Gordons, 1 R.E.) – very sad indeed – supposed that some careless Tommy knocked his pipe out on some loose powder or something. (One R.E.Sapper injured). Lyell – who was nominally in charge had a marvellous escape – he saw this particular party doing something wrong in the way they were building their stuff up etc., and ran over to stop them and got the explosion full in the face at 5 paces! He was hurled insensible 25 yards over the rocks and is still deaf but otherwise uninjured. The poor fellows who were injured had the most fearful wounds, whole cartridges – case and bullet – driven into their bodies etc etc., pieces of cases forced through their backs and out between the ribs. Thank God I wasn't on duty at the time. But as we haven't heard the verdict of the Court of Enquiry yet – I mustn't attribute the blame to anyone particular.

We have just heard that we are going to rail right back to Pretoria and probably trek out Rustenberg way again!! Gen. Hamilton & Staff have gone, and only the Royal Scots and Gordons and some Artillery etc., are left here – with Smith Dorrien in command. However from all accounts they are having so many collisions along the line that it may be some days before we get away after all. Amongst other trophies from the Boer laager I have a packet of Prussian needle gun ammunition made in 1859 – and as used in the Franco German war of '70. They burnt or destroyed numbers of rifles here.

Mon Oct 1 Fearfully close all day – one of my old troop horses – marched from De Aar – died during the night from exhaustion consequent on having a day or two's rest. They keep going alright day after day – but after some thousand miles or so it is dangerous to rest them, as they often seize the chance to die – poor old thing – he had done yeoman service for his country. I surveyed up the Selati Railway today and saw thousands of pounds worth of plant and rails etc., rotting by the contractors sheds. It seems to be a question what we shall do with the Pretoria, Komati Poort line – either confiscate it and repair it or else take down all the temporary bridges, paralyse the district and let it rot and use some British seaport for the Transvaal. We certainly shall not do permanent repairs for the benefit of the double-dyed Netherlands Railway Co (supposed neutral) nor shall we rely on supplies through Portuguese ground, except perhaps for a garrison here – fed from Lourenço Marques. But we cannot garrison all this hill and fever district perpetually. I fancy the latest is to confiscate the line on account of their obvious want of neutrality (the Netherlands Co, I mean) who have been practically 100 per

cent the mainstay of the Transvaal transport – and so can be outed as enemies. Had a bad dust storm last night – worse than the old Modder River ones. I may post this via Lourenço Marques as safer and quicker – via Suez and Mediterranean.
Best love to all – I am still in splendid health and spirits thank Heaven.

From your ever loving son Eric E.B. Wilson

P.S. What has <u>Jack</u> been gazetted to?

Komati Poort   **Friday 12th October 1900**
Temperature yesterday 105° in the shade

My dear Father

I hope you got my last letter safely – posted via Lourenço Marques on October 4th. No further home mails received here. As you will see, we are still at Komati – have been here just 16 days, and are likely to remain for <u>some time</u> – possibly a month or two months, as all available R.E. have been turned on to building huts and making roads etc., for a permanent garrison here of about 5 or 600 men – and hutting them will take time, as all material has to be railed from Lourenço M. All the troops of the Guards and XIX Brigades have returned Pretoria-wards now except the Royal Scots who are to be first permanent garrison with ½ battalion here and ½ at Kaap Muiden – a little way back – the junction for Barberton.
We have also here some mounted scouts, a few guns etc., and 1 section each of 7th and 9th Cos. R.E. and all the 12th Co R.E. – and 70 native pioneers.
It is very pleasant here at present. Spring is just changing to summer and trees coming out nicely – but though cooler today it has been most oppressive lately and will be stifling in a few days. This is considered the most unhealthy place in S.Africa in the rains – which are just beginning – but I fancy our men are fairly seasoned now – though perhaps a bit too run down to resist much fever. I have finished my rough survey of the neighbourhood – as much as I shall do, viz about 18 square miles. I had great fun exploring around in the bush and have found several good places for a bit of shooting when time allows.

Partridges common but not pheasant. At present there are any amount of wild buck of different kinds about, also panther, jackal, hippopotamus and crocodile in the river and lion a bit up North – about 15 or 20 miles. The only day I had a carbine with me when surveying some miles from camp. I got a shot at a fine buck some way off in the thick bush, but missed him and couldn't get in another shot – the bush is so thick that you may be only 20 yards from all sorts of things without being able to get in a shot. I fear that a permanent garrison here will soon drive the game further afield, so now is really the time if one had the chance.

I was down at Ressano Garcia last week – the first station over the Portuguese frontier and made friends with a funny old Portuguese Major – the Commandant there – and got leave to explore a bit along their side of the frontier – we talked vile French to each other as a medium of conversation, it was most amusing!

I sent you a copy of the 'local paper' a few days ago – it has some news in English. We heard last night that the elections were about 350 to 180 which was good news – to date.

We have taken over two fine bungalows for the R.E. now. We live in one and the men in the other – and have procured beds etc., from other empty houses and are quite comfortable at last. Plenty of food and stores procurable also here now – from Lourenço M. but very dear of course. One of the 12th Co. officers was down in Lourenço a few days ago, and saw Kruger sitting outside the consul's house, as bold as brass, with a Portuguese guard over him! I daresay he has sailed for Europe by now, It seems an awful shame that we cannot bag him!

On the 9th Capt. Coffin and I rode out and up the Selati railway to see how much rolling stock was still left. We have cleared about 5 miles of trucks away and sent them off with troops going west – but there are still some 5 or 6 miles solid of trucks and carriages awaiting removal.

We struck off into the bush after going about 7 miles and came back along the Crocodile River to camp. We saw 3 hinds and a fine buck but could not get a shot at them.

On the 10th – Kruger's birthday – 75 – we were putting in a new siding at the foot of the hills on the E. of the river for the use of the new permanent camp which is on the Western slope of the Lebombo Mountains overlooking the 'Poort' where the combined Komati and Crocodile rivers run through towards the coast.

The 11th was the anniversary of the commencement of hostilities – and it seems to me like five and twenty years ago at least! I suppose another year or so ought to see the end of it! By then we shall have a practically new army out! as all the old warriors will have been invalided home or otherwise disposed of. I believe all the volunteers are going home by degrees, and the Guards, and a few other favoured regiments. I haven't heard yet if the 7th Co: is for home or to stop out here for service – but there won't be any hurry either way. You may be sure that as surely as we are the first in the field to make ready the way, so surely shall we be the last out of it after we have made everyone comfortable and fixed them up.

I suppose Raymond has succeeded in getting home for the elections? I have seen and heard nothing of him since we met at Naauwpoort. My section that left Wynberg in Sep '99 – one officer and 45 rank and file – musters at our journey's end(?) one officer and 20 r. & f. – not bad considering all that we have been through – with scarcely a pause or rest – and no chance of men left sick rejoining again. Of horses that left Wynberg with me – I brought Fusilier and Bill Sykes (the Cape pony) and one riding and four draught troop horses, of these 7, only one of the draught horses are with me today! Though of course their places have been filled by remnants at different times. The one draught horse I think has fairly earned his daily keep by now!! But though of minished numbers the quality is very different, I brought 45 vacant minded boys away from Wynberg with me and now have 20 bronzed and salted men instead, which makes a lot of difference. I fear that all our heavy baggage – English uniform and clothes, packed away in the rainy season at Wynberg will be hopelessly ruined by now – if we ever get them again!

I expect I should find Wynberg a very different place from the pretty hill village it was when we went there in Aug '99 – since they have had thousands of sick there and large hospitals. I left my camera in Bloemfontein with our heavy stores. I wish I had it here now as there is plenty to take around the Poort. The mails I have yet to receive approximately left England: June 29, July 6, 13, 20, Aug 3, 24, 31, Sep 7, and following mails – I have received July 27, Aug 10, 17, (the last). The homeward mails from here are like the best cricketers "they go off every now and then" and also occasionally "come on again". You can picture us for the present at any rate, building wooden bungalows on the slopes of the Lebombo and frequently mopping our heated brows!

Best love to all from your ever loving son Eric E.B. Wilson

By the time a reply comes to this it will be close on Christmas.

P.S. I have several pieces of the Ladysmith 'Long Tom' Boer 6 inch gun which they tried to destroy before leaving here – also pieces of 6 in. shell if I can get them home.

Komati Poort   Friday 26th October 1900

My dearest Father

I have at last received some wandering mails once more – namely Aug 3 and 24 and Sep 13 – from you. Also from Moonie Aug 30. For all of which many thanks. I think it was a criminal piece of carelessness on the part of the War Office and I should most certainly claim my travelling expenses to and from Southampton.

I hope you got my last two letters from here- both forwarded via Lourenço Marques as safer and quicker! though the postage 100 reis = about 3 d is rather excessive. I have practically no news for you – we are very quietly but busily engaged all day in building and road making, the heat is very excessive but the troops keep very well.

I have been occupied chiefly in building two large stables for mules lately – and our next job is to be the Officer's Mess. There are 7 R.E. Officers at present with the 12th Co. and our two sections of 7th and 9th Co. Of these Buckle and Nation were my term at Woolwich – the other four are a Major Graham Thomson, and 3 Captains Clifford Coffin, Schreiber and Craven. We work in couples – Craven and I are doing Stables and Mess, and take day on day off in superintending.

I have regained touch with my Company who were till recently at Heilbron – but now once more at Bloemfontein – where we left our heavy baggage in April – our real heavy effects of course are still in the R.E. store at Wynberg – viz- home uniform – civilian clothes – in fact everything, as we, unlike the "Field Force" came out here to live here and not merely to fight and return – but whether the 7th Co. will be retained for service I am unable to say as yet. I am practically a certainty for it as I have had an unusually long spell of home service (5 years) but in any case if all goes well I shall get about four months leave.

We are already getting accounts of all the welcomes etc extended to the returning troops and rather hope the public will have expended its energy before the bulk gets back.

I feel there will be much of the feeling condemned in Matt. XX 12 to overcome in settling accounts over the war, and it does seem rather hard not to grudge reward to men to come out in charge of drafts etc at this time of day – however "to count the game above the prize" is pretty sound of everything worth doing in this life isn't it?

I also heard from Rowland last mail in reply to one I sent long ago. He wonders if I produced the account of the 'Cronje' hunt'- a feat which I must modestly disclaim – though I have never discovered who the 'Harrovian' was. I incline to Lt.Carlyon – North Staffs as the one I met in Johannesburg. I should put him at about 33.

I see the volatile Spencer Churchill has been returned for Oldham. I well remember in Harrow days preparing some work with– no – it must have been borrowing a book from him in his room in the "small" house, which for the moment I forget the master of – just below Bos's on the hill – before he got into Welldon's – and he produced a beautiful photograph of Lady Randolph for my inspection. I see <u>she</u> has married a Cornwallis West, a curious match isn't it? I saw a goodish bit of Churchill and his cousin Marlboro' during the main advance as they attached themselves to Ian Hamilton's staff.

Capt Clifford Coffin R.E. who is with us now has a wife residing in Camberley, Aunt Lily may know her.

'Steinakers' Horse' a local corps, are giving an open air sing song tonight.

Much love to all from your ever loving son Eric E.B. Wilson.

Komati Poort   **Thursday 8th November 1900**

My dearest Father

I fear that rather a long gap may have elapsed since my last letter of Oct 27 but have little news to record at present. The last letter from you was dated Sep 21 when you were just off to the auction at Cotton. We are still very busy all day in various parts of the place – the huts are growing apace – and we have finished several blocks of large stables for mules etc.

At present I am sinking a well, or trying to, through solid rock to supply water to a steam pump independently of the river – which at this season is thick and muddy in the extreme, though when we first arrived it was 'low' and beautifully clear and sweet.

We had a sanitary commission round here taking notes lately under a Col. Notter R.A.M.C. with a view to reporting on the place as a camp, as so much is always heard of its unhealthiness. We persuaded the medico that if they would only recommend the West Coast special <u>pay</u>, the place would become much healthier and well sought after!!

Coffin, our skipper, has gone up the line to visit Kaap Muiden and some other stations just along here to report on the sanitation to the Chief Engineer – the chief sign of the 20th century seems to be that every alternative person is inspecting and reporting on the health, wealth affairs and sanitation of the other half.

On Wed Oct 31 we got news from Lourenço that some boers were collecting to attack this place for the sake of the food etc, but nothing has been heard of them except a party of 4 boer despatch riders were met by some of our scouts trying to get over the frontier with despatches. We shot one dead, wounded another and captured all four horses – two men escaping on foot.

We also got the despatches which were from Steyn to the Dutch Consul at Lourenço and no doubt useful to our intelligence dept at Pretoria where they were sent.

Steinakers' Horse were the scouts in question, a most useful body of rough and ready colonials who patrol the frontier for miles each side of this.

On Nov 2 – it was wet most of the day – the 12th Co had a horse knocked through the big girder bridge over the Komati by an engine – the bridge is a railway one only – but can be negotiated by horsemen in single file when <u>clear</u> and as it is our only link with our new camp on the Lebombo Mountains it is in constant use by pack mules etc. I have nearly been caught on it once or twice by a train when riding over.

Sat Nov 3 was a regular wash out all day and we did not leave camp. I worked at a fair copy of my rough survey of the place as the C.R.E. wanted to send it to the Chief Engineer (Gen. Elliot Wood).

Col. Douglas of the Royal Scots went away on sick leave to Lourenço (uncle of the Douglas of my batch) and has since been invalided – leaving Graham Thomson the Maj, of 12th Co – Camp Commandant. I see that the young Douglas also has got home invalided – but know no details of his injuries.

After the heavy rain the two rivers have swollen enormously and are now vast muddy torrents several hundred yards wide,

On Nov 6th I was working this side of the river at some stables, in the afternoon I visited Steinaker's Horse and had some sharp shooting with them off their stoep (verandah) at rocks in the river etc 800 yds below us. I was also given a fine piece of hippopotamus hide which will make a cutting whip (sjambok) and a walking stick.

Yesterday I was well sinking and lunched with 12th Co.

Nation has gone down to Lourenço to inspect some timber. I am one of the few who has not been down yet – but I hope to go down to draw money for paying men presently.

I expect to discharge my groom George Whitecross soon – he has served me very faithfully since '97 and followed me through the war and is now naturally anxious to get home again. I hope to get him a passage as temporary servant to some officers returning home.

My little band of Sappers is gradually dwindling – I have only some 18 with me now of the original 50 – though several have fallen away sick and found me again later, in between the various expeditions since we entered Pretoria.

I still have my invaluable Corporal Colin Stewart, a man of exceptional education and resource and who has done very well all through, he is now under orders to return by Feb to join a class for Military Foremen of Works which will grade him as a sergeant major straight from corporal.

According to latest advice 7th Co are at Bloemfontein but are poor hands at answering communications addressed to them. The headquarters of 7th Co have never been in the Transvaal yet! So I have had a fair bit of luck all round. There is a lot more to do here yet after building the huts, they talk of putting down new steam pump etc to supply the camp on the hills – this would mean more well sinking and much time.

I expect we shall see Christmas here yet! However we have a roof over our heads and enough to eat and what more can one expect in wartime!

Happy and Dick, the big horse and colonial pony from Johannesburg are both still alive and well. The horse I may add has the most mournful expression you ever saw on an animal hence his name. I think I told you that all the 5

troop horses had died at last – so my tool cart at present is like a service without a parson – full of good intentions (and tools) but no one to guide it to the 'right place'. However I hope it will be rail from this on – one never knows though.
Shall post this here today as I shall not be going Ressano way.
I am glad to hear good accounts of M. and H.
Much love to all – I hope mother is teaching Algie to shoot!

From your ever loving son Eric E.B. Wilson

P.S. The 12th Co have a monkey who is great friends with me – he springs on to my shoulder – tips my helmet on one side and begins to look for . . . say wild game – yesterday however he stole a partridge feather out of the puggaree of my helmet which I prized as I had kept it since Paardeburg. He is a monkey of considerable education – there are plenty about wild – but harder than De Wet to catch!

I left De Aar – November 13th 1899 with –

        48 – N. C. O's and Sappers
         4 – Drivers
         1 – Civilian servant
         1 – Officer
        54

Komati Poort – November 21st 1900 –

Trades as under		–	Now present (14)	
Carpenters, Cabinet makers, Wheelwrights	15	–	5	
Masons, Bricklayers	9	–	3	
Smiths, Farriers	5	–	2	1 gone sick today (Partridge)
Plumbers	–	4	–	2
Painters	–	3	–	2
Fitters	–	2	–	nil
Telegraphists	–	2	–	nil
Clerk	–	1	–	nil
Draughtsman	–	1	–	1	gone home since photo
Engine Driver	–	1	–	nil
Saddler	–	1	–	1
Tailor	–	1	–	nil
Slater	–	1	–	1
Cooper	–	1	–	nil
Boot maker	–	1	–	nil
		48		16

Komati Poort   Wednesday 21st November 1900

My dearest Father

I fear you will be awaiting a letter from me rather anxiously – we have been so busy that the time seems to slip by very rapidly – out to work at 6.30 a.m. and back at dusk does not leave much time for letter writing.

I have received no letters since yours of Sept. 21st – the mails seem to be hanging fire a bit as far as I am concerned.

Nov 8th. I was well sinking all day – slow work through solid rock – we are trying to get an independent supply of water, as the rivers are vast muddy torrents now that the rains are on us. We have had a lot of rain and thunderstorms lately – making the place very humid and rank and hot – and malaria is beginning to get hold of the troops by degrees – at the moment of writing to you (7.45 p.m.) in shirt and trousers, the perspiration is streaming down my back! Clifford Coffin our captain, is lying in the next room very bad with malarial fever, but the doctor thinks he is on the mend.

On Nov 9th – I was riding around all day looking after various jobs – fixing up a bathroom for the hospital – building stables for Mounted Infantry – cleaning out the 'town' reservoir, well sinking etc.

Nov 10. I was across the river up on the hills again at the new camp seeing about the building of the Officers Mess House. Whitecross – my man who has been with me since '97 left for home after having been right through the campaign – I did not care to detain him (a civilian) against his will in a place like this – so paid him up, got him a free passage to Cape Town and he undertook the rest.

Sun Nov 11th – we had a holiday – Church Parade 8 a.m. conducted by our only padre – the presbyterian attached to the Royal Scots – an earnest but not a fluent speaker.

Jack Nation of 12th Co and Elsner the R.E. doctor came round to see us – the latter took a snapshot of my poor little section – of which I am able to send you a print. Also a key and some information about the men. I figure with a Mauser Carbine and captured Boer bandolier – my weapon since June – before that I carried a Lee Metford Carbine and Revolver. In the background you see one of the hundreds of railway trucks burnt out by the boers before flying.

The terrier Nell has stuck to us since Johannesburg and produced 4 pups (I think) on my birthday up North of Pienaars River. What these men could not tell you about hard marching, hard work short grub, and muddy water would not cover a sixpence. I feel almost ashamed of being their leader –

Names; Trade; and Age

#	Name	Age	#	Name	Age
1 Driver	Wentworth	24	11 Lance Corporal Plumber	Boyd	35
2 Sapper Bricklayer	Sheehy	20	12 Lance Corporal Slater	Davis	24
3 Sapper Bricklayer	Scrimshaw	28.5	13 Sapper Carpenter	Doyle	24.5
4 Sapper Smith	Peel	20	14 Sapper Smith	Partridge	24
5 Sapper Bricklayer	Purchase	20	15 Sapper Carpenter	Barnham	20
6 Sapper Cabinet Maker	Buckeridge	24	16 Sapper Carpenter	Beckett	22
7 Sapper Painter	Campbell	26	17 Sapper Carpenter	Waldron	20
8 Corporal Draughtsman	Colin Stewart	26	18 Sapper Saddler	Brown	24
9 Sapper Bricklayer	Clarke	20	19 Your humble servant Lieut. of Engineers	E.E.B.H-W	24.5
10 2nd Corporal Plumber	Pengilly	29			

Key to No 1

```
        2
    1       3      16      14
          5     4 18    19         13
                  6   8        15
                    7        11
                         9        12
                           10
                                    Dog
                                    Nell
```

The inscription on the two leather cases is no 2 sec: 7th Field Co: R.E. - (Nov 13 '99) De Aar to Komati Poort (Nov 13 '00) (2000 miles on foot) on horseback and usually a bit better off for grub – but I think they are proud of their survival and are ready for another rubber if need be.

Have just heard that 8 more officers have gone sick today – 2 Royal Scots and 1 R.A. This only leaves the Scots 3 Officers for duty with half a battalion – (normally some 14 Officers or so.) But they are going to be relieved by some some fresh battalion of good strength – so it won't matter much. The R.E. of course will be left here till they are carried away sick one by one To resume my diary – On Nov 12 I was ordered to Kaap Muiden station to see into their water supply and if possible start them well digging – I got there at 9.30 p.m. after a lucky journey in Leggett R.E.'s saloon – he is one of the railway swells and lives in his private saloon – anyway he stood me a good dinner – which was better that a hunk of bread and jam – in an open truck, the actual conveyance by rail. A railway company R.E. is undoubtedly the unit to have seen this show with – no long marching and starvation and inclement weather and sleeping in mire but always living on a train – the officers in a saloon, plenty of very hard work indeed, and most excellent work – but plenty of grub to do it on and a dry bed after it which is after all a great thing. Leggett however is one of the Assistant Directors of the Imperial Military Railways and a very clever fellow at railway work.

Arrived at Kaap Muiden I slept comfortably on the platform and under a roof.

After an early breakfast I walked up to the Royal Scots camp (the other ½ Battalion) to see the O.C. but no-one was up – however later on they appeared and I spent the morning walking round with a Capt. Gardiner looking at the river etc. Got a wire to look in at Hector Spruit on the way back. Train back at 5.30 p.m. arr: Hector Spruit 7 p.m. and looked up my old friend Audrey Pratt of the Scots, the Officer in charge of the station and detachment there. A.C. Pratt was in Stogden's and has a brother in the service. You may remember that I dined with him at Edinboro' Castle in '97 when doing an engineering tour from Chatham. Well, Pratt was delighted to see me – put me up on his verandah and next morning we rode down to the Crocodile River (2 miles) inspected the pumping station etc., and collected some pieces of boer guns thrown into the river here and broken up on the banks.

On return to camp I found no trains would run to Komati at all that day, so in the afternoon we went out into the bush with our guns and a native, we each had a shot at buck without a kill – mine was full gallop at 70 yards. He also shot at partridge and I at hare – with a bullet, a hard shot – so though empty handed we enjoyed our walk.

Next day I trained at 10 a.m. back to Komati.

Nov 16 I was up on the hills again and found great progress with the buildings, and Coffin who had been away also, to Barberton to get money for paying men, returned.

Nov 17 I was working on defences but had to leave off for rain and storm. Coffin down with fever.

Sunday 18th one year since my section after marching 80 miles in 5 days arrived at Orange River from De Aar, to rejoin the 7th Co. Service and a rest – principally sleep! Very hot.

19th Continued defences – curious thing that all energies had been directed for nearly two months on building huts before even the most trivial defences were commenced – however we are well entrenched on all sides now – but I don't anticipate trouble – though 'si vis pacem etc.'

Met Addison of my term, who was passing through for a jaunt to Lourenço Marques from Pretoria – a long trip.

20th Much rain – one year since the Kimberley relief column started from Orange River to attack the boers at Belmont (23rd). I wonder if another year will see the end of it – I hope so. The vastness of the country makes flight and concealment of marauding bands so easy that it will be some time before all is clear, though we seem to capture and kill a few most days in the parts still infested by guerillas.

It will be about Christmas when you get this – so all sorts of good wishes to the noble house of Wilson. I am quite fit and well at present thank God – and thanks to the excellent constitution you appear to have endowed me with, though my dear Mother encased it in rather fragile clay. Still I cannot expect immunity from fever here in the long run, except by great good fortune.

Much love to all at home from your ever loving son Eric E.B. Wilson.

Komati Poort Saturday 1st December 1900

My dearest Mums

Many thanks for your nice long letter which reached me in record time considering how far we are from Cape Town. It was dated Nov 2 and got to Komati Poort Nov 30! I have also received letters from Phar dated Oct 19 and 26 – so am quite up to date. I also received enclosed envelope which may interest you – I hope Christian De Wet enjoyed reading the letter – tho' I think he might have put it back again!
You must have had a great gathering of the clans at Lowestoft – the children however must have been like mice in the House of Lords – unless they met some other juveniles there!
I hope Cousin Annie is better I was sorry to hear she was not well.
The Captain Fraser that Father asks about is in the 7th Co – he took Boileau's place when the latter got a job on Ian Hamilton's staff. Fraser leaves today, though, I understand, for the Staff College at home – lucky man. I hope you have heard from me now since Nov 6 – The next few letters went via Delagoa Bay and the Suez Canal as being nearer, but latterly I have been posting via Cape Town again as it is more convenient to get at for posting. They have opened a field P.Office here now – so one can get stamps again.
Fancy you spotting the marriage of Miss Davies in the E. Anglian. I have seen no account of it yet – though she wrote and told me ages ago that she was going to marry in Oct:– she is the elder of the two and I suppose now 22. The younger – Freda is 20 – they were both excellent friends of mine at the Curragh – but I know nothing of the man Palmer – I think his name is – perhaps he has pints of biscuit money? They have both been most kind to me in sending papers – etc and writing frequently during the war.
I have heard no more of Fusilier – nor do I expect to – but I have got a claim for £35 for horse to replace him – approved by authorities, and it has gone forward to the Paymaster some 3 weeks now without response.
We are in hopes of being ordered back to the 7th Co again soon, as the building here is practically finished – we have built a regular hamlet here since we came. The 7th Co are at Bloemfontein – and there is more fighting going on thereabouts at present than anywhere, and the more fighting we can get these gentle farmers to do the quicker it will be over. I think about next June or so <u>ought</u> to see the war nearly over, one cannot tell though.
The country is so <u>vast</u> that there is bound to be tumult in some remote corner or other unless we can slay the last boer and root out the last farm.

If they had only the sense to surrender when they found they were thoroughly defeated they would have been living in peace and quiet such as they never dreamt of now – but the riff raff element – foreigners – colonial adventurers – rebels etc – have only the war to exist on for food and occupation – so go about in bands of bandits attacking small posts and flying before the first force that arrives. As Punch said recently – "It's like chasing rats with a traction engine!

On Nov 23 (Battle of Belmont '99) I went up the line to Kaap Muiden about 40 miles as the bridge was reported damaged by flood – however it proved a false alarm and took me till the 26th to send and receive and receive explanatory wires and get back here.

Kaap Muiden though higher is quite as bad as this place for fever and mosquitoes, I was half murdered by them! Men have been going down fast with malaria here – however the Yorks have relieved the Royal Scots here so we have some fresh blood which will take some time to go under. Capt. Coffin R.E. has been very bad with fever but has now got away on the hospital train which makes trips to cart away our invalids at frequent intervals. I have now very few men left.

I have been working on the defences here recently – and am now busy making plans etc – to forward to Gen. Stevenson who commands us and Barberton district.

Nov 25 and 28 were Graspan and Modder River battles, and 29 the day I rode Fusilier into the heart of the boer position in the early morning to find it evacuated in the night. The 12th Co R.E. who are also here, are, I think, to move to Barberton shortly – we were to have gone with them – but the C.R.E. have agitated to return us to our companies for 'repairs'!! which we sadly need. I expect when this reaches you, you will be busy with the black draughts and bilious pills to counteract the effects of too much Christmas on the children!

You will find enclosed a cheque for 21/= which I hope you will expend for the benefit of the small birds as a small Xmas present from Eggie.

I dare not send anything of value through the post in these troublous times, I do not see many newspapers except by chance or those sent to other officers. I get a Spectator from Uncle Rowland pretty frequently – I see Raymond and Uncle Walter, and Henry Greene of Shrewsbury, who took me back to Harrow after Grandfather's funeral, are all in the new parliament. Send me an account of Miss Davies' wedding in case I do not see it. One of the few pleasures of the poor soldier man consists in seeing his friends launched into the troubled sea of matrimonial (!) happiness!

I expect a lot of returned invalids and wounded will be out again soon and help to finish this interminable campaign. It must be very nice for you and the children having Mr Turner so adjacent. I hope Father and all are in flourishing health – as this leaves me.

Best love from your affectionate Eggie.

Pretoria   Sunday 9th December 1900

My dearest Father

Back here again for the fifth and possibly the last time – on Dec 3 we got orders to leave Komati for Pretoria and not sorry to get away safely without fever or other ills of that most unhealthy place.
Tomorrow I leave here to rejoin my company after an absence of seven months – we leave early and hope to reach Bloemfontein – barring break downs and boers in about 3 days.
On Dec 3 – I saw off Buckle and Lyell and half our 'commandos' on the first train from Komati at 6 a.m. and followed with the rest at 3 p.m. We reached Kaap Muiden that night and stopped there.
On the 4th we resumed our journey at 8 a.m. and reached Waterval Boven at 5 p.m. after traversing the most superb scenery in the Transvaal – up the Krocodile River Valley between enormous rocky mountains which we had marched over on the way out. At Waterval Onder the valley ends in a precipitous cul-de-sac the river falling a great height in a fine fall from here to Waterval Boven about 4 miles. We climbed up out of the gorge by means of a rack railway and cog wheel engines rising at one in twenty, or up a yard in every twenty yards, finally diving through the crest of the mountain by about 500 yards of tunnel and emerging on the huge rolling plateau of the 'high veldt' – some 6000 feet above Komati Poort!
We halted for the night at Waterval Boven where I met Newcombe R.E. one of the Railway men who was living in a fine furnished bungalow in the village 'taken over' from some absconding Hollander official of the late railway staff. We proceeded next morning at 5.30 a.m. – I forgot to say I dined with

Newcombe with the unheard of surroundings of tablecloth, napkin, glass to drink from instead of a mug, and a carpet under foot!!

During the night Moir, Adjutant of the Royal Scots arrived with 80 men en route to join Mounted Infantry in Pretoria – so we proceeded, a strong party to meet train wreckers and marauders.

At Godwan River we got back into familiar country – this being where we left the rail in marching out via Kaapsche Hoop and Barberton. At Machadodorp it commenced raining and continued till we reached Pau Station – here we were told that a large party of boers had been seen near the line that morning and so proceeded with all decks cleared for action – rifles loaded and ammunition handy – but saw no one and steamed into Middleburg about noon and had an hours halt to water the animals on the train etc. We reached Brugspruit that night, one of my natives having rolled off the train en route – presumably asleep. I wired back for him as he was seen walking back to Middleburg along the rail, and there's no 'stop!conductor' on a troop train to pick up absentees!

This part of the journey was done in great comfort in Newcombe's private coach, with every luxury, as he spends most of his time touring the line in the course of his work.

At Brugspruit was a detachment of the Buffs with whom Moir and I dined – and went on at 5 a.m. At Balmoral the next station (the scene of the terrible storm in July – when we first marched there after our tour round the N.E. of Pretoria) I met Col Barker – our late C.R.E. 1X Div. who is now Brigadier General commanding Communications from Pretoria to Middleburg. He was delighted to see me – turned out in his pyjamas to give me a cup of tea and thrust a handful of cigarettes into my hands just as the train whistled off.

We reached Pretoria safely after doing 300 miles in 3 days – it took us 27 to march it going out. Buckle met me at the station and took us out to camp at the N.E. corner of the town on Johnson's Kopje where we found some R.E. volunteers encamped who had been ordered in to prepare to return home! but had been kept some two months here to date and likely to stop many more before the war approaches an end.

At present, as a native chief very aptly remarked, the English hold the towns and the railways and the boers hold the country! and this task alone swallows up almost the entire force out here in garrisons at every town and station. It is like a ten acre farmer in Redgrave trying to farm Germany by postal correspondence, trying to administer and pacify this enormous country as long as any boers like or are able to prowl about in small armed bodies attacking small points and flying from large forces – however there is one certainty – they must all collapse in time when their food and ammunition run out and their farms destroyed.

There is no doubt we were much too lenient when we first occupied the country, the boers mistook it for weakness and conciliation – two things they only interpret in one way. and we were treating them far over their heads – forgetting they were only savages in the refinements of civilization as yet.

On Friday Buckle and I interviewed the Engineer in Chief (G.M.Wood) and reported our arrival – he was interested in hearing of progress at Komati etc – and I think rather surprised at seeing us after 2½ months in that death trap.

Yesterday (8th) I was in the town arranging with the Railway Staff Officer about the move on Monday. In the afternoon I went over to the Imperial Yeomanry Hospital and saw Elsner R.A.M.E, who is recovering from Komati Fever (the officer who took the photo I sent you recently) and Coffin R.E. who was not making very good progress. The band of the Lincolns was playing on the terrace of the house which has a splendid view all over Pretoria. I also saw Phillips of 7th Fusiliers who used to keep wicket at the Curragh, he was recovering from dysentery.

Today Sunday – we had company service at 8 a.m. – and in the p.m. played the Newcastle and Durham Volunteer Engineers at Cricket – I think you will not find it difficult to understand that when we do get a Sunday without work it often becomes our day of recreation as well as rest. I enclose a copy of the score – by which you will see a good margin in our favour.

The native Macè is an exceptionally useful player – bowls and bats. I think he learnt at a mission school.

I hope Mother got my last letter from Komati. I hope to write next from Bloemfontein, all well.

Much love and all good wishes for another year, and a new Century of Peace and prosperity, and a steady termination to this deluge of Blood.

Ever your loving son Eric E.B. Wilson

First Newcastle & Durham Volunteer Engineers v Ian Hamiltons Composites Field Co:R.E.

Corp. Purvis		b. Wilson	5	Lce Corp Davis	b.Tate	22
Sap. Paul	c. Wilson	b. Davis	9	Driver Ives	b. Purvis	5
Lt. Pollard	c. Sheehy	b. Wilson	0	Native Mate	c. Paul b. Pollard	9
Sap. Harrison		c&b Wilson	0	Lieut. Wilson	c. Summers b. Purvis	10
Lt. Price		b. Davis	2	Driver North	st: Paul b. Harrison	4
Sap. Summers		c&b Wilson	0	Sap Lee	st: Paul b Tate	4
Sgt. Thomas	c. Wilson	b. Davis	0	2nd Corp Pengilly	c. Anderson b. Harrison	0
Sap. Anderson		b. Davis	2	Sap. Barnham	l.b.w. b. Anderson	21
Sgt. Pescod		b. Wilson	0	Lce Corp Whelan	b. Purvis	7
Sap. Tate		not out	8	Sap. Sheehy	run out	4
Sap. Laverick		b. Davis	2	Sap.Waldron	not out	0
Extras			7	Extras		10
		Total	35		Total	96

Played on Johnson's Kopje, Pretoria. Dec. 9th 1900

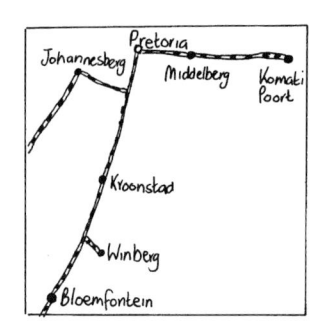

Bloemfontein, Orange River Colony   Sunday 23rd December 1900

My dearest Father

Here I am again – after various wanderings once more with the headquarters of the 7th Co. I have got a letter from you dated Nov 23 and one from Moonie Nov 28 by the last two mails. Some letters apparently sent forward by the company to Komati Poort are still in the post, but will no doubt return south in time.

Give Algie my best love and wishes for Jan 3 – he has not to wait long in the new Century for a birthday. I hope he is quite well of his chill.

On Monday Dec 10 the break up of the composite Field Company came at last and Buckle and I severed forces after 5 months cooperation.

I left Pretoria with my little band at 10 a.m – two having suddenly fallen ill at the station – to their intense misery had to be left in hospital – however two rejoined one there who had fallen away earlier, keeping my number (16) the same. We had a long delay at Irene where floods had caused a bad washaway of an embankment – and reached Elandsfontein Junction at 3 p.m. Here I met several old friends who had been there ever since July.

We moved on again at 4.15 and the rest of the journey to Bloemfontein was absolutely new to us, as of course we marched up West of Johannesburg and all over the place coming up. We reached the Vaal River at dark and stayed the night at Viljoen's Drift station. At Meyerton, just north – we passed the Ist Cavalry Brigade encamped. An officer told me that J.R.White was there but I did not see him.

<u>Tues Dec 11</u> (Magersfontein '99) we moved on at 4.30 a.m. and reached Smaldeel junction by sunset – and stopped for the night. Country very open and plain like that we marched through, except near the Rhenoster River. We passed many signs of the various raids and attacks and train wreckings carried out by De Wet at different times and passed many a little group of white crosses by the line out in the veldt marking those who fell in the attacks. The whole line is of course strongly held right through – men at every bridge station – it is this which absorbs nearly our whole force, having to hold so many hundreds of line day after day.

Wed Dec 12 Went on at 4 a.m. and dawdled on via Brandfort Karrie and Glen, arriving at Bloemfontein about 11 a.m. without attacks or mishaps en route – except the death of my poor old horse Happy – who had carried me from Modder River to Komati and I fear brought the horse sickness away with him – it was terrible there. The horse died about ½ an hour before we got in, leaving me only the Johannesburg pony 'Dick' – who was, however very plump and fit.

I met Barrington R.E. up the line – I last saw him when we acted together in 'Chiselling' at Chatham in '96 or 7. We were met at the station by four horses to pull up our toolcart – that I had wired on for – and soon unloaded our other wagons and baggage and marched up to Camp.

We found the 7th Co camped under a hill to the N.W. of the town about 1½ miles from our old camp in March which was slightly S.W. Everything here is fearfully dried up and dusty after the long green grass in the Transvaal – as the rains have not begun here yet – and although this is midsummer here we find it quite cool, almost chilly, after Komati Poort and its steaming heat night and day.

The change has had a bad effect on our animals – of 20 mules which arrived – seven died like lightning though in appearance robust and shining – the vet says lung sickness from sudden change of temperature. My pony Dick has nearly died – he has been taken into veterinary hospital and not likely to recover – so I am horseless!

Well in camp I found Maj. Haggitt our new C.O and Henriques the volunteer sub. and nos 3 and 4 sections. Johnson is still up at Potchefstroom with No 1, and Musgrave was away down the line laying mines to blow up trespassers and rail cutters and succeeded in severely injuring his own hand by an untoward explosion.

Haggitt is a first rate chap – a Suffolk man – owns property at Thurston – asked me if I was a Redgrave Wilson – knows all the Bury people – Uncle Rowland – and Walter, the Partridges etc etc and lives for shooting and fishing. He met Bertie and Muriel in Corsica last year and knows Bertie well. I found things fairly quiet here – not too much worry – and have practically been having a good rest –as Haggitt intended I should.

However amongst my kit left here I found several distressing deficiencies. My camera and many rolls of (to me) valuable photos taken during the war – specimens of rare boer ammunitions, fuzes, etc – all clean gone. The miserable Quarter Master Sergeant who has been here the whole time in charge of everything protests complete ignorance.

On Wed 19th Musgrave came back for two days and has now gone off again to Norvals Pont to see about some huts there. He proposes to take on some job under the O.R.C. Police I fancy – some R.E. work which will give him a good billet out here for several years.

Most days we ride or drive round the various works the men are employed on, we have a very handy cape cart which runs well with a pair of transport ponies, they are like a dog cart only with a pole for a pair and a hood.

The 20th Co R.E. under C.S Wilson are camped next door. He has one 2nd Lt (Hordern) and one volunteer(Thomson) with him – we are to dine with them at the Club on Xmas Day. We have a nice tin shed for a mess room here – separated by a very deep Longa from the camp, over which we cross by a single plank – a fearsome walk in the dark!

I cannot give you much news of the fighting – it is pretty general and constant in various places – some boers got into the Cape Colony lately and tried anew to fan up rebellion but I think they are being kept well in hand.

De Wet is still at large – in spite of all the hairbreadth escapes he has had and the vast numbers of columns that have set out to <u>really</u> round him up.

The general opinion is that we can settle down to another 10 or 12 months of general uncertainty and devote it to more attempts to corner these slippery marauders. I have no wish to go on trek again if it can be helped!

Much love and all sorts of good wishes for the new century.

I hope we shall meet ere 1901 is through.

Ever your loving son Eric E.B. Wilson

The townspeople here have subscribed handsomely for the men's Xmas fare – over £1000 – it works out at about 2/= a head.

Haggett was employed in War Office before the war and is a most clever officer.

Fraser the captain has gone home to Staff College. I daresay ere now you have met some of the thousands of luxurious loungers who have found their way home by various means.

I have just read Churchill's book 'Ian Hamilton's March.' You <u>must</u> get it – a very faithful account of our doings and wanderings – and wherever you read 19th Brigade Gordons, Cornwalls, Shropshires and Canadians <u>I was not far off</u>.

I inspected many of the incidents depicted <u>with</u> Churchill himself notably the Zand River and Doorn Kop fights.

Bloemfontein   Sunday 30th December 1900

My dearest Father

This is undoubtedly the last letter I shall write you during the 19th Century. The mails are working very well now – we get out home letters on Sat p.m. or Sunday a.m. and the mail goes out at 8 p.m. on Sunday – so you will see that one day further North would just make them get their mails wrong. Since I last wrote (23rd) I have received 3 letters from you – Nov 9 and 16 which had been to Komati Poort to look for me and then back – and today I received one from you Dec 7th – only 23 days in transit. Many thanks for all – also the cuttings of R.M.A. football etc. I got a good mail in this week, cards and letters from several friends – a letter from Joe Durnford – who tells me he is going to marry in Jan. in spite of my repeated warnings! and that he had fully counted on me to be at home to help him through. He says he will only feel half married if I am not there to act as best man!
I heard from my late man George Whitecross to say that he had got a passage home on the 'Chicago'- about Nov 24th I think. I also got a charming letter and card from Lady Jenner at the Curragh and similar good wishes from Aunt Amy and others.
I am very glad indeed to hear that Jimmy Hales has got appointed A.C.F – I should think he would make an excellent soldiers 'padre' as he is a good sportsman and understands life from the point of view of those he will talk to. I hope Cousin Annie is better, it must be very trying for her to have to compete with ill health after such an active life.
I was very interested to hear about the operations to the Hinderclay tower – it would be a pity if it fell down – as a landmark from a soldiers point of view it is one, which in company with many other of our country towers, would be fought very shy of when artillery were about, as it would be the first thing they would try their guns on! to get the range for bursting their shells!!
I fear I haven't got very much news for you – even on the spot one can never hear anything, as our 'intelligence' people have at last found out that a secret that 3 people know might as well be the headline of the morning's news at once.
We believe that great activity continues in parts – we know that parties of boers still hold a footing in the Cape Colony – and the general impression is that we have another 12 months or more of harrassing work before us.
As regards the 7th Co: we are still (and likely to be) the sort of Bloemfontein head quarter Co: of R.E. and the men are daily occupied according to their trades. We also have detachments up and down the line doing odd jobs.

The next big job here will be the permanent hutting and barracks for the garrison. It is to come out from home ready for erection – but railway transport will not be able to bring it up from the coast until trains can run at night. They have decided on a very nice site for the permanent military camp on a farm called 'Tempe' about 2½ miles from the market place and under some fine sheltering hills.

We are busy boring for the water supply and have already got quite enough. I expect the 7th Co: will be for further Foreign Service here as they are filling us up with drafts and odds and ends from Balloon section etc, so that one's individual chance of returning home will consist of the ordinary 'leave of absence' as soon as peace is fairly established. By the end of 1901 I shall have six months leave due apart from any leave granted as a special reward for active service.

Best love to all – Ever your loving son Eric.

Bloemfontein   Sunday 6th January 1901

My dearest Father

By this week's mail I got two letters from you – one Oct 12 that had been wandering about, the other Dec 14 – so I expect I am pretty well up to date now. From the Oct letter I learn that Muriel and a Miss Shaw were staying with you, and you had been touring the latter round the country.
I also got news of many relations and friends – Villiers seems to be on his feet alright – Frank I should say might find something better going on here in about a years time. He might do worse than join one of the local mounted corps and try for a commission – starts at 5/= a day, horse, food and forage found – if he is keen on a bit of rough work and looking after self and horse without help.
I suppose Herbert Bryant has duly arrived ere now – I shouldn't mind a month or two of England for a change – though one cannot complain of absence when it has not yet reached two years. In your last letter (Dec 14) you hoped soon to hear I was away from Komati Poort – while you were writing that I had just arrived at Bloemfontein!
Last Monday I had to prosecute at a Court Martial – the largest batch of prisoners I have ever seen – about 20 or so, nearly all 'Xmas drunks' – which though not a ferocious crime in peace time is a very serious one on active service naturally.
We had 2 men up before it – both got 21 days Imprisonment with Hard Labour – a light sentence for the offence – the last cases got six months. Luckily for these men Lord Kitchener published a remission of all sentences (except serious crimes) unexpired on Dec 31 – "in consequence of the gallantry of their comrades in the field". These men were sentenced on Dec 31 and so got off scot free – except for the entry in their documents which of course would be against them at a future trial.
There has not been much going on here besides routine – and minor works of a more or less peaceful nature.
The 20th Co: R.E. under Capt C.S. Wilson marched out on Friday to Thaba Nchu (40 miles) with a view to running a barbed wire fence across all roads and gaps between there and Ladybrand on the Basuto border – to impede marauders passing N or South.
Several days this week I spent as president of a board of 3 officers to enquire into the loss of certain stores, arms, equipment etc lost or expended on active service, with a view to adjusting ledgers etc and deciding on whom – 'Public' or individual the cost of replacing them should fall – needless to say the

'Public' usually come out at the bottom on these occasions, as nearly all the stores are actually expended during operations in the field.

On Wednesday we were trying a new pair of ponies in the Cape Cart (a sort of dog cart), 2 wheeled with a pole, and they bolted before they were fully harnessed in – they took the cart over some fearful dongas and rocks before they upset – but no damage resulted except to the cart which had to go into the wheelwrights shop for repairs.

Yesterday we had some native sports – great fun – we employ about 130 natives on the public works. The high jump, of all things, caused the most amusement both to black and white – all were keen enough but deficient in science – some sprung off both feet like diving off a diving board, some simply hurled themselves into the air and fell sprawling yards beyond the jump! I nearly died with laughing – I think the best man accomplished about 4ft 6 in.

We also had sack, 3 legged and running races – a mule race for the drivers – tug of war and throwing the Knob Kerry at bottles – the prizes were pipes, shirts, tobacco etc – and they were all delighted – the proceeds wound up with a grand native war dance in about 80 phases!

Finally they sang God save the Queen in Kaffir to the English tune – the harmony was wonderfully good – tho' the words were not intelligible to the audience!

You may remember my telling you that after our assault on the laager at Paardeburg, Lord Roberts came round to the camp and addressed the company on parade and that I, among others, lying asleep under a wagon tired out after our nights' work, did not hear the speech first hand.

By the same token it occurred to me later that practically the only men who were on parade were those who had been left in camp the night before and had not taken part in the night attack, and that those who had were lying about, like myself, dead to the world and also did not hear the words meant for them.

Well, recently here amongst some old papers, I came across the C.R.E's official log of that day in which he makes the following entry, which will tell you the substance of Lord Roberts' address:–

> Feb 27............ "Lord Roberts rode round to our camp in the afternoon and addressing the 7th Company congratulated them on the gallant manner in which they had thrown up a trench within 80 yards of the enemy; that the section of the Canadians and the Royal Engineers by which a lodgement had been effected on the flank of the enemy's position had <u>undoubtedly caused</u> Cronje to abandon further resistance and surrender unconditionally, and he complimented the company on the rôle they had played as Engineers and Soldiers......."

This is the height of the summer here now and the thermometer ranges from 85° to 110° daily in the shade – but it is so dry and dusty even within a few hours after a thunder-deluge – that one does not feel the heat at all in the way it is felt in the humid country round Komati Poort.

We have a 2nd Lt. Hordern messing with us now, from 20th Co: while they are absent.

Lt: Col: Buston C.R.E. is in Engineer charge from the Vaal to the Orange River and has 3 R.E. co's to work it – 7th, 20th, and 38th, the latter having headquarters at Kroonstad.

Musgrave of our co: is still down at Norval's Pont putting up huts etc. McClintock is with MacDonald in the Cape Colony on intelligence work – and Johnson and No I section are still at Potchefstroom or thereabouts in the Transvaal. Fraser our Captain has gone home to the Staff College.

I saw in the 'Standard' that Raymond had been attending dinners and making speeches – a terrible ordeal except for the professional politician it always seems to me – certainly not the soldiers' rôle – he gets 6/10d a day or whatever it is to do his work and there is, or should be, an end of it.

I have no patience with men like Churchill, unless they have some genuine patriotic ambition behind it all – perhaps he has – but he doesn't fail to let the public know his opinion on every subject under the stars – for what it may be worth.

Best love to all at home from your ever loving son Eric E.B. Wilson

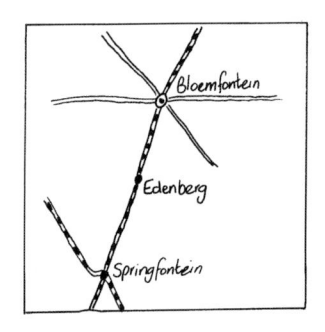

Bloemfontein   **Sunday 13th January 1901**

My dearest Father

Our last mail came in on Friday but as I was away for the day, down the line, and our Sgt. Major in a fit of officiousness, without asking anyone when I was returning – reposted my letters to a wayside station down country –I am unable to answer any of them this mail – and doubt whether doubt whether I shall see them back in less than a week!

I have been fairly busy this week – working on an extension of the telegraph out to "Fisher's Farm" some four miles out of the town where we have a large government horse farm and remount depôt – and they want to be able to telephone in and out hence the new line – I hope to have it open in a day or two.

On Friday I went down the line to a station called Edenburg, with two men and some stores, to see about putting up a blockhouse there for the defence of a bridge. I stayed the night at a very fair little hotel for these parts – and wartime – 'Potgeisters' and slept for one night with the luxury of a bed and sheets!

On Saturday I saw work started – got out plans and wired for materials etc not obtainable on the spot – left the two R.E's in charge and came back by the mail to Bloemfontein arriving 4.10 p.m. – walked up to camp to find in my few hours' absence the Sergt. Major had sent my weeks mail down to Edenburg on his own initiative! So I was disappointed of being able to answer any letters this mail.

This morning I took the men to the Cathedral 10.30 a.m. – the Bishop preached, a white-bearded and pleasant-spoken old man – I don't know his name. He preached on changing the dull things around us (water) into subjects of interest (wine) by taking interest in our surroundings and obliterating self.

At 5.30 p.m. today I am attending the funeral of poor Elkington, of ours, who died in hospital, the 7th Co are furnishing the escort (40 men for a subaltern) and the available subalterns (4) of similar rank to deceased walk as pall-bearers – other officers attending follow as mourners.

Absolutely no news all this week – we are in complete darkness as to what goes on elsewhere as the authorities never issue any news now.

I have got a most satisfactory settlement for the loss of my two original horses, Fusilier and Bill Sykes. For the former I have permission to select an animal from the Remounts here to the value of £50 though I doubt if they have an animal of that value! For the latter I have got £25 in cash – what I gave for him! I see that Lieutenants are to get 7½ £5 shares 'bounty' for the show = £37.10s less 37/6d income tax deducted before payment!!

Captains get £60 – Majors £80 – both good rises above Lieut: <u>All volunteer officers get £100</u> in addition. though it has been a heavy loss to many – leaving employment for so long.

I hope to be able to clear off all the bills – uniform etc now. I have an account at Standard Bank, Bloemfontein where I bank all allowances etc drawn out here – for your information – and Cox credits me 10/10d per diem at home- but I fancy I have pretty well drawn up to that since we have been out here as everything is about double price. Eggs at present 4/6d a dozen.

Best love to all ever your loving son Eric E.B. Wilson.

Bloemfontein, Orange River Colony　　　　　Sunday 20th January 1901

My dearest Father

Very many thanks for two letters received this week – Dec 21 and 28th – the former after a trip to Edenburgh and back. I also heard from Uncle Rowland by this mail and curiously enough he also enclosed the cutting about the presentation to Raymond. It was curious you getting your letter of July 6th back – of course they would have been unable to readdress it out here.
I am glad Corp. Bryant got home safely and was so kindly received – the Protectorate Regiment I have not met – but I know they had some roughish times of it.
I see by the R.E. Journal that Col. Hasted, who has taken the Brook House was in the old Madras R.E. – is married – first commission 9th Dec 1853 and retired in 1890.
I am glad you had a good gathering at Uncle Georges on Xmas Day. I imagined it was where you would be dining.
I expect Miss Colkett will enjoy her visit to Muriel. I am sorry to hear that Aunt Minnie has been poorly again – but I expect she is as cheerful as ever, whatever attacks her!
I went down the line to Edenburgh again on Thursday and tried to get back the same day but as they don't run trains after 7 p.m. we had to stop the night at Kaap Spruit – 14 miles S. of here where we arrived at 6.30 p.m. – it seemed rather a piece of red tape not letting the train run through under the very noses of our outposts – because it might possibly arrive at 7.5 or so! However I had a very pleasant little dinner with 2 officers of Norfolk Militia there – <u>one</u> of whom was the young <u>Steward</u> who used to stay with the Kennaways and was in Welsford's house at Harrow – he spotted me but I didn't recognise him – he seemed very pleased and kept murmuring "how odd" etc most of the evening!!
Yesterday we had a company cricket match and got beaten by the Army Labour Depôt by 150 to 50 – we are not strong – I did not do well – I bowled one, and hooked a wide to leg into my wicket the third ball for 0.
This morning I marched the men to the Cathedral.
Last night I dined with Moore A.S.C. an old Curragh friend and Pigott D.S.O., A.S.C. late of Cruikshank's – a cousin of the Upchers and a good chap all round. They have a bungalow in the town – near their work – supplies etc, chiefly office work – after dinner we went to the local theatre and saw two pieces – "Brothers" and "Jane" – the latter a most amusing 3 act comedy.

[1918] →
10 - DSO.
7 - CMG.
1 and CB. OBE.
CB. MVO.
CIE.

CMG. DSO.
CB. CMG. DSO.
CMG. DSO
CMG. DSO

P.G. GRANT. O. WILKINSON. W.E. BARRON. T.W. ROSE. R.S. McCLINTOCK. F. RHEUSH... M.S.LC... L.C. JACKSON CMG. DSO.
C.F. HADDON. L.E. MILLINGTON. R.F.A. BUTLER. W. ELLIS. DSO. E.B. WILSON. OBE.
CB. CMG. DSO OBE CMG. DSO MVO. CIE. CMG. DSO. O.E.J. BURFORD.
— SKIPWITH. DOUGLAS. (Sir) DSO.
1914 (Sir)
†

18. R.E. Second Lieutenants commissioned August 1895.

The wind and tempests of dust are very trying living under canvas – all one's boots, clothes and food are always full of sand and dust – but the rains should begin soon and all will be slosh for a month or so.
I got an invitation to Joe Durnford's wedding for Feb 5th today and replied to "Lieut Col and Mrs Ford's" invitation with regret – the girls' name is Bessie Muriel Ford so she only has to add "Durn"!
I wrote to Joe D. and chaffed him a bit about her caring a 'durn' for him!

Best love to all at home from your ever loving son Eric E.B. Wilson

Bloemfontein Club   **Sunday 27th January 1901**

My dearest Father

Your letter of Jan 4 reached me on Friday. I hope you found all well at Nether Hall. We have had a very depressing week since we got news of the Queen's death – at about 4 p.m. on Wednesday- all flags are now at half mast etc.
The old Bishop preached a very good sermon today and many of the ladies in the Cathedral were in tears.
We had a very rough day on Thursday – a gale of dust and wind in the morning followed by a deluge in the afternoon – which was very refreshing however – and in the evening the most lovely calm – and what the Bishop referred to this morning as "surely the grandest rainbow since the time of the great deluge."
We have been fairly busy lately – I usually have about a ten or twelve mile ride round in the morning visiting the works on outposts and defences – which are more or less my province at present.
I expect I shall have another run down to Edenburg this week to see how they are getting on there.
We are absolutely without news of any sort of the operations – I doubt if any one here could tell you for certain where 1000 of the 200,000 troops out here are or what they are doing – so well do the staff keep their movements and doings concealed.
We hope however that the chief Boer leaders still in the field are seriously considering a display of discretion at last – they are known to have had a

conference recently – Gen. Hunter has gone home from commanding here and Gen. Tucker has taken over.

Send me out a set of new stamps the moment they are issued with the King's head on them.

I am handling a nice young horse about 15.1 that I have temporarily drawn from the Remounts – if I think he will turn out well I shall keep him to replace Fusilier – he is very green at present but a perfect gentleman in manner.

Much love to all Ever your loving son Eric E.B. Wilson

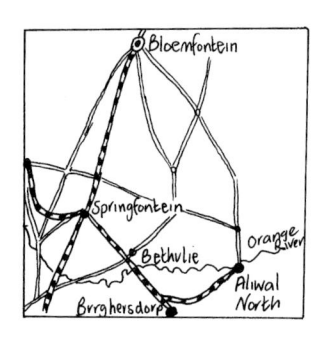

MRS H.C. ROBERTS
PROPRIETRESS
Telegrams "Balmoral",

Hotel Balmoral
Aliwal North
Cape Colony
Sunday 10th February 1901

My dearest Father

You are accustomed by now to the sudden appearance of letters from unexpected places from me!

I left Bloemfontein with four sappers and a quantity of explosives etc for Bethulie on the Orange River on the 2nd Feb by rail, arriving on the 3rd. My precise mission I was not aware of till my arrival, when I found I was to organize two parties to proceed East and West along the Orange River, placing 'mines' and explosives etc at the various drifts or possible fords, more as a moral than practical way of intimidating marauders from crossing the river into Cape Colony. The two parties set out early on the 4th, having been up all through the night obtaining wagons and supplies etc. 2nd Lieut Evans and a few men started East – and I and a few scouts of Bethulies M.I. one ox wagon and one capecart, with 10 days supplies started West.

We had a very enjoyable time on the whole and I put down a lot of mechanical mines with trip wires and other arrangements at the most frequented drifts, 'setting' these mines I may add is the most dangerous operation one can be called on to perform and for a few seconds when connecting up the wires which are to pull the trigger so to speak – one is very literally carrying one's life in one's hand. However we worked along by degrees – having several bad places to get our ox wagon over which necessitated off loading every article on it and carrying it all (about 3,000 lb) from midstream to shore before the bullocks could pull the wagon over.

We had two very wet nights too – but did not come across any of the enemy which was something – as we were very easy prey had we been discovered! On the Wednesday I met Musgrave who had been sent out East from Norval's Pont to meet me and so shorten my journey – we met and exchanged notes and turned back – I arrived again at Bethulie Bridge on the Thursday night – inspecting all the mines I had put down going out. Two of them had been exploded by stray cattle – in one case a horse had walked into it and been literally blown inside out – the body lying about 15 yards away from the mine. Of course we also warned the farmers in the neighbourhood – more for the moral effect their alarmist reports would spread to brother boer than to save their cattle as they will get compensation for them.

We did very well too in the egg, milk and butter line – and I drank one of the first glasses of fresh milk I have had for a twelvemonth!

On returning to Bethulie I found sheaves of telegrams from various generals anxious for reports of our movements and wanting details etc. My only hope is that they are not under the delusion that a mine is an impassable obstacle – as beyond the moral effect of not knowing how many more there may be about, and possibly with luck blowing up one man or horse, there is nothing to prevent determined men crossing – but I presume they can work that out for themselves – I am only the Engineer who puts the mischief down to order!

I dined at Bethulie Bridge with the 4th Cheshires (Militia) and there met a Major Willie Woodward who used to shoot a lot with Harry Horsfall – he was a splendid host and did a lot for me.

I next got a wire without any further instructions than to proceed to Aliwal North at once, and here I arrived last night with my 5 men by rail after a night's delay at Burghersdorp. From here two officers have just started out East again on a similar job and I was rather relieved to find I was not for it. I found (between you and me) that I had been wired for by Gen. MacDonald on McClintock's suggestion (the subaltern of our Company, who is doing Intelligence officer to MacD.) as he had said I could be found a useful job no doubt and he wanted to see me again and thought I should like to see Aliwal North!!

So I dined with them last night – Gen. MacD., his brigade Major, McClintock and self – four of us. MacD. was most cheery and amusing though I believe he is not always so. I fancy he intends sending me along the river checking the rather inaccurate Military map we have and inspecting mines etc en route – which would not be unpleasant work though rather jumpy as there are a lot of boers down here now.

Anyway I am to wait here until I am told to start – so I am having my meals in this by no means badly equipped hotel. Just before I began this letter a subaltern of the Grenadier Guards was playing the piano to himself – most magnificently – he must be very fond of it I should judge – and one doesn't often hear music nowadays.

I had not seen McClintock since the fight at Welkom (Vet River) in May – he seems well, and wanted to know all about Komati Poort etc and reviled his misfortune in never having crossed the Vaal.

I cannot say quite what operations are pending, the boers foregathered in the best force they could muster and once more came south, and several columns are after them and everyone is waiting to see where they are going to try to force the river. They have about eaten out the free state and are desperate now to get loose in ones and twos amongst the fertile farms of Cape Colony where they can loot and feed to their hearts content, as it is well nigh impossible country from its vast extent to fritter troops about chasing small parties – and there comes the crux – and who can guess the solution?

Best love to all from your ever loving son Eric E.B. Wilson

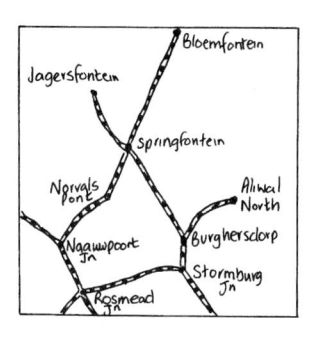

Bloemfontein   **Saturday 16th February 1901**

My dearest Father

I got back here alright from Aliwal, whence I last wrote, on Tuesday – and found two letters awaiting me – one from Mother of Jan 11 and from you Jan 18.
This weeks mail <u>should</u> be to hand by now and I hear of some who have got their letters, but <u>all</u> the bags do not appear to be up yet.
You seem to have been having a fair round of gaiety for the children. I hope Dr. Hannagan's services will not have to be requisitioned in consequence though I have vague recollections of mysterious visits to Dr Amyott after similar orgies in early days!
Haggitt who was also out on a different portion of the river has returned here, we met in Aliwal North and dined at the Hotel.
I had a curious meeting at that same hotel. Last Sunday I had noticed a quiet looking civilian feeding there, whose face somehow recalled my recollection but on close inspection I decided I did not know him – that evening after dinner we were sitting outside the hotel and he came up to me and said "Is your name Eric Wilson?" I said it was, but I could not recall the speaker's name which he gave next as – Mervyn Bosworth Smith.
It appeared from his account that he had been trading for some time in Basutoland – had tired of it as unprofitable and had come down to Aliwal with a view to enlisting in one of the colonial corps! He told me Pouty was doing well as an officer in the Basuto Police and that <u>he</u> had also been offered a commission in the Police but did not care for it.
He had grown up a fine strong man – not unlike Bos. himself. I remembered him last as a small boy who stammered – he has quite got over this now.
He told me there was to be a great R.B.S. house supper in July – and expected most of the Bos. boys would try to get home for it – Pouty and Gerard and Alan etc.
They had a tremendous storm while I was away from here – the stream through the town rose 15 feet and washed up level with the girders of the bridges which span it – but it all dies down within an hour of the rain ceasing.
Coming back I travelled viâ Burghersdorp – Stormburg Junction – Rosmead Junction – Naauwpoort Junction and Norvals Pont – where I met Musgrave

again – I travelled with a colonial office – Smitherman – who ran on foot into Mafeking through Boer and British lines without detection, spent 3 days giving B.P. news of the outside world, and got safely out again – of course with British connivance this time. A splendid fellow and full of confidence – now doing Intelligence work collecting news from his trained scouts and spies etc.

I am very sorry to hear of Olga Gilbert Smith's illness.

Just heard that nearly all DeWet's waggons of ammunition etc have fallen into our hands. You will note from his route that he fought shy of all our mined drifts to the S.E. of the O.R.C.

Best love to all Ever your loving son Eric

Bloemfontein　　　　　　　　　　　　　　　　　Saturday 2nd March 1901

My dearest Father

The mails lately have not been very punctual in arriving, and the incoming now usually arrives after the outgoings. Your last received was dated Feb 1st tho' I believe this weeks mail is in the town tho' not ready for delivery. I had another trip down the line on Tuesday last to a small siding just north of Jagersfontein Rd, Van Lyls Spruit – where we are building blockhouses – back the same day as far as Kaffir River where I had to get off and stay the night in order to inspect similar works.

At Edenburgh coming up I had an interview with Gen. Hart, who is commanding the lines of communication from here to Norval's Pont. I rather fancy that this Gen. Hart is none other than the Col. Hart who used to command Arthur's battalion – but this I am not sure of.

At Kaffir River I dined with the Headquarters of the Norfolk Militia under Major Beale.

I heard also that Capt. (Richard) Bagge was with them but posted on detachment down the line so I have not met him.

On Wednesday no train passed up till 2 p.m. when I got as far as Kaal Spruit and again left the train to arrange some works with Calverly, the Capt. Norf. Mil, in charge.

I got into Bloemfontein by 6 p.m. picking up another up train soon afterwards, on which I found Harold Tuck coming up from Riet River to draw Pay at the Bank for his men. I took him up to our camp and dined him and also put him up in my tent and he left after breakfast next day.

Now I am just off again – tomorrow – Sunday. I have to get to Jagersfontein Road to see into some question of water supply which has arisen there and several other jobs on the way up, one which will entail getting off at a small station and trolleying to an intermediate point, then a walk of a mile or so into the country, with a chance of an encounter with our friends the enemy, as it is a locality that has always been infested by small parties of them.

Wednesday last was the great anniversary of Cronje's surrender – so that his army have now spent 12 months in ?captivity at St Helena and elsewhere. The general feeling here is that the air is clearing a little and report says that Louis Botha is negotiating for terms in the Transvaal after being chivied by French right across the country.

DeWets incursion to Cape Colony has proved a failure and he is making desperate efforts to get his men back here again – pressed by columns on all sides – of course the vast extent of the ground covered makes actual capture a remote possibility as escape is easy – however the end must come by the slow method of attrition at last.

Much love – ever your loving son Eric E.B. Wilson

Bloemfontein Club   Sunday 10th March 1901

My dearest Father

I have just received yours of Feb 15th which arrived last night – I also heard from Joe Durnford, who reports himself duly married – and returned to Chatham on the 5th. F. D. Logan R.A. acted as best man for him in my absence – you may remember him as being in the Shop cricket and football teams same year as myself – a very good fellow and a mutual friend of Durnford and mine. I am very sorry to hear the sad end of Driver – I should not at all have liked to assist in the surgery – though I have many a time been an unwilling witness of the most horribly damaged humanity.

I am glad to have obtained a place in the Despatches though with our vast force in the field there must be thousands better entitled to mention after all it is only a question of opportunity, the last bugler out from home might at any moment find himself <u>compelled</u> to earn a V.C. which many would desire in a lifetime of campaigning without getting the golden <u>opportunity</u>.

Last Sunday I had to go down the line once again on a tour of inspection, which took me to Jagersfontein Road and other intermediate stations. I am off again tomorrow – I think to Bethulie this time.

Coming up last week I journeyed some of the way on one of the armoured trains under a Capt Nanton R.E. and on it met a certain Campbell of the Cape Garrison Artillery. I was sitting in his carriage talking to him and saw several photos etc tacked round the walls – amongst them one of Jack Lake and his wife – he turned out to be a brother of the two Miss Campbells I met at Orpington and I fancy, through the Dallam Tower Wilsons, a connection of ours.

While on the armoured train I had to get off and climb some hills about a mile from the line on which the General wanted some mines laid – as boers were in the habit of rendezvousing there to watch the line and fire on trains.

I got out there with 6 men escort and arranged places for the mines, and then we had to lie down and await the return of the armoured train, which had gone on to the next station to cross a down train.

Meanwhile a party of six boers not knowing we were there came galloping over the veldt towards our hill and we all got ready to give them a bolt from the blue – before however they came within shot, a picket of ours nearly 2 miles away spotted them and foolishly fired at them at an absurd distance and frightened them off, as they turned and galloped like smoke at once – and we could have blown them out of the saddle in another 5 minutes.

Haggitt and Pigott and I went to see "Still waters run deep" at the town hall here last night. It was not bad.
The weather has broken for rain now and will be followed by winter.

Much love from your ever loving son Eric E.B. Wilson.

Bloemfontein Club   **Friday 15th March 1901**

My dearest Father

Many thanks for yours of Feb 13. I am glad that you are pleased at the "mention in despatches" – I am as you may imagine – more than proud to appear in Lord Roberts own list of officers, of whom he says: "I confidently recommend those I have named to be to the favourable consideration of H.M. Government." Which in plain English means that the Government are requested by Lord Roberts to reward them. I have seen the gazette and reports, and just skimming through I make out about 40 R.E. officers all told from Kitchener and Sir Chas Warren downwards and of these some 12 are subalterns – of whom 3 are deceased and of the remainder five senior and three junior to me – but this is only a rough glance – no doubt the R.E. Journal for March will have correct extracts of the corps.
This list moreover will be enormously swelled on the conclusion of the campaign when there will probably be enormous departmental lists furnished by heads of departments – and generals – which will probably add a great many more R.E., however it is very nice being in the list of those mentioned in the heat of the fray in the good old hammer and tong days!
A year ago today since we entered Bloemfontein – it seems a lifetime!
Last Monday I went down the line on tour of inspection of defences as far as Bethulie, calling at Springfontein, Jagersfontein Rd, Van Zyls Spruit, Krugers, Edenburg etc., etc., on the way back.
Near Van Zyls Spruit I was driving in a cart over the veldt and picked up a collie (?) pup about three weeks old – miles from a house – how it got there I cannot imagine – anyhow I brought it back to Bloemfontein and it is thriving well – a well marked dog to be called Van Zyl.

I am off again south tomorrow – Sat – to Norvals Pont this time – where I shall meet Musgrave – returning next day.

I hear we have two new 2nd subalterns posted to 7th. Co:– Chevenix Trench and Ellis rather a bother at this time of a campaign – as they have so much to learn that instead of lessening work for us they may increase it for want of instruction.

This will make us 1 major and 5 subalterns of wh: I shall be the senior sub and take the place of captain in the Co: as our real establishment is 1 maj 1 capt 4 subs.

Haggitt and I went to a good organ recital lately at the cathedral.

There seems some prospect of Louis Botha surrendering soon. I fancy two of his (!) conditions are – no black to have a vote, and that we will make a money grant to farmers to start again – but of course no suggestion from the Boer side will carry any weight unless it happens to concur with the chiefs decision.

Much love to all – Ever your loving son Eric E.B. Wilson

Bloemfontein   Sunday 24th March 1901

My dearest Father

The mails have been delayed this week by a break down to the boat – we hear, so we shall probably receive two by the same post this week. The last from you were two very well written epistles from Michael and Amy – with a covering note from you addressed by Mother, a regular family affair!!
I tried to find <u>Dye</u> – I got wind of him at the convalescent camp where they told me he was a <u>Sergt</u> in the 8th Hussars – but had left the camp for duty with the Military Police – exact whereabouts unknown – so he appears to be alright.
We have been reinforced by two 2nd Lieuts: <u>straight</u> from Chatham after a course of <u>one</u> year following 18 months at <u>Woolwich</u>!! They seem to be turning out officers like German toys, by the gross, at present. One has joined us here – Chenevix Trench – a nice bright boy – with a big intellect and a not athletic frame – age 19 but looks about 15. The other, Ellis has gone up to Johnson and No 1 section at Potchefstroom.
Last Saturday I went by rail to Norval's Pont where I saw Musgrave and dined with him at the doctor's mess where he lives – he tells me his mother was extravagantly delighted at his being mentioned by Lord Roberts – and talks of coming out to the Cape. The whole family as you know only consists of Lady M. and A.D. and H. the two sons – the elder in the R.H.A. in India.
On Sunday – north to Springfontein where I was to meet Col. Buston C.R.E. from Bloemfontein and arrange about some additional works there and start them.
Monday the C.R.E. was off early and I out early marking out work we had decided on, started the various parties and got back here in the p.m.
On the train (up mail) in which I came were Lord Harris (Col:) A.A.G. for Yeomanry, and (Capt:) F.S.Jackson (Lancs: Militia). Jackson hailed me the length of the platform at Edenburgh where we stopped awhile – we last met at the Curragh where he used to stay with his sister Mrs Capt. Harper (R.E.) and seemed to be in pretty fair health and spirits – his regiment are at Zand River – a lonely and undesirable point up the line S. of Kroonstad.
Haggitt has gone off down the line now with the C.R.E. to see to about some more requirements, there is no end to the work.
Prisoners continue to stream in steadily from the various columns operating throughout the country – I think the total bag for February was over 1500.

The number of genuine Burghers who are writing, agitating and beseeching for peace to their fellows in arms increases also daily but seem to have little effect. However the process of attrition is thinning them down surely if slowly. Though I cannot see why we should feed thousands of their women and whelps and so make the it easier for them to prolong the bloodshed misery.

Ever your loving son Eric E.B. Wilson

Bloemfontein Club   **Sunday 31st March 1901**

My dearest Father

Your letter of Mar. 8th arrived yesterday. The mail for the week before, which was delayed by a break down at sea, has not arrived yet.
I am very sorry to hear of the death of Bertie Henniker – Charlie will now I suppose succeed to the barony.
We have not yet heard the result of the Boat Race, which I believe was rowed yesterday.
I see that the Suffolk hounds met at the "Hepper Mulberry" on the 12th – I suppose they worked over to Hinderclay.
From the results in the Varsity Sports, which I see in "this" weeks Field – Oxford appear to have the jumps and weights at their mercy – hurdles and sprints as usual fairly open – and distances to Cambridge.
Nothing much doing this week – or rather no break to the continuity of pretty heavy work.
On Thursday I went down the line to Riet River and thence rode, with a Capt. Barrett of Norfolk Mil: (H. Tuck's captain) (did not meet H. Tuck) about 2½ miles on horse to site some defences for a bridge, back to lunch at Riet River and by rail here same night.
At present I am under standing instructions to go to Cape Town to enquire into and see after, the state of our baggage, stores etc left there in Sept '99 and reported to be suffering, not only from long neglect, but also from too much attention, at the hands of gentry ordered home sick or otherwise, to

whom the opportunity of replenishing his wardrobe at the expense of the absent might prove too strong.

The C.R.E has been very good in letting me go and has left it entirely to me as regards when I start and return – entre nous – a legitimate method of getting a few days change of air and rest combined with an object in the way of duty.

I fully expect to find all my baggage looted and valuables gone but qui viora verra.

I may start Tues or Wed and get Easter Day at Cape Town – I see they are sending R.E. reinforcements out whole new companies – for erecting the garrisons, huts etc., etc., so I fear that means that every R.E. will be kept out, as long as he can stand up, for the next year or two – as there will be a lot of work to do.

Much love and all good wishes for Easter,
from your ever loving son Eric E.B. Wilson

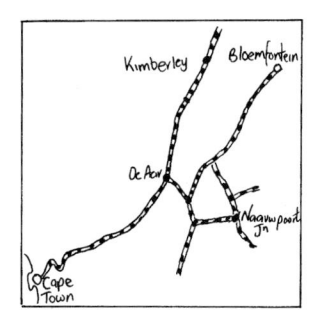

The Castle, Cape Town   Tuesday 9th April 1901

My dearest Father

Once more, after nearly 20 months, I find myself writing to you from the R.A. and R.E. Mess at Cape Town. I told you in my last letter that I might be coming down – I left Bloemfontein on Thursday and we came right through – passing through De Aar in the early hours of Good Friday and down over the vast open Karroo – reaching Cape Town about 9 a.m. on Saturday, just 47 hours journey. It seemed very strange seeing the familiar Bay and shipping and town just as it was in the far prehistoric days before the war – each day of which so full of incident and tension makes the time seem more like a cycle of years than of days.

My primary object here being to overhaul our company stores and baggage, which has been lying untended in a store shed at Wynberg since Sept '99. I sought out Capt. Burnaby R.E, in charge of 'Base Details' R.E. – odds and ends of men from companies up country who have come down sick and not yet returned.

I went down with him on Sat afternoon to Wynberg and walked up to the Camp – where he had some business – during which I went over the Store containing our baggage etc and found it in fairly good condition but in some chaos. We decided to have it all removed to Fort Knokke – his headquarters here – and where the baggage of all other R.E. companies is stored – so that it would be under his eye and also easier to get at for men coming down country and going straight on board ship.

Traction engine and trucks go out for it by road tomorrow (Wed) and I shall stay to see it housed here – as I was told to take my time and not hurry back sooner than I liked – to enable me also to get a breath of sea air!

While at Wynberg I walked all over the old camp and found very little change – in spite of the enormous hospital work which had been carried on there.

Here and there, where we had roads and clearings in old days, the ground was all overgrown with dense from disuse of former tracks etc.

Walking back to the station I looked in at Coghill's Hotel – where we first billeted on arrival, and a place where many hundreds of visitors had been passing through weekly – I had scarcely walked in when a voice said –

How are you Mr Wilson – I thought you must have been lost long ago! This was a small negro waiter of incredible age – who has been head servant there for several years and spotted me at once – asked after Col Kincaid and Capt Boileau etc etc and seemed to have followed every move of the war since we had left the hotel nearly two years before.

We got back to Cape Town soon after 5 and I went to call on the Morris' – he still being C.R.E. but unfortunately found them out. In the Mess here I found a younger brother of Charles R.E. – and R.S. McClintock of my batch – just come out after going through the Ashanti campaign and getting a promise of brevet promotion. He put me up in his room in the castle and we had great talks over old times. There are several other R.E. and R.A. officers in the mess also – some temporarily quartered here – others passing through.

On Sunday (Easter) morning I went to St George's Cathedral where we had a choral service and celebration, lasting from 10.30 to 1. o'clock and I was enabled to return humble thanks to the Almighty God for having safely brought me through great dangers (and) to hear once more the story of the great promise of a life to come. During the celebration the choir chanted the lovely hymn Peace – perfect Peace, and I fancy the verse "with loved ones far away – in Jesus keeping we are safe – and they" brought tears to the eyes of others besides myself,

In the afternoon Burnaby drove a Maj Hawkins R.E., (just landed in command of the 46th Co R.E.) and myself round to see some new defences outside the town and from one or two places lovely views of the town and bay were obtained.

Yesterday in the afternoon McClintock and I went up to the gardens and museum where I was anxious to identify several kinds of buck and antelope and other animals I had seen in the life up country.

We then went out by electric tram to Rondebosch and I took him to call on two families I had known well here before – but alas – the Strubens were away from home and the Jacksons had returned to England recently so we returned empty!

Today I shall probably go down to Wynburg with Barnaby again, to arrange about labour for loading up our stores for removal tomorrow.

Many thanks for March mag: The mail is in here today – but I shall have to chase it to Bloemfontein to get my letters. I heard from Muriel with congratulations on my selection for favourable mention and I heard not long since from Cousin Nellie.

Much love from your ever loving Son

I travelled as far as De Aar with Wilfred Gutch now a Lieut of Yeomanry – he said he met you at Cambridge some while back.

The Castle, Cape Town				Monday 15th April 1901

My dearest Father

I write again from here just before returning to Bloemfontein.
I completed the removal of all our baggage and stores – three road-trucks full, from Wynburg to Fort Knokke, which is on the foreshore here at Cape Town, and is used for depôt for all R.E. units up country – and have had it all overhauled labelled and stacked so that any individual man ordered down country or home will have no difficulty in getting his kit from the storeman, instead of having to go 9 miles out to Wynberg and rummage everything upside down to find anything – as there was no storeman in charge there.
I reported completion on Saturday and Col Morris said I could go back on Monday (tonight) if I can get off – the routine of getting a ticket – a seat in the mail – ones baggage disinfected from plague – etc etc is something fabulous, and entails personal visits to about a dozen different offices!
Yesterday I met (Lt Col) F.C.Heath R.E. who has been isolated as commandant of Hoopstad for the past 8 months, and has just run down here for a day or two. He reports well of his people at Redlands etc – and tells me Mrs Helsham Jones is at Mentone. I called on Col and Miss Morris also – and had tea and listened to some excellent music. On Thursday a party of us went to the Opera House and saw a play of Wilson Barrett's "Quo Vadis" – a good piece, of the time of Nero and the burning of Rome.
I hope to find two mails awaiting me at Bloemfontein.
We have had some good games of squash racquets here in a court built in the castle ditch – a very good one.
I was walking round the castle ditch the other day studying the building of the massive old ramparts and saw an inscription which I daresay is not often noticed – as it is rather faintly cut on a stone high up.

It read "   1663   "
LVDOVICVS

I should rather like to know who Mr Ludovic of that period was!
There is a subaltern of gunners – Green, here – son of Col A.O. Green R.E. who draws magnificently. He showed me a book of sketches cartoons etc done by him – he makes quite an income from it – and draws topical cartoons of DeWet etc for Cape papers.
I hope to write to you next from Bloemfontein. I shall probably see Musgrave on the way up at Norval's Pont. I came across my name in Angus Hamilton's

"Siege of Mafeking" page 25 lately – referring to the handful of troops at De Aar in Sep '99.

Best love to all Ever your loving son Eric E.B. Wilson

Bloemfontein Club   Saturday 20th April 1901

My dearest Father

I returned safely from Cape Town – arriving here on Thursday last. I found awaiting me letters from you of March 14th and 22nd and yesterday received one of March 29th – a goodly budget for one week! I also got an invitation to a farewell House supper at Harrow, and a short note from Bos: hoping I might be home in time for it – July 11th – which I have answered this mail.
I am delighted to hear such good news of Helen and her daughter. What a pleasure it will be to her if the child lives – she was always a motherly child from early years.
I had some good games of squash racquets in the court in the Castle ditch at Cape Town.
I am sorry the new tenant at Garboldisham is such an undesirable one – as it makes a great difference in a small corner of the country like ours.
I hope Frank will be able to secure himself a good position in Jamaica now that he has started so well. How will the new tax on sugar affect his prospects I wonder.
I heard from Muriel in London, this mail also – she had met Raymond and Uncle Walter in the same hotel – and seems well, and enjoyed her time at Pau. Many thanks for the account of the racquet finals.
I have seen a great deal of the Highland Light Infantry out here – we were with them at Paardeburg and elsewhere.
I think the rains are pretty well over here now and we shall soon be having cold nights and frost – at present it is warm and pleasant.
A new section of R.E.Volunteers has joined us, and the old one under Henriques has sailed for home. The new lot are being kept at Norvals Pont at present.

I found the puppy Van Zyl immensely grown during my absence at Cape Town and he simply whined and leapt with delight when I returned, he has evidently decided that I am his master, the first human being to handle him when he was wandering on the veldt – though many of the men and cooks feed him and pet him.

We had a great game of football yesterday – scratch sides – we had a match on but it fell through. I am quite stiff today.

Sapper Brown, of my section, died in hospital during my absence- a good fellow – he had never been the same since our hard times with Ian Hamilton and the long stay at Komati Poort.

Best love to all Ever your loving son Eric E.B. Wilson

Bloemfontein   Saturday 27th April 1901

My dearest Father   6 p.m.

Your last letter dated Mar 29th.

The mail this week has come in but contains no letters for me – which is unfortunate as I am just off with a column for another trek.

I expect we shall be away the best part of a month or five weeks so you must not expect much in the way of letters for a while, as we shall be quite away from the railway.

As far as I can make out we are going pretty well due West at first, establishing police posts etc at various places, and working round to Petrusberg which you will find on the map. There I fancy, a largish garrison is to be established, and I shall have to supervise their arrangements for defence etc – and then come back here with some convoy or other, as chance may offer.

My party consists of 5 R.E. and 60 Natives – Major Massy R.A. is commanding the column. We 'rendezvous-ed' about 2 miles out of the town this afternoon and after seeing my party camped have ridden in again to dine with the 7th Coy and shall go out again afterwards to sleep with the column. We march at 8 a.m. tomorrow – Sunday.

We have with us a party of telegraph R.E. who are going to put up wire as we proceed, and I shall assist with my natives etc – until we reach the various posts where the natives will be required to work on defences.

I have seen the list of clasps they are going to issue with the medal – I make out that according to the conditions I shall get five viz :–

1. Belmont (C.C.)   2. Modder River (C.C.)   3. Paardeburg (O.R.C)
4. Driefontein (O.R.C)   5. Johannesburg (Transvaal)

Unfortunately – by the conditions – the possession of a "battle clasp" in any colony precludes getting the "general" clasp for each colony – viz Transvaal O.R.C, Cape and Natal – each of which have a clasp to cover other engagements or even merely being stationed in any of them, so that a great many people who (may) have never seen a shot fired but have just been stationed in either Colony can obtain, say, three clasps easily.

Boileau will get six as he was at Diamond Hill – which Smith Dorrien's Brigade just missed by going to Elandsfontein in June '00. Haggitt will also get six as he was with 6th Division which qualifies him for Kimberley Relief, and Methuen's column do not get Kimberley Relief. We estimate that General French will get the largest number possible for one man, either eight or nine, very few others will exceed 5 or 6.

Musgrave is with us for a day or two, and McClintock is due tonight both for a short stay only, so we have a great reunion before we separate again. Will you please write to Helen for me and tell her how pleased I am to hear that she and her daughter are flourishing – I have been too busy and may not be able to write for some while now.

Best love to all from ever your affectionate son Eric E.B. Wilson

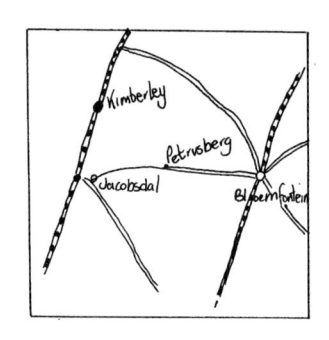

Petrusberg, Orange River Colony　　　　　　　　**Sunday 12th May 1901**

My dearest Father

Have just heard that a convoy in going into Bloemfontein tonight – so snatch a moment to report all well and fearfully busy from sunrise to sunset. As there is every probability of this being intercepted by the enemy between here and Bloemfontein I cannot give you any details of work going on.
We left Bloemfontein on April 28th – a strong column of Royal Irish Rifles, South African Constabulary and guns – and marched via Bains Vlie, Daniels Kuil, Strydon's Pan, Abrams Kraal, Driefontein, and Kaatdorn Put to here, about 95 miles in all. We stopped a day or two at some of the places and established strong posts of S.A.Constabulary which I had to plan and fortify.
We had several brushes with the enemy – and two or three men and some horses hit, the men all slight wounds. At Abrams Kraal we shelled them out of some hills, at Driefontein we had a smart go at them over the old battlefield and cleared about 150 of them out of the same hills as last year, and coming in here we twice came into action and cleared small parties away, who fled wildly in all directions, after firing a few shots.
The town of Petrusberg was almost deserted – 3 sick boers and a doctor and a few women and children being the inhabitants – however we got some useful stores and material from the town. We are now camped on a farm about a mile from town with a strong position and lots of water and supplies etc. The S.A.C. go out from here and clear up horses and stock from adjacent farms and dispense or capture small parties of the enemy.
I have seen no letters or papers for some time now – but we are in telegraphic communication with Bloemfontein and hear the war news.
They have been doing good work all round lately – some 300 to 400 boers were killed captured or disposed of last week – the rest will soon realize that they have nothing to fear from peace and will gradually come in.
We have with us a telegraph section under Lawson (attached R.E.) – they have done splendid work. L. and I mess together and have a common camp for our men.
I don't think I have had so much to do single-handed and so few men to do it as the last fortnight ever since the early days at De Aar!

I have not been out of my boots for the last ten days! However it is just the work and life that suits me best and I am very fit thank God. I hope some of the society soldiers and gilded skunks who slipped off home as the hardest time was coming on are feeling sufficiently foolish now!

Best love to all Ever you loving son Eric E.B. Wilson

Petrusberg Orange River Colony Monday 27th May 1901

My dearest Father

A convoy has just come in through Bloemfontein – a great event – and brought besides supplies – mails. I hasten to send you a line as the same wagons are returning tomorrow and mail bag closes tonight. I got letters from you dated April 12 and 19 – and a book of Harrow, by J.F. Williams, for which many thanks. Also a book and note from Helen – and a paper re sale of Montgreenan to sign as a trustee of the marriage contract.
I am sorry to hear of the death of Montgomerie.
I expect this will reach you somewhere in the West of England if your tour is not over by the time it arrives. Many Happy Returns of the 4th June when you should be 58?
The following day will be the anniversary of our triumphant but tattered entry into Pretoria! when it was absolutely necessary that some of the men should march well in the <u>inner files</u> of the column, going through the town!
Both your letters are so full of interesting things that I cannot refer to all in detail.
On May 24th I obtained a half holiday for my 60 Basutos who have been working on the defences etc here under my 3 R.E.s from 7th Co: and made them give three cheers for the King which they did most heartily!
My work is nearly complete here now and I expect to return to Bloemfontein any time after the end of this month, as escort or opportunity offers.
We have completely transformed the farm and hills we are occupying – with defences, buildings, roads, fences, wells, etc etc, and most of the houses in the

old hamlet of Petrusberg have contributed their quota of furniture, windows, doors, planks, tanks, fencing etc, etc.

I fear our brother boer would not recognise his happy home readily now!

We call the camp Belfort – and the farm where Major Massy R.A. and headquarters are, Waterford. I dined with Major M. on the 24th, we had a great party – Major O'Leary commanding the R. Irish Rifles here and Apthorpe of the S.A. Constabulary and several others helped to demolish a stout pair of fowls and a neck of mutton with song and music to follow.

Lawson of the Telegraph with whom I mess and camp is son of the incumbent of Sudborough in Northampton and a good fellow – he is having an easy time now – all his telegraphs and telephones once fixed up.

Our mess stores are running low – as we did not anticipate so long an absence from our respective headquarters.

We are now out of butter and soups! But L. got a case of 1 dozen Whisky by this convoy!

I am busy building ovens, and as we got a lot of flour this convoy – we hope in a day or two to replace hard biscuit once more by bread. Such is life on the veldt, when what you at home no doubt regard as almost valueless items of daily life – become of the most vital interest!

I see Bertie got £55,000 for Mountgreenan – not a bad little sum and equals some £1800 per annum at 3½%.

Although I believe long since published, no one here has yet seen the long list of C.B.'s and D.S.O's etc., which we hear have been published – and no doubt chiefly absorbed by the various Staff Officers. Very little, in a large campaign like this, will find its way to the regimental officers.

I must close now – with much love to all at home – and best birthday wishes also to poor Moonie on the 16th

from your ever loving son Eric E.B. Wilson

P.S. It will probably be a long time before another convoy leaves.

Bloemfontein   Thursday 13th June 1901

My dearest Father

Once more in Bloemfontein – but only for a moment. I got in from our six weeks on the veldt, on the 11th, marching in from Emmaus – 64 miles in three marches – doing 16, 22, and 26 the last day – not bad going.
We went out from Petrusberg to Emmaus on June 3rd – 12 miles, with only 1½ companies of Infantry, and had some fighting en route – one man of Royal Irish Rifles being shot in nine places and killed.
We were supposed to be stopping a gap – for a big drive – i.e. we were "in the butts" – and ten columns from different directions drove boers on to us – I think the total bag was 180 boers when I left – being wired to return to Bloemfontein. I had to slip through from Emmaus to Petrusberg in the dead of night – freezing cold and only three men as escort – however we dodged through and reached Petrusberg at 8 a.m.
There I found a letter from you of May 3rd and a parcel of warm things from Mother – which were <u>most</u> opportune – the red mittens "from Amy" came straight out of the parcel on to my frozen wrists – also a scarf – the other things warmed my poor men.
At 11 a.m. same day a column under Major Marshall left for Bloemfontein and I accompanied them 'as a passenger' as I was wanted back here – my party leaving on foot the next day with Major Massy's column – and should be in tomorrow – Petrusberg being handed over to the S.A.Constabulary – after we have spent 5 weeks making it impregnable and building forts, wells, roads, ovens, tin houses etc etc.
I am off tomorrow to Springfontein Junction where I relieve Musgrave, who is joining the S.A.C. 'Pioneer troop.'
My work there will be erection of numberless blockhouses on the line and running up by horse, trolly or train as opportunity offers – the distance of the stretch of line is about 35 miles – I sent my groom and horses off tonight and follow by mail tomorrow.
You will be quite safe to <u>address</u> c/o Railway – no – I think you better stick to "Bloemfontein" – it only means 2 days later – going up and coming down – though I shall probably be <u>at least</u> 2 or 3 months at S. – or even to end of war, as it is a big centre for work and needs as R.E. officer on the spot.
I have seen Gen. Colvile's Despatch about Paardeberg though Roberts had <u>already extracted</u> names and mentioned them.
Colvile is very eulogistic of 7th Co R.E. I am glad to see. However in regard to rewards I fear the Lt Cols and Majors are getting all those that <u>usually</u> fall to

the Capts and subalterns – everything being on such a big scale. So far no one but Staff Officers and special cases have been rewarded – 'Regimental' rewards have not been entered upon.

Kincaid and Boileau have already got brevet promotion as staff officers. I expect they will get further reward over Paardeberg in the regimental lists. The 7th Co by being all over the country in small parties will do well in the aggregate of "clasps" – I make out that in the company there have been earned no fewer than 12 different clasps – the greatest number to one individual being 6, which will be borne by I think four or five men – Boileau gets six, (with Diamond Hill) also his groom!! I doubt if any unit of the Field Force will show a bigger total than 7th Co R.E.

Many thanks for parcel of magazines and Conference Lecture by T.H.W. – in which I was most interested.

I have also received since I returned a letter from you of May 17th from Cornwall – describing reception of Pole Carew – who was with us at Belmont – Modder River – Poplar Grove – Bloemfontein and Belfast – Komati Poort.

I had tea with him one day at Modder River, when bearer of some message. I hope you enjoyed your Cornwall and West of England tour. Michael is seeing a lot of the old country that is quite "terra incognita" to me!

Must stop now – with much love to all
from your ever loving son Eric E.B. Wilson

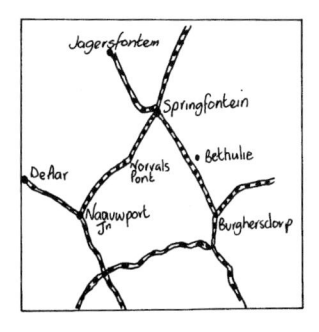

Springfontein Junction, Orange River Colony Saturday 22nd June 1901
Our shortest day
Sun rises 6.52 a.m.
sets 5.12 p.m.

My dearest Father

Here I am firmly installed for the time with a great deal of work on hand. I have spent all last week running all over the line between here and Norvals Pont and Bethulie.

My work at present all lies in the triangle formed by the two railways and the river.

We are busy putting up numbers of block houses – quite close together, all along the railway and this entails a lot of organising in the way of despatching materials, food and men, to a number of places, to arrive at the right time – so that one party does not get double rations and another a double allowance of nails for their supplies!!

Then I have to be constantly at each place myself to choose new sites and check progress etc, generally involving a walk of some miles from mid-veldt into the next station.

Musgrave who was working here has now gone North to work with B.P's constabulary and form a Pioneer Troop, start workshops etc., a job I considered deeply at one time, but as it meant signing on for 3 years more I shied off!

I have been very fortunate here in getting a room in a house pro: tem: which Dr Clarke the Railway doctor lives in – and had kindly put at my disposal, entirely as a guest when he could easily let for £15 a month. However I am building a little shed to form an R.E. office and bunk for O.C.R.E., and when it is finished I shall not trespass on Clarke's hospitality any longer.

I have so much office work and writing and books etc to keep going, and no clerk, that it is impossible to do it in a windy tent with dust storms or rain going.

I was down at Bethulie this week and saw Willie Woodward in hospital – he has been very ill but is now better. Perhaps you remember him – he used to shoot a lot with Horsfall.

Springfontein in Orange River Colony 1901

I met Fox on the up mail also – just out again – you said the Walkers had met him abroad. We had a great talk over De Aar times!

Two nights this week I have been at Norvals Pont, where a lot of work is going on – there I stay with the doctors at No 10 Hospital – a rare good lot too – I met another Carlyon R.A.M.C. – brother of the one I met at Johannesburg and great nephew of Edmund Carlyon – a nice fellow – he has seen a lot of Trissie C.

Many thanks for yours of May 24 also cuttings re Remenham and other cricketers etc.

I expect another mail tomorrow forwarded from Bloemfontein.

Aunt Amy writes to tell me that George has passed well off the Brittania – which must be a great joy to her and Uncle R. I have had no time to write to them yet and I owe so many letters.

We have had heavy rain last two days – most unusual at this season, and a godsend for filling the ponds and dams in the dry weather.

My big horse was stolen last night during my absence by some prowling blackguard, and I had mounted men out all day searching for him – luckily he was branded 7RE on the hoof, they found him, late this evening – with three other 'picked' horses concealed in some hills, evidently with a view to making off tonight – as there was no one near him we could not detect the thief and I was glad to get him back.

Much love to all – Ever your loving son –
I got some magazines from you last post.

Springfontein, Orange River Colony   Sunday 30th June 1901

My dearest Father

By last mail I received two letters from you :– dated May 10th and 31st. The former had been right out to Petrusberg by ox convoy and back to look for me! I gave Carlyon at Norval's Pont all your news about Uncle Edmund –he expressed great surprise at his trip to Gibraltar etc., C. was rather poorly when I last saw him – in bed with a slight influenza – but I think nothing much. This morning I met Major R. Smythies – 1st Cousin once removed, he has been here a long time with the South Lancs Militia, but we have never met hitherto. He accosted me with the enquiry if I was any relation to Mrs Machell-Smythe! He himself bears a striking resemblance to Uncle W. on rather a smaller scale. They are just off home (today) as they have been relieved by the 5th Lancs fusiliers – so you might soon meet him.

I am glad you found all well at Uncle Charlie's – fancy your never having met Mr. Phipps before! He was very kind to me last time I was there. Evie Phipps the eldest girl I remember as a most charming girl – but I do not think I have seen her for nearly four years now! I quite expected to hear that she had married over and over again. I am sorry to hear that Aunt Minnie was not very grand – I do so long to see her again. Fancy Frank being at home again at last – I hope he will wait till I come back!

I have a lot of work to do with Arthur's old Colonel (now Major Gen) Fitzroy-Hart C.B., C.M.G. – I don't fancy he was much beloved in the East Surrey's however he is a good old chap where fighting and work are concerned.

I got a very nice note from Dr Conan Doyle last mail – he lives near Haslemere, I saw him there when I was with Muriel, and again out here – I wrote to him a few minor corrections on points of fact within my knowledge, with regard to his book "The Great Boer War". He says:– "some of which shall certainly be incorporated in my final edition"

I also heard from Muriel last mail from Murrayfield, Edinboro' – she seems very well and happy I think. She promises me a photo of the boy – see that she sends it will you! as I am most anxious to see it.

I am still staying with Clarke, the Railway Medical Officer and my office is progressing favourably but hanging fire a bit for want of material at present. Haggitt comes down here on Monday to go over the line to Bethulie, which is the next piece we are going to blockhouse along. We shall probably trolley down on Tuesday, about 30 miles altogether.

Last week Clarke and I went out twice with his 3 greyhounds – one day we had two short runs after hare but lost both – the other day we had two splendid runs – killing the first – the second going to ground after about a mile at full gallop.

On Wednesday I was at Norval's Pont for the night and dined and slept with the R.A.M.C.

With the new militia battalion here has arrived a certain Bowring – a great friend of Harry Horsfall's – I think he shared the shooting one year with him did he not? He seemed very pleased to see me and I entertained him their first evening and had a great talk over old Redgrave shooting days.

Best love to all from your ever loving son Eric E.B. Wilson

Springfontein, Orange River Colony   **Sunday 7th July 1901**

My dearest Father

I was just settling down to write to you, and turning over your letter of June 7th when my man came in with this weeks' mail – June 14th – a day earlier than usual! Another coincidence that did not coincide, as the Irishman would put it, occurred today – I had a very heavy day's writing making up Native Labour Accounts etc for June – amounting to something like £170, in small sums, and was wishing I had a clerk to do some of my writing for me when the door opened and a Sapper appeared – Well who are you? I said – Please Sir I'm corporal Chipperfield that Major Haggitt sent down by train today from Bloemfontein to act as Clerk in your office!!

Many thanks for your last two letters and cuttings re cricket and the late E.E. Bowen.

I am sorry you have been disappointed of Helen's visit.

It was curious your hearing of the engagement of the eldest Phipps girl so soon after your visit – I think the M. F. H. will be a lucky man – as Evie P was decidedly the finest character of the party, as I remember them.

I am very sorry to hear that Mrs Methold is ill – I hope she is recovering now – please remember me to them all next time you see any of them?

I have just completed my work on the Springfontein – Norvals Pont line and the next three weeks will find me busy travelling up and down the Springfontein – Bethulie section.

Haggitt was down last week and stayed two nights with me and we trollied down to Bethulie, 30 miles between 9.30 a.m. and 12.30 – stopping at about a dozen places to choose sites for blockhouses on the railway. As we were nearing Bethulie we were walking along the veldt looking out for a covey of partridges, reported in the neighbourhood – when up jumped a 'stembuck', one of the smaller deer.

Haggitt knocked it over fairly at 40 yards with a charge of no 5 shot – but it jumped up again and made off over a kopje – I hurriedly fired with a rifle I was carrying and missed it – gave chase and knelt down and fired again bringing it down with a broken leg, when we secured it. We didn't see the partridges however.

We stayed one night at Bethulie inspecting work there and returned the next day. I am off at daybreak tomorrow that way again but hope to be back in the evening.

My house is almost finished now. I got two windows from Bloemfontein today and a keg of paint – I hope to move in on Tuesday. I call it a 'house' – but at home it would probably be mistaken for a garden tool shed but as things go here it is much to be preferred to the open veldt.

Much love to all from your ever loving son Eric

P.S. If you want a really good amusing and life like book to read get "Some Experiences of an Irish R.M. It brought back Co Kildare very vividly to me.

Springfontein   Saturday 13th July 1901

My dearest Father

I am inditing my weekly epistle on Dr Clarke's typewriter which is rather a novelty!
This week's mail is not yet to hand – due tomorrow.
Last week I was down at Norval's Pont, starting a party at roofing two fine stone block-houses we have just built there. While there I met one John Gillespie – the engineer who originally built the railway, quite one of the old Pioneers of the country and a most interesting man to speak to, as he has explored and shot all over Africa.
On my way back I caught a momentary glimpse of Richard Bagge, going South on a troop train, but we only had time for a mutual glance of recognition.
My little tin mansion being at last completed, I have moved over from Clarke's hospitable abode, and slept for the first time there last night.
At the present moment I am waiting for a wire from General Hart to go down the Bethulie line with more block-houses: I have three parties working there.
We (the 7th Field Company R.E.) complete two years of foreign service tomorrow, and 643 days of RED WAR!!
It is almost a year since you had the false alarm that I was coming home, is it not?
Several militia battalions have left for home lately, and fresh ones come out – the terror of all, as they see a BOER in every ant-hill, and a commando in every flock of sheep, and are always firing in all directions, by far exceeding the danger from the bullets of the enemy!
When is the Redgrave flower show to come off this year?
I hear Harry Horsfall is thinking of leaving Worcester in September and wants to find another place in Norfolk, but cannot hear of one at present. His stepmother still occupies the family house near Northampton I believe.
Van Zyl, my Kaffir puppy is growing an enormous dog, and is not yet four months old. He follows me everywhere when I am riding round the works.
It is eleven years this month since I came to Cotton from Harrow, to see you marry Miss Turner.
Have you any news from Moonie yet?
I suppose Bos:'s farewell house supper is now a thing of the past?
I met today the younger Beale, of Colbecks, the elder one was more my contemporary, and rowed, I think, in the Cambridge boat. Or am I thinking of H. AGame, another Colerite?

I see the cricket match was a drawn game – somewhat in favour of Cambridge, who still lead on the total. The Borderers season will, I suppose be now in full swing. I shall soon forget which end of a bat to get hold of I fear.

The days are getting visibly longer here, though we still get sharp frosts at night.

Well now I must bring my first effort at writing with a machine to a close, I am rather proud of the success of my maiden effort.

Much love to all from your ever loving son Eric E.B. Wilson.

Springfontein, Orange River Colony   Sunday 21st July 1901

My dearest Father

Yours of June 28th arrived last night – two days earlier than usual. I am glad Peter continues to make runs – his cricket education certainly commenced early enough in his life to make a first class performer of him!

I am afraid Helen will be very much upset over the sad death of Cicely Henniker.

Last week I did a good bit of travelling – going twice to Bethulie and once to Norval's Pont. Coming back from Bethulie last Monday I travelled up with a very nice man, a Captain Campbell 9th Lancers, who had been with us in all the early part of the campaign, round Orange River Bridge way – he had just been down to the Coast on 3 weeks leave to meet his wife from home. I think he has brought her to Aliwal North to stay for a while.

We arrived very late at Springfontein so I took him over and put him up in my shanty for the night and he went on to Edenburg next day. He owned <u>and</u> rode 'The Soarer' who won the Grand National in '96!!

I think the 9th Lancers have had the hardest campaigning of any regiment in the empire, having been really at the forefront on the march and in all the subsequent 'hunts' after the bands of brigands still at large, right away from the start.

I think they nearly all get 7 clasps – they get Relief of Kimberley and Diamond Hill in addition to my 5. Poor Major Jenner my Curragh friend is terribly sick at having been out of it all when his regiment have done such a lot.

Tuesday I went down to Norval's Pont to pay Native Labourers their wages – they average 1/4d per day and their rations – but will not work more than a month or two in the year, as this earns them enough money to take it easy for the rest of the year – or until they want a little more money – or a new wife! On Friday I went again to Bethulie, putting up new block-houses along the railway.

We found the telegraph cut and a pole down at one place, so I had it temporarily mended etc until the proper repairs could be done by the armoured train party who came down soon afterwards.

No signs of the boers however – they often lie in wait after a job of this kind to have a shot at the repairing party who they know will soon be on the spot.

Yesterday I combined much pleasure and a little business by trolleying down to Jantjesfontein – 8 miles from here, with Dr Clarke and Mr Growdon the Permanent Way Inspector.

We left the line with shot guns and 3 natives as beaters, carrying rifles in case we came across "big" game(!) and walked a good 20 miles over kopje and veldt – finishing up at the trolley at about 5 p.m. – our bag being 8 partridges and 7 hares – not bad for the country where 5 miles walk for a partridge is easy going – Growdon got most of the shooting and is a dead first class shot – from the left shoulder – never misses anything within 50 yards – quite one of the old colonial stock who save and reload the same 50 brass cartridge cases all their lives!

At one period of the day the armoured train came along and halted on the line in a most suspicious way – we thought they had spotted us and took us for boers – Clarke and Growdon of course being in civilian attire – as they had a 12 pr on the train we decided that prevention was better than cure, so hastened to put a good stout kopje between ourselves and them, and lay low till they had passed on up the line.

In the evening I dined with Dumaresq and Simpson – the Railway Staff Officer and Station Staff Officer – and their Irish cook Riley gave us a capital dinner – two gunners and Clarke were also there.

After dinner six officers of the South African Light Horse came in and we had a great and musical evening – Dumaresq being a first rate violinist and one of the S.A.L.H. at the piano.

What with our long day's shooting and long night's noise and smoking I am decidedly sleepy this morning!

There is a large southward move of troops – so we expect to hear of great activity in the Colony shortly. I have just heard that when Broadwood surprised the town of Reitz lately and caught many 'officials' of Steyn's entourage – that Steyn himself only escaped in his shirt and trousers and that one of our men – (not R.E.) – I fancy an officer, had <u>six</u> shots at him with his revolver from five to eighty yards while he was running for his horse! It makes my mouth water! What a chance! and Steyn is a good broad target – I think I would cut my hand off if I missed him like that – just think what a difference it would make to closing the war. However it may be only a yarn – the fact remains that Steyn only just escaped capture. Will you send me out a magazine called 'The Wide World' – it is publishing Conan Doyles "Great Boer War" in serial by monthly instalments – and I rather want to see his accounts of certain phases of the campaign – as I fancy he has revised a lot since he brought his book out.

Much love to all from your ever loving son Eric E.B. Wilson

Springfontein   Sunday 28th July 1901

My dearest Father

Just got yours of the 5th inst: many thanks.
I have had such a terrible amount of office correspondence to get through today, (Sunday and all) that I am not sure if this will catch the English mail, I hope so.
You should have got also some educational papers I sent off during the week. I have been very busy lately on routine and engineer works.
I was down at Bethulie on Tuesday and back same night – I picked up a fine old Dutch flint lock elephant gun, of incredible length and calibre – what the boers call a "roer" (pronounced roor).
On Thursday we had a visit from General Tucker and his staff and I had to ride round all the defences and explain everything to him – he was quite amiable and pleasant – usually his language is something awful!
On Friday I went down to Norval's Pont to attend to that end of my "parish" and found a great ball on for that night – but I shied off going and had a quiet evening in the Hospital Mess with Arthur Carlyon and a few other non-dancing men! I met Harold Tuck – I think he graced the ball in the evening too.
I got back last night after various stopping and en route to visit works.
This afternoon one Tisdall Royal Irish Rifles arrived, en route for England to join the Irish Guards, a great friend of mine during the Petrusberg trek. He plays the violin magnificently and entertained us sometime with it.
Tomorrow I am off at streak of dawn to Bethulie to pay some of my men and visit some works.
We have had intense cold lately at night. One feels it more and more each winter – and this is my third – they say one's blood gets thinner – I know that it takes four blankets, a skin 'karross' and a great coat to keep me warm at night nowadays!
I am reading Sir H.Colviles "Work of the IXth Division" it is most interesting. I for one think he has been treated vilely.

Ever your loving son Eric E.B. Wilson

Springfontein   Sunday 4th August 1901

My dearest Father

Mail not to hand this week yet.

Nothing much to record for last week.

On Monday I trollied down to Bethulie bridge – 28 miles in 2¼ hours – taking mails etc for my party working there. Found good progress with the works, blockhouses etc – lunched with the 4th Cheshires at their mess – an old farm house near the river.

Caught train up again at 3.30 p.m. which did not arrive Springfontein till past 8 o'clock!

Monday night we had a very sharp frost and all Tuesday the usual gale of dust and wind from N.W.

Rode round various works in progress in the camp – we are busy building several new houses for the hospital – viz – Surgery, x-ray room etc etc. In the p.m. 4 civilian carpenters arrived from Bloemfontein to assist in this work and having brought nothing with them except what they stood in, I had to fit them out with blankets, kettles, a native cook etc etc to sustain life in them! They "understood" that everything was going to be provided for them – a very unsound rule to work on in this country!

On Wednesday usual round in a.m. – also sent off 7 water tanks to various blockhouses etc on the line which were short of storage for water.

Generals Hart, C. Knox, and B. Hamilton were all in, through, or around Springfontein during the day.

In p.m. had a game of football for 'Railway' v. 'Hospital' – we lost by 1 – 2, but the gale and dust prevented any concerted mode of action, in addition to the referee (a 'Hospital' man) giving us 25 minutes with the wind and 45 against it, as his idea of "half times". In the evening I dined with one Jackson, vet: dept: at Strausz's farm, where the remount establishment focuses – a fine old Dutch farm, with the usual oleographs of the Kaiser and family and other German prints.

On Saturday – Waterhouse – (I think of Marshalls) passed through from home after 15 months invalided – to rejoin his regiment – some highland battalion. He was very badly wounded in one of the earlier fights – shot through the temple and other places and has quite lost the sight of his left eye and the lid is closed permanently etc – such a pity as he was a very good-looking boy.

McInnes D.S.O., R.E., has just turned up to stay the night with me, bound for Bethulie, so must close now.

Much love from your ever loving son Eric E.B. Wilson

Springfontein   Sunday 11th August 1901

My dearest Father

Mail is late again this week, though I have now arranged with P.O. at Cape Town to forward my letters direct here.

Major Haggitt is down for a day or two, and he and I trollied down to Bethulie yesterday, visiting all the blockhouses etc en route.

Tomorrow we go to Norvals Pont in a similar manner.

I think I forgot to tell you that Mervyn Bos: passed through here recently on his way home again, though I think he intends to come out again later.

I have not yet heard the result of Harrow v. Eton: Do you remember what a long time the news took to reach me last year?

We are all hoping great things of Kitchener's latest 'notice' – viz: that all leaders, commandants, and 'men of influence' (v. elastic term!) who have not surrendered by September 15th, will be deported for life when caught.

Also that the Dutch families will not be fed free after that date but payment recovered by the confiscation and sale of burghers property. I think that will touch a few tender spots.

In between my excursions last week I had another game of football, when we defeated a team of Mounted Infantry by 4 – 1.

It is nearly two months since last rain fell, we are getting very dusty indeed now. By the time this reaches you I expect the first shots of the partridge campaign will have been fired. I see that Frank has undertaken to conquer the fen this year!

H.Tuck and R.Bagge are both at Norvals Pont now, and though in my many visits I always meet the former, I have never yet managed to come across the latter!

The cold weather has broken now and nights are much warmer.

There will be a good many useful (stock) farms for sale when all is over, and men with capital will get the best bargains by buying early – good farms run about 15/= to 20/= an acre to buy outright – usual size about 3000 acres – but a lot depends on the water.

I have got a collection of ten different boer firearms adorning the walls of my hut now, I hope to succeed in bringing them home some day.

Much love from your ever loving son Eric E.B. Wilson

Springfontein   Sunday 18th August 1901

My dearest Father

Your last to hand dated July 19th enclosing menu of 'Show' received on 13th inst: the actual day of Show – so I was able to figure you at the moment having steam rides in the Park! Though from previous reminiscences I fancy the poor sec: has a good deal of trotting about to do on his stoutest boots. I hope all went off with good success.

I am glad Moonie is safely through with another of the old stock – I have just received from Bertie, a photo of Robert the eldest – a most intelligent looking child – who I should think will be quite abreast of the scientific times he has made his appearance in. He reminds me very much of Muriel as I remember her at Cheltenham.

I also heard from the parish clerk last week and am writing to her.

I have now heard in yours that Harrow won easily by 10 wickets, which is most satisfactory.

Things are going very nicely in the reduction of outstanding burghers; great captures have been made the last few weeks, and I think Kitchener's proclamation will have a strong effect in bringing sight to the blinder ones.

We have had great activity round here, as Kritzinger has been driven out of the Cape Colony by Gorringe & Co and has been flying in all directions round here and well hammered by armoured trains and blockhouses – he will now have to collect his payments somewhere and scratch his head for food and raiment, as this country wouldn't support a chicken for a week now, it has been so cleared and harried.

Last Monday I trollied down with Haggitt to Norvals Pont, inspecting every blockhouse and post en route.

We dined at the Hospital and returned at 4 a.m. next morning – H. going straight on to Bloemfontein.

On Wednesday I rode down the line to see about some work done on a fort, and in the afternoon played again for Railway v. M.I. and we won 1 – 0 after a good game.

On Friday I was down at Norvals Pont again and returned yesterday.

Tomorrow I visit Bethulie to pay my men there.

Last Thursday Lerothodi the Basuto Chieftain passed through with his suite, to meet the Duke of York at Cape Town, and present him with a white ox – a token of friendship etc.

Much love to all from your ever loving son Eric E.B. Wilson

Love to
Rowland 33?
Leonard 26?
Frank 25?
Villiers 24?
Piers 19?

Springfontein   Saturday 31st August 1901

My dearest Father

I fear you did not hear from me last mail as I was on the train for three consecutive days before mail. We have had a great rush of work lately and shall have pressure for some time to come. They are running the blockhouse system for all it is worth and are now doubling them all along – i.e. halving the distance between – which has suddenly thrown the construction of over thirty more on to my section of the railway, and this means much travelling, arranging, moving and rationing of the various building parties.

A blockhouse, I may add is a sort of bullet proof summer house with double walls, the space between being filled like a sandwich with broken small stone to make it bullet proof – and has loopholes all round for a dozen or so men to shoot from. The new scheme will bring them some 1400 yards only apart – so that each has only to look after some 700 yards each side of it. If they cannot prevent boers crossing a chain of these blockhouses then I think the garrison had better take to croquet or marbles!

Of course the value of these chains of these blockhouses is obvious in a large country like this as it acts like a 'stock yard' for the pursueing columns to round up the scattered parties of desperadoes and drive them on to a chain of blockhouses – when in their desperation alas they too often succeed in breaking through, with a toll taken by the fire from the men in the b-houses.

Your last received bore date Aug 9th and arrived on 30th – the one before arriving on the 26th – my birthday. The reason I only had four days to wait is that, after repeated applications, the Cape Town P.O. have at last started addressing me 'Springfontein', thus avoiding 3 days lost in going to Bloemfontein and coming back from 7th Co. I have received a fine consignment of local papers lately from you and Uncle Rowland which are of great interest to me. Also a bundle of Magazines. Don't forget to send me "The Wide World Magazine" if you can get it; as I am anxious to read Conan Doyle's revised edition of "The Great Boer War" which is appearing serially in it.

I hope some nice people will take the Hall. It has always been a (secret) ambition of mine should I ever succeed in acquiring enough money to rent the Redgrave shooting and Hall, if still in the market whenever the day might come! But I fear the army is the wrong place to amass coin in!! At the present moment I fancy I am about as rich as I have ever been! I don't owe a penny in the world and (I think) have a credit of nearly £150 – however when I ever left for home the expenses of restocking my uniforms and other millstones of civilization would soon make that look small I fear! However I have just remembered that I <u>do</u> owe Uncle Walter £50 and must write to him about repayment!

I am very sorry to hear such poor harvest accounts as our prosperity in Suffolk is bound up with the land almost entirely.

Much love to all from your ever loving son Eric E.B. Wilson

I had a great birthday dinner on 26th shared with a young Norman Herbert of 5th Fusiliers, who happened to be here and also to become <u>21</u> on the 26th – one of the few I have met who had same birthday.

<u>Our guests</u>: Colonel Carleton (Commandant) Lt. Dumaresq (Ry St: Officer) Lt. Stack (S.O. to Comm.) Lt Westmacott 5th Fusiliers, Lt Simpson R.F.A, Dr Geo. Clarke, 2nd Lt Norman Herbert and yours truly – 8.

Norvals Pont, Cape Colony   Sunday 8th September 1901

My dearest Father

I nearly missed this mail, as I have been on the train up and down my section of the line the last two days – putting up more blockhouses – and put in here for the night yesterday, dining and sleeping at the Doctor's Mess, No 10 General Hospital.

There is little of interest to record this week: the dryest and dustiest time of the year is with us now. Not a blade of grass on the veldt and dams and streams all at lowest ebb; and continuous heavy dust storms – all day long.

The capture of Lotter's Commando is the feature of the week: they seem to have been thoroughly brought to bay in a corner, as it is most unusual for a party of boers to fight long enough to have 12 killed and 45 wounded. Captain Coffin R.E. was through Springfontein last week: you may remember he was O.C. of the Composite R.E. Company I was with in the Eastern Transvaal.

I last saw him dangerously ill of malarial fever at Komati Poort, but he seems very fairly well now. He occasionally has returns of fever, but they say that K.P. 'fever' remains in the system for life.

McClintock of my company was also at Springfontein for a day – he is at present working just North of me on the railway.

Russell R.E. a Lieut. who lives here and works along the Orange River mining drifts and setting 'booby traps' similar to those we first started in March last – had a narrow shave of being caught last week – he had just visited a drift on the river and, to their mutual surprise, found himself face to face with Lategan's Commando of 180 boers! He sprang on his horse and made a dash for it and got some way off before they hit his horse, which fell with him, he continued on foot and finally reached a comparatively safe spot.

Six boers who tried to gallop round and head him off – he dispersed by emptying the magazine of his rifle into them – he managed to stick to his gun all through.

He finally reached Colesberg Bridge 25 miles off, on foot and finding a column there promptly led them back to go for Lategan, who put up a bit of a fight and fled – not before Russell's cape cart, kit and saddlery, which had been left at a farm near where he was working, had been set fire to and destroyed.

The boers must have shot vilely, as Russell is one of the biggest men in the Corps, about 15 stone and 6ft 3. Had they caught him I have no doubt they would have murdered him, as they dread our dynamite traps above all things.

Much love from your ever loving son Eric E.B. Wilson

Springfontein, Orange River Colony　　　　　　　Friday 13th September 1901

My dearest Father

Since last mail I have received yours of Aug 16 and 23. I am very glad to hear how successful the Great Park Fete was – it must be a great relief to you that it turned out so well – and is also over!
I really must become a little sceptical of the severe depression in East Anglia of today if they can produce over £200 for the asking! But then on the other hand I am quite sure that we can produce a staff for organizing this class of thing, which would give a long start to less experienced officials under any conditions. I hope none of you are suffering from chills on the subsidence of the afterglow!
Your next letter written with a determined energy in the middle of the night, (which I am quite sure your eldest son will be unable to emulate at 58 years of age) describes an anticipated trip to Felixstowe – which I hope was enjoyed by all the party.
I am very glad to hear that there is a chance of Cicely being married at Redgrave. I only wish I might be home in time to see fair play! as Rowly would say!
It seems a long while ago since Muriel Barbara plighted her troth in the old church. I hope I shall meet Jimmy Hales somewhere out here – I should think he would make a capital fighting parson – I always think it would have suited you so well – though possibly from always expounding the Word to a very moderate thinking class of male flock one would not always see perhaps so much good work resulting as in what I might term a "General Practice."
I hope you enjoyed your cricket at Garboldisham: though I can hardly imagine the old ground without Cookson and his old Carthusian blazer casting a fiercely critical eye on a defaulting plantain on the pitch!
My news this week is meagre. A large move of troops to the North of the O.R.C. appears to have a view of picking up the scent of the obdurate Mr

T. Steyn and his ragged retainers and giving them scant repose till such time as they can be caught napping or go nap and chuck it up.

Prisoners continue to be caught freely in batches of 2 to 30 – one wonders really what the fighting population of the two republics really can have been.

I cannot think – that with Foreign Mercenaries – they can have had less than 120,000 men under arms at different times – Thank God they – like the race horse – were ignorant of their strength when we were weak.

Ever your loving son Eric E.B. Wilson

Lawson with whom I worked and fed with at Petrusberg has just come in. He will be surprised to see me!

Norval's Pont   Sunday 22nd September 1901

My dearest Father

I received a letter from you dated 30th Aug: just as I was leaving Springfontein yesterday, and am I think just able to catch mail here – so am writing in my office here before returning to Springfontein.

After the very heavy rain we had for 3 days the earth has sprung in one bound into its summer suit – and today is a beautiful still sunny day, which reminds me of many such in the past two years whose stillness was broken by the crash of guns and musketry and the galloping of horses.

Every contrast in this country is a violent one – no 'graduality' about it. The ground is abrupt in its changes of feature – and the water courses have sharp cut banks – and the seasons come and go in 24 hours! One day the streams are running ten feet deep with a roar all over the country and the next hour they are dry – perhaps for three months!

It is a very fascinating country from its very uncouthness, there is absolutely no limit to its frank boldness – no peeping through hedges over glens, and turning round corners and coming on nooks and dingles! – you can climb on to the nearest kopje and gaze over five hundred square miles by turning round!

I expect you will have great doings at Cicely's wedding. I meant to write this mail to her but think next mail will be the first I can get now.

My work is still along the railway – I have to be constantly moving about to keep some 150 men employed, at high pressure, and arranging for their daily food, clothing, supply of tools and materials for their work, and even the personal delivery of letters and papers which arrive for them! But I simply revel in the work, as there is always some tangible result to show for it!

The reduction of the numbers of irreconcilables still at large goes steadily on – some 1000 or so are accounted for each month – and they say there are still 10,000 at large in small parties. As their numbers decrease of course the difficulty of catching them gets greater when you have to locate them and chase them over an area about the size of Central Europe!

The occasional snaps they make at small parties of our men are only the hasty kick on the shins which the stout merchant gets from the gutter boy who flies for his life at once! But they cost the lives of good men alas out here.

Much love to all at home from your ever loving son Eric E.B. Wilson

POST OFFICE TELEGRAPHS

Handed in at: Victoria London to Brighton South Coast Railway
To: Wilson Redgrave Rectory Botesdale
At: 8.59 a.m.
Received at: 9.40 a.m.
Office Stamp: BOTESDALE 10.30 a.m. SP 28 01
Message: Hearty congratulations 0n Eric's D.S.O.
From: Bertie

Handed in at: Cambridge
To: Holt Wilson Redgrave Rectory Botesdale
At: 9.37 a.m.
Received at: 10.32 a.m.
Office Stamp: BOTESDALE 10.30 a.m. SP 28 01
Message: Hearty congratulations on Eric's D.S.O

Handed in at: Regent's Park Road
To: Rev Holt Wilson Redgrave Botesdale
At: 12.37 p.m.
Received at: 1.11 p.m.
Office Stamp: BOTESDALE 10.30 a.m. SP 28 01
Message: Congratulations on Eric's D.S.O
From: Wilson London

Handed in at: Warminster
To: Wilson Redgrave Rectory Botesdale
At: 4.33 p.m.
Received at: 5.10 p.m.
Office Stamp: BOTESDALE 10.30 a.m. SP28 01
Message: Congratulating you on Eric's distinction
From: Charles

Springfontein, Orange River Colony   Monday 30th September 1901

My dearest Father

Many thanks for yours of September 6th – also for two charming epistles from Michael and Amicia – also for the account of R.B.S. final House Supper – also for a very acceptable parcel of magazines.

Nothing much to record this week – busy as ever – and plenty of work waiting in hand! Had two trips to Norvals Pont – during one of which photo overleaf was taken, and which I hope will reach you safely. I have sent prints to M: and H: also.

Summer is on us – quite warm and inclining to heat again.

I have six small patches of flower beds which I dug up in odd moments and see signs of a good crop of mealies (maize) and of oats! So I also have the right to style myself a farmer! and hope there will not be a severe agricultural depression in my neighbourhood this year!

Things are drifting to the inevitable end – about 900 –1000 boers are caught as each fortnight goes by – one wonders where they all come from! We had no idea of the numbers they must have had in the field at the start.

Thank God I am still well and fit – weight 11st: 12 in light kit – and looking forward to a few days off duty some time in the dim future!

By the way – if any good news should at any time appear in an Honours and rewards gazette, use the cable. Lieut. Wilson R.E. Springfontein is the shortest address that will get me – this entre nous.

Best love from your ever loving son Eric E.B. Wilson

P.S. Congratulations on your Robin Hood like performance.

	Oct: 11th 1899	days
See enclosed picture of E.E.B.W. on the	Cape Colony	155
seven hundred and nineteenth day of	Orange Free State	100
the Boer War	Transvaal	199
1899 – 1900 – 1901	Orange River Colony	265
Aet: 26 – weight 11 st: 12 lbs	to Sep: 30th 1901	719

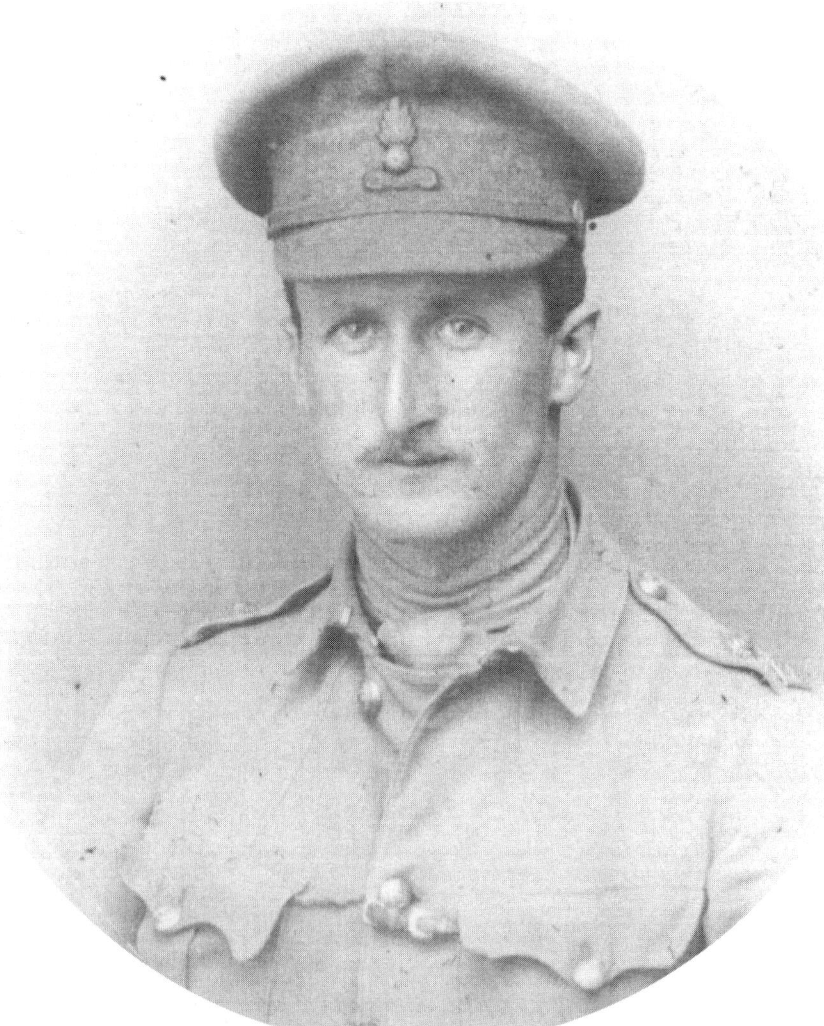

Springfontein, Orange River Colony   Saturday 5th October 1901

My dearest Father

Many thanks for your letter of Sep 12/13 to hand in good time. I was much interested in the account of Thomas Holt Murrays visit to Redgrave – does he wish to wrest the property 'vi et (Washington) armis' from Cousin George ?! I have met so many Americans and Canadians out here that I have been fired with a great desire to visit America some time, to see what their life really is like.
Many thanks also for Duncan Tovey's article on rifle clubs. He appears to be a man of many parts.
My mail this week consisted of two envelopes addressed by you and two by Muriel – yours dated 9th and 13th – M's 9th and 10th! Her first was spontaneous and 2nd to say that a letter had just arrived from me.

Handed in at Cape Town 2.10 p.m.
(diverted from Bloemfontein)
Received Springfontein 3.9 p.m.
To Lt Wilson
7th Co R.E.; Sfn
E. 29797 1st Oct: heartiest congratulations
London 30th Sep

One thing only is clear to me – that something in the nature of good fortune has fallen to me, but whether an unexpected relative has bequeathed me a fortune, or I have been promoted to Field Marshal, is shrouded in mystery, I shall no doubt experience the pangs of unsatisfied anticipation for some three weeks!
However; for what we have received, thank God.
If it should by any chance turn out to be which is I think, my most reasonable speculation, that I have been made a Companion of the Distinguished Service Order, it would be the proudest moment of my life; since I made 60 odd runs against Dublin University in '98 ,when they had one of the strongest sides I have ever played against!!
There is great satisfaction that the man Broeksma has been shot – it has been vipers of his class – cringing under our protection and secretly working sedition and inflammation – that has done more to keep this struggle

lingering on a diseased and cowardly existence, with neither manly opposition nor honourable submission, than ever the scurrilous and poisoned effusions of men like Stead and Laboucher at home. If the nation, at home, was not so sunken in a corporate inertness and impotence, due to a complacency and indifference to all that did not immediately threaten them with an empty stomach; we should never have tolerated the existence of men of this class for five minutes.

I have a far more tolerant sympathy with the Colonial rebels than with these men. They at least are Dutch, and armed rebellion, open and unaffected, has always been the crime of princes not of paltroons and vipers – though it is equally desirable that, for the good of the state, death should be the penalty common to both crimes.

McClintock paid me a short visit yesterday from Bloemfontein and we ran down through the line to Norvals Pont inspecting various works of offence and defence.

Haggitt is up in Heilbron neighbourhood organising some new scheme of blockhouses etc.

Johnson is still in or near Potchefstroom, Musgrave in Johannesburg and Trench our new subaltern, round by Kimberley! So we are well split up still. 7th Co have not been all together since April 1900 now.

Best love to all from your ever loving son Eric E.B. Wilson

Springfontein   Saturday 12th October 1901

My dearest Father

Many thanks for your letter of Sept 20th – just arrived.
I am very sorry indeed to hear that Alan Bos: was in charge of the boat that was lost, I had seen an account of it but not the name of the officer.
Please thank Aunt Amy on my behalf for the papers which arrive regularly and which pass through many hands after mine!
By the same mail I have heard from Col. Cockburn, my old chief at the Curragh, who writes an interesting letter of general Corps news from Aix-le-Bains. He has definitely retired now, as they would not let him come out here – but is I fancy possessed of fair means besides his pension.
Last week I made several trips to Norvals Pont – on my return on the 10th I found two letters which had practically arrived simultaneously, offering me congratulations on the D.S.O. and incidentally forming my first my first notification of the fact.
Since then I have had so many congratulations from friends of all ranks – the most practical of which was that tendered by McClintock of my Company – (himself a D.S.O.) who with terse comment, enclosed me a piece of the ribbon of the Order, thus enabling me to wear it as soon as I liked.
Possibly the intense pleasure it has given me is only exceeded by that which I hope it has afforded you, and all who are interested in my welfare.
I fancy that the necessary leverage at Army Head Quarters was applied by General Smith-Dorrien – with whom, as you know, I was the only R.E.Officer from Bloemfontein to Pretoria. So perhaps I owe him a debt of gratitude as well as well as to my hard working men who did so well for me and all. I have not yet seen the full list – I am very anxious to see what other R.E. Officers have received preferment.
Last night we had some local excitement – a few boers with apparently no object except mischief – fired on two of the outlying forts and the bullets for a while were flying over the Camp freely – we turned out at about 10 p.m. and manned our corner of the defences and slept in the open once more – and curiously for the time of year – there was a very sharp frost! No one on either side appears to have been hit – and no trace of boers remained when our Scouts went out at daybreak.
Previous to the alarm I was dining with Jesse A.S.C. the Transport officer, as were also Col Carleton and the station staff and our post-prandial music was abruptly stopped by the familiar rifle shot.

Love to all from your ever loving son Eric E.B. Wilson

Springfontein   Sunday 20th October 1901

My dearest Father

Many thanks for yours of 27th Sep. I hope the wedding went off well – I should have liked to be present at the family gathering.

It was very sad for poor old Bos: Alan's death on the Cobra. From the accounts I have seen it would appear that he died at his post in the manner that forms the best traditions of the Navy, might have had a chance of saving himself – as the Boats Engineer who stood by his side appears to have done at the last.

You seem to have had a good round of Harvest addresses all over the Eastern Counties! I hope you found Cousin Bob and all well.

I should like to see the Harrow Calendar which you say is just out. I remember the one for '81-'91 coming out while I was there.

We are well into the hot weather now, and the flies promise to be above the average in their billions and pertinacity. Food and drink have to be kept under cloths until the last moment, and even en passage to your mouth generally receive the attentions of a score of flies!

I made one trip to Bethulie Bridge and one to Norvals Pont last week. We are busy now connecting up blockhouses by telephone, which makes a great difference in getting reports in from out districts.

Since I last wrote the Commandant has taken me into his mess, and we are very comfortable, Col. Carleton Commandant – Lt Stack (Staff officer to Commandant) – Lt Dumaresq Railway Staff officer, Lt Simpson R.F.A. Intelligence Officer and myself – five in all.

We had quite a good concert etc given by the Supply Depôt (A.S.C.) on Friday, 3 violins 2 mandolins 2 clarinets and flute and pianist made a good orchestra.

One comic vocalist sang a good topical (parody) song about "There's a home for you with me" and a verse in which DeWet is reputed to say:–

> "I'm very fond of t.Y's
> As long as they bring supplies
> There's a home for them with me" etc

Caused much amusement! I enclose the programme.

I have had the first letter by post from England re D.S.O. from Sholto Douglas (of my batch) dated 28 Sep – (being employed in the War Office I expect he got an "early view" of the gazette!)

He says. "in time for the mail to congratulate you on your well-earned D.S.O. I am awfully glad old man, and its some compensation for having been kept out such a beast of a time!"

Much love to all at home from your ever loving son Eric E.B. Wilson

Springfontein Orange River Colony   Saturday 26th October 1901

My dearest Father

Your letter of congratulation arrived on the 24th in quick time – 20 days.
I am very glad you are pleased, and that others have been kind enough to express pleasure, my pleasure of course is very great, as the Distinguished Service Order is an absolutely invaluable military asset for a subaltern who wants to get on, and often leads to congenial after – employment vice undesirable billets etc.
I have had several letters of congratulation from home, namely Helen, Lady Jenner, Mr Sholto Douglas R.E.; G.E.J. Durnford R.E.; R.Q. Henriques Vol. R.E. late attached 7th Co; and T.H.W.- six by English mail and several from up country here – all of which I have industriously answered.
I had an earlier one, before the gazette came out, from Gen. Smith-Dorrien, saying that the War Office had mentioned their intention of including my name for a D.S.O. and "he sincerely hoped I might get it" – which was as good as a congratulation. This of course quite confidential; as rather a personal matter, which Gen. S-D. naturally would not like to be mentioned.
I notice you hadn't steeled your heart to put it after my name yet!! It is quite usual, and follows the name immediately, just as M.P., C.B. etc etc, and preceding corps or regiment.
I don't expect the old Fort Wilson at De Aar is still standing, as with change of times defences etc have been pushed much further out from the town and so on – it served its purpose when needed however – and no doubt, if still up, is known to the present garrison as No 3 post or so on – there is little continuity of nomenclature in earthworks during a campaign, as the men who hold them change so frequently.

I am going to try and hunt up Jimmy Hales. If he is at Edenburg I can easily get to him as it is quite near, up the line. I expect to run up to Bloemfontein on the 29th for a day, just to see Haggitt and report general progress etc down this way. I have not been there since June.

I had an afternoon's cricket (?) this week of a sort and made 10 runs out of a total of 36 all out! They also had two concerts of sorts, which were very fair and passed an evening pleasantly.

I have also to report that at last I have seen Richard Bagge – at Norvals Pont and had a great talk with him. He asked repeatedly after you etc and is getting quite the stout captain and a trifle bald, and seems very fit. He has also got the D.S.O. – I was glad to see. They have awarded a certain number to the Militia Battalions, to a few of their senior officers; and although not usually as a recognition of any particularly active service, are a very complimentary one, and a recompense for the terribly dull and trying time they have had sitting on the railway by the month together looking out over the barren landscape. I came in for a great dinner at Norvals Pont – given by my friend Col Peard R.A.M.C. Principal Medical officer of No X Hospital in honour of his C.M.G. There I met a certain nursing Sister Barwell – of Norwich – who to my surprise said that, if my name was Eric Wilson, she knew my sisters extremely well! We had a great East Anglian chat – I think I remember the name – tell me all about them – this Miss Barwell is a very pleasant person of about 30 I should think – I wonder I have never discovered her identity before as I have often been down at Norvals Pont. It was very curious that absolutely the first Nursing Sister, not only in that Camp, but in any camp that I have made the acquaintance of out here, should hail from Norwich and know M. and H. well.

I can also report H.Tuck as fit and well and quite the old seasoned warrior now – though I don't think many of the Norfolks have seen men trying to kill each other dead often – I hope and trust I shall never have to witness it again either.

The enclosed was received this mail from "Debrett" and is rather amusing; as I don't know in the least what they want (except to sell their books.) I send it on to you for disposal.

We had a smart rain last night and everything is fresh again and dust down for a few hours.

The Dutch Refugees are averaging 8 – 10 deaths a day from enteric, pneumonia, measles, etc, etc. I cannot conceive why they don't move the whole camp down to the coast, where it would be cheaper to feed them and less trouble, much healthier for them and for us, and a great source of anxiety removed as to their spying and treacherous propensities.

I suppose the powers that be are, as usual, afraid of Exeter Hall and Stead, who would talk about "exiles" and "prisoners of war" if they were transferred to the the Cape Colony Coast!!

Don't forget about the Wide World Magazine if you have a chance of getting the nos: with Conan Doyle's History of the War in it, as various <u>facts</u> etc were supplied to him <u>by me</u> and I want to see what he makes of them.

Much love to all – mind and convey my best thanks to any you meet or write to, who have so kindly expressed pleasure at my preferment.

Ever your loving son Eric E.B. Wilson

Springfontein   **Sunday 10th November 1901**

My dearest Father

I am glad that Cicely's wedding went off well – Redgrave has had its share of pageants I think this year!

We are favoured today with an unusually virulent dust storm, which covers everything with a thick layer of red earth.

I had one ½ day of cricket last week playing for the Railway club v. A.S.Corps. The bowling was good on either side, the A.S.C. having an old Lancaster pro: – Proctor – who is still very useful with the ball.

The scores were A.S.C. – 45 and 46: Railway (Pirates Club) – 40: – won on 1st Inns by 5 runs by A.S.C. – I think we should have won if the game had been finished. I contributed 20 to our 40 – the only double figure.

On Thursday I went down the line with Col. Carleton on a special inspection tour to Bethulie Bridge – we stopped and inspected every blockhouse (about 30) en route, and got back by 6 p.m.

On Saturday – the King's Birthday – we had a great sports meeting for the troops, which I think went off with great swing.

I filled the office, which I know you would have volunteered for, of "Clerk of the Course" and of his duties you are able to estimate for a long day.

In this case it consisted in practicality – drafting and arranging the programme, the prizes, the conditions, the sequence of events, taking all entries at the post, arranging heats, getting competitors marshalled at the start, taking down winners at the finish, marking out the course, erecting and supplying the various properties and the thousand and one things which go to make up an Athletic Meeting.

I don't wish to claim an undue share of the work, as all filled their allotted posts admirably, and the day was voted one of the best military meetings.

Some irresponsible person in the crowd, after the prize distribution and usual cheers, roared for "three cheers for Lieut. Wilson", which given heartily as they were, were both embarrassing and gratifying.

The most amusing events were the blindfold wheelbarrow race (won by an R.E. pair) the V.C. race in which after "beating off the enemy" (two bottles) a dummy had to be carried ¼ mile round the course – some competitors in their haste were very ungentle with their wounded dummies, one man coming a fearful purler and alighting on top of the dummies' head!

The Native high jump was exceedingly funny also, as they mostly sprang off both feet simultaneously and fell on their heads!

The Warriors race handicap evoked considerable interest and was won by a gunner with 6 clasps.

The Native ¼ mile finished down the hurdle course, and needless to say it was crash and spill over every single hurdle in turn!

In the Officers donkey race, after about a quarter of an hour spent in securing the mokes, a fair start was made – bareback and no bridle – (steer with the donkey's ears!)

Nelson of Royal Sussex was first past the post, Simpson R.A. and myself following close on him; our donkeys refusing to part company and proceeding pari passu the whole way, and as my right knee was firmly locked behind his left knee – he was placed 2nd and I 3rd!!

Most of the others proceeded along routes only familiar to the donkies!!

The heats for the tug of war were:–

I.	R. Irish Fusiliers)	R.I.F. 2–0)			
	Army Ser. Corps)				
II.	Insp Mil. Rail.y)	R. Sx 2–0)	R.I.F. 2–0)		
	Royal Sussex)			R.I.F. 2–1)	
III	Royal Engineers)	R.E. 2–0)	R.F.A. 2–0)		
	Mounted Infantry)				
IV	Bye)	R.F.A)			
	Royal Fd. Arty)				

It was considered very creditable the R.E. winning a pull, as we had only 15 men to choose 10 from – and all very light. The Programme was completed exactly to schedule time, and in the evening a most successful Camp Concert was held in the open with a large force of volunteer artistes and musicians which kept us going till 10 p.m.

There is some talk of a cricket team from the Bloemfontein Club (Ramblers) touring round this way, I think we can give them a game here. We have Sinclair, one of the English South African Team, just returned, here and several other useful players.

You will soon be at your coldest, we at our hottest – next month.

Much love to all Ever your loving son Eric E.B. Wilson

P.S. An officer, who until two days ago was a stranger to me, came up after the Sports and said that when he next had an athletic meeting at his ancestral abode, he would telegraph all over the world for me to come and organise it for him! (Thus does an hereditary instinct assert itself!!)

Springfontein   Sunday 17th November 1901

My dearest Father

Just as I was sitting down to write this, a parcel containing 18 walnuts arrived, to which you refer in your letter of the 25th Oct. as having grown on the tree which I planted 14 years ago. As I have not tasted a walnut for over two years, they will make a pleasant variation to our board this evening.

We have Col. Murray – the new Principal Medical Officer of the Hospital here, coming to dine with us also.

It is very hot indeed here now – but at our altitude – 4937 feet above the sea, is nice and cool at nights. You will see from enclosed rough diagram, that we are the highest point on the railway between the Orange River and the Vaal. The heights in the sketch are distorted uniformly about seven hundred fold more acutely than they really are – relatively to the distance traversed – in order to be self explanatory to the eye. Practically from Edenburgh to the Vaal is open undulating country, and from here to the Orange River very broken and hilly.

Talking of Edenburg, I wrote to Jimmy Hales there, and received a reply from the centre of the Transvaal! – where he appears to be accompanying some column now. He reported well.

Harold Tuck – lucky young beggar – has gone home to be appointed to the 1st Battalion Norfolks – now serving in India – where I suppose he will proceed after a short leave. He has had, in common with his regiment, a dreary time out here – their scope of service extending from Bloemfontein to the Orange River in small detachments – with no fighting – only the deadly weariness of always anticipating it.

We had a number of Boers – some 400 under Brand – in our neighbourhood this week, prowling around for scraps of food – but the columns have chased them to the four winds again, and they are once more in ones and twos – absolutely heartbreaking to catch.

The Transvaalers seem to have been making great efforts to play the game properly, i.e. collecting in numbers sufficient to give them the chance of scuppering one of our small columns and then dispersing again. The attempt on Benson's column was a bad repulse for them, but cost us very dearly also. I think next winter (April–Aug) will see great numbers acknowledge themselves beaten.

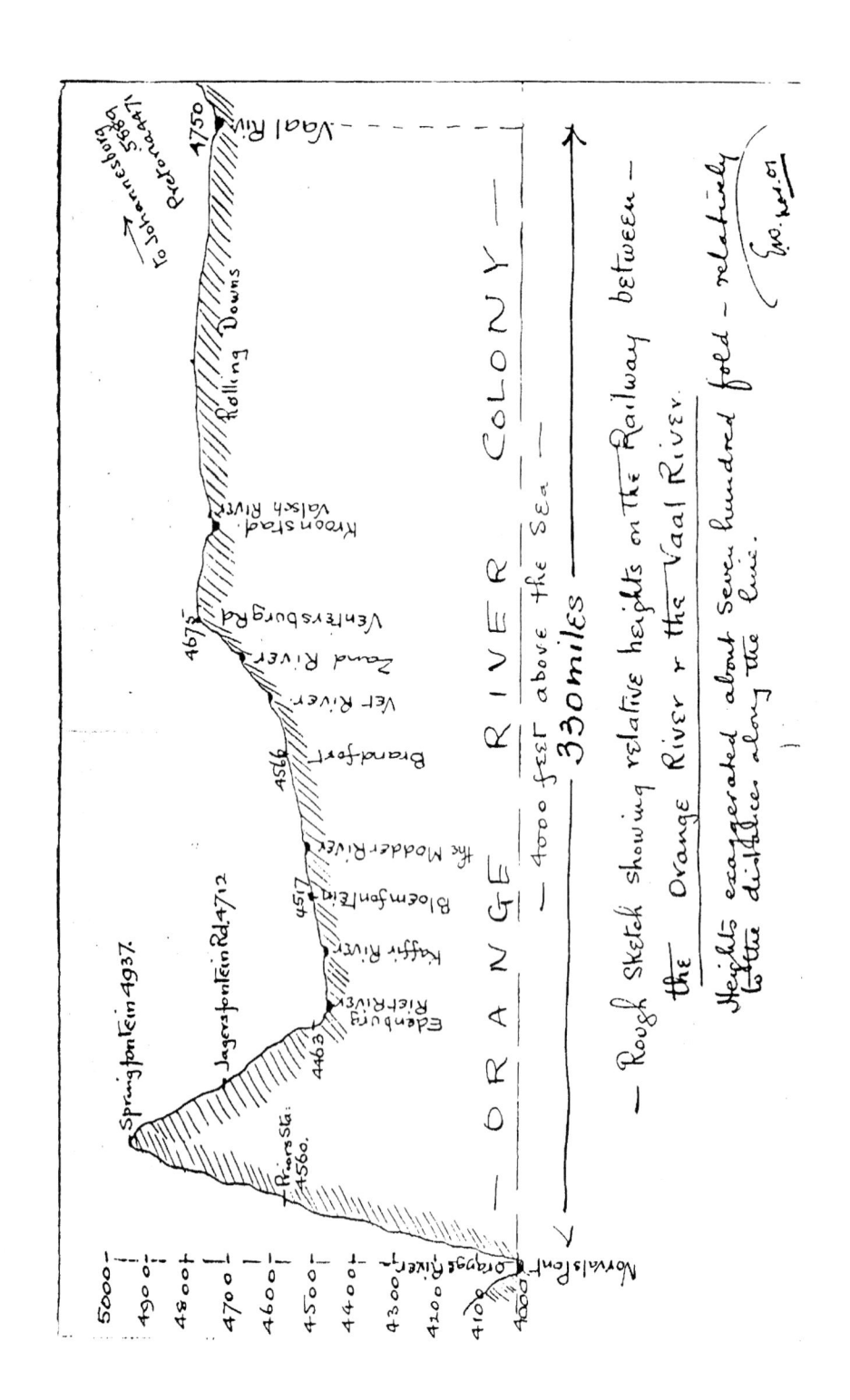

Rough Sketch showing relative heights on the Railway between the Orange River & the Vaal River.

Heights exaggerated about seven hundred fold — relatively to the distance along the line.

Geo. Ker. 01

— ORANGE RIVER COLONY —
— 4000 feet above the Sea —
— 330 miles —

The balance now stands roughly as I should estimate it:–

Combined Boer forces at the zenith of the war	110,000	These are only fancy figures and would be
Captured and prisoners	50,000	roughly handled by
Killed, died etc	20,000	professional statist-
Mercenaries who have fled the country	12,500	icians but I think they
In the country on parole and in Refugee camps	20,000	have a certain bearing on the actual numbers
	102,500	
Still in the field	7,500	
	110,000	

McClintock was down here for one night this week – and I went to Norvals Pont on Thursday, returning Friday. No cricket this week – as the neighbourhood has been rather warlike!

Best love to all from you ever loving son Eric E.B. Wilson

R.E. Journal for Nov leaves by this mail.

Springfontein   Saturday 23rd November 1901

My dearest Father

Your last letter arrived precisely on the 21st day after being written – it is not often letters arrive in the same month as sent. I also received a Diss Express, with an account of Cicely's wedding. I fear the letter I wrote her, (enclosing a small tribute) must have been late for the ceremony, as I see it does not figure in the Catalogue!

I have received today the R.E. Journal for November in which I see myself in the lists in front of "D.S.O.!" The first in our "batch", at any rate – I think there only two junior to me on the Corps – Greig and Mackworth – I also figure out that at the present rate of promotions, I shall be 31 ere a Captain, 38 for Major and 49 for Lieut. Col: if I survive to attain any or all of these ranks. We are a long way behind the rest of the Army now. Men who failed for Woolwich when I passed – have long been Captains via Sandhurst or Militia – and all my standing in the Artillery (DuPort, Geoff Stowell etc) are Captains!

However there may be a relief of the congestion after the war, as many of the senior officers may feel they have had enough soldiering, and take their modest pensions without further thirst for glory! and then one may overtake other Captains, who will perforce be years in that rank, as this spasmodic promotion always lands men for years in some rank or other.

We have had a most blessed shower of rain today which has cleaned the Camp and will bring on my lettuces etc.

McClintock was down for a night this week and we both dined with J.L.Jesse, the Transport Officer, who looks after the wagon and animal department of the Depôt and replaces old and worn out carts and animals for 'columns' when they put us in here to refit.

I have not been down to Norvals Pont since I received your last letter but will enquire about the local men, though they are almost sure to be out in blockhouses up the line somewhere, as there are very few of the Nofolk Militia at Norvals Pont.

I see the 21st Lancers (surely the very last Cavalry Regiment at home?) are to come out. They must have been chafing all through the war – but now they will be alright – they will get the same medal etc as all of us and no one will be the wiser. They cannot get the clasps however.

If the War Office only knew how much T.A. prizes his medal – what a symbol of hardship and companionship with Death it has been – as different from the trumpery campaigns of the last 50 years – they would not be so liberal at hurling it at adipose Aldermen etc of the City of London, who at the best have only voted trust funds to supply volunteers. The men were so savage when they saw that! No cricket this week and plenty of work.

Much love to all from your ever loving son Eric E.B. Wilson

Springfontein Orange River Colony   Sunday 1st December 1901

My dearest Father

Your letter of November 8th just to hand – it will be some time before we get the next mail as the Dunnottar Castle has broken down, and the letters etc have been transferred to the Lismore Castle, expected at Cape Town about the 10th inst:, I have also received the Nov. magazine.
This being the last mail which can possibly catch you before Christmas, I must herein wish you, and all near you, at home, the extra happiness which is always associated with the season. I am enclosing a small cheque, of which I wish Mother to expend half for the benefit of the youngsters, with best wished from their brother Eggie! and the other half I should like you to expend on small creature comforts for those most deserving of them in the parish – preferably on those whose names figure in your "bread dole book"! I also heard from Cicely last mail – a very bright letter of thanks for my letter of good wishes on her marriage.
Also from Aunt Amy – a long letter – of congratulation on the D.S.O. etc. By the same token I completed one year of seniority in the "Order" on the 29th November, as the award bears date Nov 29th 1900, – though it was not gazetted till nearly a year later.
A (non-military) friend was asking the other day what the difference was between the circumstances governing the award of 1. the V.C., 2. the D.S.O. and 3. the D.C.M., meaning of course the circumstances in principle, (as alas here as in all mortal favours influence, favouritism etc have far too

much to say) – well the best simile is borrowed by considering war as a game of cricket – as "Active Service" is of course the "sine quâ non".
1. The V.C. is open to all men who wear the King's Uniform, and may be said to be awarded to anyone who makes a brilliant innings of 200 not out – sometimes two innings of 150 may secure it! – well – 2. The D.S.O. (open to Officers only) is awarded to those who record <u>an average</u> of 50, throughout the season, or perhaps two seasons! and the (3) Distinguished Conduct Medal (open only to men) is usually awarded to men who score a good individual innings of say 100 – sometimes for a season's average of 30. There you have the principle of the award of the three most coveted Military recognitions.
Unfortunately those in the "ring" too often see things like C.B.s awarded to rich militia Colonels who have sat down within reach of a bottle of champagne for a few months, D.S.O.s awarded to frail young Dukes who have condescended to be present in a country where war is in progress – or worse still – to Militia Officers who have never heard or seen a blow given in anger or a shot fired to kill – because it "encourages the Militia to come forward don't you know" etc etc.
Please don't quote these latter private expressions of opinion, dad!!
I have had my District extended to Edenburg northwards now – I see by my various lists etc that I have upwards of 170 Forts, Redoubts, Blockhouses, Ports etc., etc., under my charge, to maintain, improve, alter etc., etc., from time to time – and of these I either designed or built about 140 myself, in months gone! under the ruling supervision of the C.R.E. and Maj. Haggitt etc – but as a rule it has been left pretty well to the R.E. Officers on the spot.
I see to my sorrow, in the papers from home this week, that in the attack on Col. Benson's column three very great friends of mine were killed outright – Thorold, Brooke and Shepherd of the King's Own Yorkshire Light Infantry, mounted Infantryman Thorold was a particular friend of mine and we shared the same bungalow at Wynberg in the dim past, before the War.
All that lot of Yorkshire Light Infantry were devils to fight, and have done magnificently through the war – they would be killed to a man, if opposed to heavier numbers in a tight corner, as they never used to dream of surrendering or retiring unless the latter was the right move for the occasion, as it sometimes is, but here their tenacity probably saved the column from disaster on a large scale.
Wed: and Thurs: this week I was down at Norvals Pont – and saw Barrett and Calverly – two Captains of Norfolk Militia – also Reggie Bagge from the train, I could not trace the local men – I suppose they were in some other companies on detachment.

Coming up on Thursday I met Gen. Ian Hamilton, who has come out again, and had a great talk with him over old days. He was pleased to remark that I looked extremely well. We also discussed Churchill's book on the "March" up the Eastern border. In the evening Col. Carleton and I dined with Captain Tomblings, Remount Officer, of VIIIth Hussars, and old Curragh friend of mine. Friday I was up the line to Edenburgh and back inspecting works etc.

I wrote to Uncle Charlie last mail, for his birthday.

They hope to get Johnson and No 1 Section back to the company directly – he has been on detachment for over a year, in the Transvaal.

Victor Brooke, 9th Lancers, who I met just out again as A.D.C. to Ian Hamilton, said he had seen Boileau quite recently, very well, and threatening to get married – he also told me that Sir W.K. Jenner Bart proposed retiring from the Service – Lady J. said something about it in a recent Curragh letter, but I did not gather that he really meant to retire.

They had some sharp fighting near Edenburgh yesterday, just after I left by rail, some boers wanted to cross the line and the blockhouses beat them back on to the column who were chasing them – haven't heard any results.

We are moving the Station Mess into another mud house tomorrow I believe – as the Commandant wants more room for his office etc.

Much love and all kinds of Christmas and New Year wishes to the family – I have no doubt you will all enjoy a good old fashioned Redgrave Xmas! Give my love to Broom Hills and Rickinghall when you foregather.

Ever your loving son Eric E.B. Wilson

Springfontein Sunday 15th December 1901

My dearest Father

Yours of November 15th received this week – delayed by the breakdown of the Dunnottar Castle. This week's mail due here on the 12th is not yet up – no reason for the delay has been discovered yet – I got quite a lot of letters by the delayed mail – one from dear old Mrs Money – who you may have heard me speak of – as the owner of the terrier 'Jack' I had for some time at Chatham – and an aunt of Sholto Douglas in my batch – to say that Jack was no more. She used to feed him so enormously that when I last saw him in '97 he was so fat I thought his demise possible at any time – but she was devotedly fond of the dog, and very kind to me in Chatham days. Douglas and I used to bicycle to them (about 22 miles down the Canterbury Road) and stay Sat: and Sunday etc. She addresses me as "Capt" Wilson now!!

I see that almost all the year junior to me at Woolwich are now running into Capt: in the Artillery – while I have precisely four years and eight months to go before I shall see promotion! – Aug 1906.

I also heard from Aunt Amy – saying she was sending me 1½ lbs of plum pudding! which I hope will arrive safely before Christmas. Also from Lady Jenner with Christmas greetings etc, and a long letter of Curragh doings and so on. Also from Frank – asking about the prospects of employment in this country. I should very much like to do something for him, but it is extremely difficult to find anything that a man straight from home can drop into. In order to find a congenial job here it is absolutely necessary to be <u>in the country</u> and look around and ask questions for a few months – and that requires capital.

The best way is of course is to get into <u>some</u> sort of military draft from home – Yeomanry, Constabulary or so on – and then there is every chance of a man getting an occupation in the country after the war – as he could probably obtain the tenancy of a government farm (forfeited burgher property etc).

I have written to Frank but I am afraid I have not given him much light on the subject. His is the hardest class in the world to find employment for – a gentleman with no definite profession. There would be no harm in his writing to the Deputy Administrator, Bloemfontein O.R. Colony – stating exactly what information he would like about the conditions under which Government farms may be taken up etc.

The life would suit him once he could get his foot in the country. But the cost of living will be very high until the war is over.

I have had a lot of running about this week – and have a great deal of work in hand and coming on – at many points in my district.

Much love to all Ever your loving son Eric E.B. Wilson

Springfontein Orange River Colony　　　　　　**Sunday 22nd December 1901**

My dearest Father

Yours of November 29th received on Friday – one day after the bulk of the mails passed North – on Thursday I got a long letter from Uncle Charlie, which must have crossed the one I wrote him a week or two back.

One of the finest items of the past week has been the wounding and capture of Kritzinger – one of the finest boer commandants, a young man of about five and twenty – who absolutely was without fear – and was considered the head and brain of the rebels in Cape Colony.

He was picking his way down to make a tour of inspection and collect some of the small bands together etc., when he showed contempt for our chains of posts once too often, and in making his way between two blockhouses was shot from shoulder blade to rib and through the thigh, and caught after riding gamely on yet another two miles. This has taken several months off the war. They appear to be doing well further North also, and catching many of the leaders lately.

The papers and book mail are not up yet, but I must thank you in advance for sending the Harrow Calendar. I shall enjoy seeing old names and recalling old faces of those days.

I well remember staying with the Surtees' at Holtby – they had two very fierce cats which lived in a wood-stack near the house, a large wooden ship which we used to sail on a pond, and ripe cherries!

I have a great pressure of work on hand now – and spent most of last week riding or railing about my district.

Springfontein from becoming almost empty has recently become quite a centre again and troops have been pouring in and out and depôts of horses, transport, supplies etc all revived into full activity again; all of which means heavy work for the R.E. who are everyone's 'factotem, guide, philosopher and friend'! 'Could you just. Would you mind lending me.... Have you got a carpenter you could spare for an hour or two Would you let your fitter see my' etc etc etc – all at once and all in a hurry day in day out! Such is Royal Engineering on service – apart from our real daily work of solidly continuing the defences, blockhouses, buildings etc etc, and everyone who wants help thinks we only exist to assist them or theirs at a moment's notice, forgetting that others have claims on our workmen etc.

Such is human nature. The hospitals are the worst offenders, and naturally the people for whom we do most, but even they ask for things that you would hardly be able to provide in London; let alone in the middle of the wilderness. I fear the calibre of the senior officers of the medical service is far below that of the average officer, both professionally and socially – they do not appear able to attract the right stamp of man to their service – though there exceptions as everywhere.

Uncle Charlie finishes his letter with "Come home safe and sound and I'll find you such a nice wife and plenty to live on!!! However I don't know what he has got up his sleeve – but I know that in a soldier's life:–

> "White hands cling to the tightened rein
> Slipping the spur from the booted heel,
> Tenderest voices cry 'Turn again,'
> Red lips tarnish the scabbarded steel,
> High hopes faint on a warm hearth-stone
> He travels the fastest who travels alone"   (R. Kipling)
>   (n'est pas?)

Ever your loving son Eric E.B. Wilson

Springfontein　　　　　　　　　　　　　　　　Monday 6th January 1902

My dearest Father

I have been forced to run it rather fine this week, and am not certain that this will catch the mail. I had to go down to Norvals Pont on the 3rd – and all the 4th – the Railway Bridge over the Orange River was under repairs and no traffic running – and I did not get back till late yesterday, which means of course that I found about 48 hours arrears of office work piled up awaiting disposal and several works in hand that required personal inspection this morning.

Your letter of the 13th December arrived on the 4th and I found it awaiting me yesterday – I am glad that Jimmy was pleased that the walnuts arrived safely. Who is going to take the Hall, now that the Walters are going?

On New Year's Eve we had a great 'dinner party' with Captain and Mrs Buckle – (the Officer in Charge of Supplies here) and they gave us a splendid feast – the first approach to civilization I have met with up country. How they do it is a mystery to us all – Every luxury under the sun from 'olives' to 'candle shades' and napkins!! At midnight – Dumaresq the Railway Staff Officer went over to the Station and started every engine whistle in the place blowing full split – you never heard such a noise – and Canon Bellamy – the Chaplain – went over to his tin church and tolled the bell vigorously! Bellamy has a 'parish' in Johannesburg in peace time I believe, and is doing military work pro: tem:.

I saw Richard Bagge D.S.O. at Norvals Pont yesterday – he seems well – I have some great waterworks on here now, we are improving the camp supply by boring and opening up some springs and laying on service by pipes etc., it will be a good job when completed.

I heard from both M. and H. last mail but have not had time to write this mail. M. does not expect to get into their new house for some time it seems.

I saw all the Scots Greys passing through Norvals Pont – straight from home – they looked a nice lot – I hope they don't go and put them in the heart of a fighting corner straight off before they have had time to learn how to fight, as the few desperadoe bands of boers still in the field are the very essence of cunning, and require handling by seasoned men to do them any harm – putting the pale faced recruit against them today is like pitting a calf like a panther.

Much love to all at home from your ever loving son Eric E.B. Wilson

PHOTOGRAPH ENCLOSED

Boring for water with the Diamond Rock Drill – (steam)

Springfontein Orange River Colony January 1902. This boring was carried down 52 feet through solid rock and tapped water at 15 feet and again at 35 feet: giving a supply of about 15,000 gallons of pure, ice cold water, per diem. The figures standing around are Surrendered Boer Prisoners. Sitting in white shirt sleeves W. Rome (in charge of Engine) Standing (in uniform) E.W.

Photo by A. Anderson, Foreman In charge of Boring.

Springfontein   Sunday 12th January 1902

My dearest Father

I am very sorry to hear that measles has appeared at Redgrave – I fear the children's Christmas festivities will suffer heavily in consequence – however the material portions of the holiday will no doubt keep till they are able to enjoy them later on.

Many thanks for the Wide World magazine which arrived safely last week and has already provided much reading. Their usual tales, which one is asked to believe as true, would almost provoke one to rename the magazine as the 'Wild Word Magazine'.

I have been twice down to Norvals Pont this week, seeing to various works, and paying my employés their weekly wage.

We have had a lot of work in connection with the Water Supply here, and I have been opening up old, and boring new sources of supply. We made a very successful strike of water on Wednesday, tapping a strong underground spring, which flows out from between two layers of rock in bountiful profusion.

The Government Water Engineer who has been working with me estimates the supply from this new source at 400,000 gallons per day! And says it is one of the finest strikes of water he has seen in this country. He says that if I had worked it out in peace time for any landowner (other than the Government) it would have been as good as £2,000 in my pocket!!

He has been boring with the steam rock-drill independently, and has made some good yielding bore holes. I am busy building a stone reservoir around the new spring to hold up a supply of water for pumping from etc. Water is more precious than gold in this country and if a gold-mining company strike water in a shaft intended to find gold, they usually stick to the water and let the gold go!

It is still exceedingly hot and dusty – with a fierce sandy wind blowing most of the day and we want rain very badly. The rains are very late this season.

I have started a brickfield here – as the ground is very favourable and the sun-dried brick is as strong as our kiln burnt brick at home if properly made – this will enable me to run up some workshops etc and get things in good shape for carrying on in the wet weather.

Much love to all from your ever loving son Eric E.B. Wilson

Your last letter to hand dated Dec 20. 01.

Springfontein   Sunday 2nd February 1902

My dearest Father

Many thanks for your letter of January 10th with enclosures of letters from the children; also King's stamps which are most interesting.

I am glad Miss Colkett is coming to us again – it will seem rather strange for her teaching the new generation – with her old pupils mothers of families!

I am very sorry to hear of the illness of Mrs Methold and Harry. I hope both are getting on well and will soon recover. Please give my best wishes to Mr Methold if you meet him.

My piece of news this week will interest Mother – Arthur Carlyon R.A.M.C., Norvals Pont has inherited some £12,000 from an obscure uncle – I thank a partner in Something, Bolitho & Co: Bankers. He is delighted; and expects to get leave home to arrange his affairs. Perhaps Mother can throw some light on it?

I have had a trip to Norvals Pont this week returning next day. Most of my time has been occupied with the Waterworks here which are shaping into a good business now and likely to stave off water troubles for some time. We are having the dryest wet season known since 1860 – odd so far.

It will be a very serious matter for the grazing lands if rain does not set in shortly, Springfontein had no rainfall for 13 months on end in the record dry year in the sixties! It should have rained, by average, on about ten days in January – and I think we only had light showers on 2 days!

I played in a game of football at 6 p.m.(!) yesterday, after work, for Springfontein Pirates v. Mounted Infantry and we defeated them by 3 – 0.

Many thanks for the Sportsman Almanac which now adorns the wall of my office!

I have received the (annual) alphabetical list of "Officers of the Corps of Royal Engineers", this includes all still living, whether serving or retired. Roughly running through it I make out that there are some 1595 still living who are serving or have retired, of these 11, or one in 145, have received the Victoria Cross; and 55, or one in 29 – the D.S.O. with of course many of the higher Commanding Officers rewards – G.C.B, G.C.M.G. etc etc.

I think the above percentage would compare very favourably with the figures for the other arms – R.A. – Cavalry and Infantry.

Best love to all at home Ever your loving son Eric E.B. Wilson

Kipling's poem "The Islanders" – has aroused considerable interest in the army – and I see from indignant letters in this weeks papers has struck deep in certain quarters – as a dear old Colonel here remarked on reading it – "Well its all the fault of the women at home – they could drive the able-bodied men into the Field quicker than any Recruiting staff – instead of the gutter bred weaklings who are called by various high sounding titles of no fighting value who are sent out in every ship."

Springfontein   Monday 10th February 1902

My dearest Father

No letters this week, but a paper from Muriel.

The columns have been doing well last week – Methuen took 131 of Delarey's men besides killing 7 and wounding 12 – and we have just heard this morning that in the last 3 days DeWet has been stripped of 283 men at a cost of 10 casualties to us.

This is very good going now-a-days considering the fugitive nature of the enemy.

I am just off to Norvals Pont to administer the monthly payments to my employés there.

Lord K. passed through here this morning going South – presumably to have a talk with French at Middleburg.

On Saturday last I had a half holiday and attended a gymkhana organised by the Royal Irish Fusiliers. In the dropping potatoes into buckets at full gallop I got one in, of three, as did three others – I do not think anyone got more. In a race in which competitors galloped 200 yards towards some ladies – chiefly Hospital Sisters – and dismounted to hand them a thread to be threaded and sewn into the man's coat – I rode the little Basuto pony Jimmy, and chiefly owing to the Sister allotted to me being a fairly calm and phlegmatic individual she had the needle threaded and sewn into my coat almost as soon as I handed her the thread! However although I got away easy first from the confusion of horses, men, women and needles, one of the big horses (all sizes) caught me up going over a jump which Jimmy didn't fancy first try and won. Jimmy did very well for 13 hands carrying 12 stone and jumping fences!

After the gymkhana I proceeded to play in a football match, the other side of the camp; where we lost a most ferocious game by 1 – 2.

I got some shakes and jars from the hard ground which make me feel "all one piece" even today – however I have been bruised once or twice before at the same game!

I believe Canon Bellamy has a concert for the Hospital Patients tomorrow evening, which will afford an evening's diversion.

The Hospitals are fairly full now with enteric and general cases from further North – this is a bad time of year for the youngsters from home.

We are busy fixing up a local telephone service all around the Camp and outposts – the place is beginning to look like a huge laundry drying ground with posts in all directions.

They have accelerated the up mail train from Cape Town by about 5 hours – when it arrives to time – so that the English Mails should be in our hands before midday on Thursdays now.

Much love to all from your ever loving son Eric E.B. Wilson

Springfontein   **Saturday 15th February 1902**

My dearest Father

Letters from you of Jan 17th and 24th have arrived since last I wrote. The former, though legibly addressed 'Springfontein' took another three days going on to Bloemfontein and back, the latter duly arrived yesterday.

Today I hear from Frank that he purposes coming out shortly – He writes from his uncle Evan James' at Ealing.

I am glad the farming is getting into such strong working order – I expect you take a great many strolls down the back meadows towards the black acre in the course of a week! You have not told me what they shot off the glebe this year – or perhaps they drove it in with some of the Russian plantation ground towards the ladie's bridge.

I am very sorry to hear of the death of Dr Hills – his departure will snap a strong link with the past for you and all of us who remember them in earlier days.

How well I remember the interest I took in Dr. Hills explaining the working of a telephone which I think he had between two establishments at the Asylum. I remember it well now: the instruments etc in use then would be quite out of date now – the telephone was a comparative novelty even then.

The last time I saw him was not long before I came out here – I afterwards went on to Cromer and spent a day or two with Cousin George and family at Cromer – all the Bury Lakes were there and Lily Charlesworth and her husband.

We had two days beautiful rain last week – but the ground was so dry and hard that it nearly all ran off – however it has freshened up the veldt around splendidly.

It is just two years since we struck out from the Railway into the Orange Free State to force our way to Bloemfontein across the wilderness.

The 18th saw Cronje brought to a halt and compelled to fight a most sanguinary battle at Paardeburg Drift while the 7th Division marched past the raging battle and calmly sat down athwart his line of retreat to Bloemfontein. By the 19th he was surrounded.

I wouldn't go through the 9 days from the 18th to the 27th again for all the D.S.O's in Europe! I can smell the carrion as I write – as General Colvile so aptly remarked; "we could at least be thankful the dead cattle weren't elephants"!!

The entry in my log for Feb 14th '00 runs: "Left Ramdam at 4.30 a.m. and marched with the Advance Guard to Waterval Drift on the Riet River – put up pumps and made approaches for carts. Great difficulty in getting the heavy transport and guns up the bank of the drift. Went to 9th Division Headquarters for orders for next day and got back to camp at 10 p.m. and lay down (!)

<u>Feb 15th</u> Marched from Waterval at 1 a.m.(!) to Wegdraai Drift along the Riet to 4 miles short of Jacobsdal – full moon and cold night – found the 7th Division here. Heard heavy firing to N. during afternoon – 6th Division engaged on the Modder – (this was covering French's dash on Kimberley).

<u>Feb 16th</u> More firing close at hand turned out to be 19th Brigade clearing Jacobsdal previously held by a small picket of Mounted Infantry who had been turned out by the Boers soon afterwards. Marched on to Jacobsdal at 5.30 a.m. Heard that our supply column following behind had been attacked and destroyed at Waterval Drift.

Reached Jacobsdal and offsaddled in the market square – then moved on to a hill to E. of the town where there was a small spring of good water. Busy fitting up pumps tanks and troughs for watering the Division, till 5 p.m. Heard that French was in Kimberley. Got two fowls in the town.

Marched on again at 9 p.m. and marched all night towards the Modder – reached Klip Drift at 5 a.m. Feb 17th and found 6th Division resting after their fight the day before – a good few wounded about.

One hour for sleep then working down at the river on water supply all day till 5 p.m. when the Division marched on again and I cantered up and rejoined them. Marched on to Paardeburg Drift which we reached at 5 a.m. Feb 18th – one hour for sleep – and down to the drift and working all day getting James' boat and rope across, transporting guns over and bringing wounded back – very heavy fighting along the river bank all day long. Nearly drowned in the flood while trying to get rope end across the river which was running 5ft deep and ten miles an hour.

Pouring with rain all day. At dusk the 7th Coy came down to the drift and marched across and I rejoined them – all soaked through to the marrow with fording the river at the Drift.

Marched a mile on the North Bank and fell down to sleep in the mud, as we stood, till daylight. This, such as it was, was the first night's "sleep" we had had since the 13th. The actual summary reading about 9 hours rest for 5 days and 60 miles marching!

However later on – before the 27th we got in the way of snatching an hours sleep while at work, when there was another officer available to take a spell at the same job. We thought it a bit hard at the time but many times since then we have had as little rest and considerably less to eat!

Mending bridges just short of Komati Poort in Sep '00 – we had 3 or 4 days absolutely on end without any sleep for the officers, who had to superintend one gang of men after another, as long as they could stand up or keep awake sitting down!

The columns have done splendidly further North this last week – catching over 700 altogether, this will make a very serious difference to the remaining freebooters, though it need not impair their cunning in hiding or flight.

If ever England is called upon to take part in another war, during the memory of the present generation, they will bear in mind that fighting means letting the blood out of your opponent until he dies; and not patting him on the back in an apologetic manner and pampering his women and children.

We had just overstepped the boundary line between comfort and luxury on the downward grade of a big nation's existence; but thank God this will stiffen the backbones of the next few generations before they drop into the inanimate and invertebrate stage again – which I hope will not be in our time.

Ever your loving son Eric E.B. Wilson

Springfontein Orange River Colony   Sunday 23rd February 1902

My dearest Father

Your letter of Jan 31st just arrived. For some reason lately they have taken to sending all my letters up to Bloemfontein and I have to await their return 2 days later: though legibly addressed "Springfontein".

I think the "7th Co" catches the sorter's eye at Cape Town and he says "Bloemfontein" and reads no further! It would be quite safe to address "Royal Engineers" Springfontein now, I think, for the present.

I received a long letter from Aunt Julia this mail also – giving news of Uncle Fred and Aunt Emily etc. She says that the dear old 'Colekins' was 92 last month and writes as clearly as ever. What a wonderful old lady

We have had the most lovely rain on and off this week: the face of the veldt has very rapidly changed from brown to green and is a great rest to the eye.

A Captain R.H. Macdonald has been posted to us, so that the 7th Co R.E. is complete in officers again now: Major Haggitt, Capt. Macdonald; Lieut. McClintock Lieut. Wilson; Lieut. Johnson and 2nd Lieut. Chenevix Trench. McClintock has, much to his delight, been sent round to Kimberley to give evidence on a question of compensation to the DeBeers Co: for material and money expended in connection with the building of the forts etc during the siege. McC. you may remember was the engineer of them all, and got his D.S.O. for their efficiency – and has often expressed a wish to revisit the beleaguered city, under normal conditions – I fancy he made several friends there also during the siege so perhaps there is a human element in it also!

Musgrave has done well for himself in taking three years employment with the new S.A. Constabulary, he has been made a (local) Constabulary Captain as regards 'rank' and draws £510 per annum!

Of course they are only too pleased to get R.E. Officers if they can, but the R.E. chiefs do not approve of parting with their carefully trained officers for this sort of work and raised many obstacles before M. could get leave to take it up.

Many thanks for the King's 6d stamp. I think I have seen them all now.

The Army Service Corps gave a very pleasant concert last night to which we all went. Dumaresq – our Railway Staff Officer here – went down to Cape Town for 10 days leave last week and I gave him some letters of introduction to nice families there. He is a very nice fellow and has a career not unlike Frank. His grandfather fought at Waterloo – his father was a Colonel in the Army – but he had to earn his own living and selected farming in New Zealand. He came out as a Sergeant in the 1st N.Z. Contingent and of course was soon given a

Commission. A very talented musician like his brother in our Corps. What he will do after the war I cannot say – as his commission is only a temporary colonial appointment and his age, 30, prohibits starting as a subaltern in the army with any prospect of pension etc.

I am shortly expecting to see Frank out. I shall try and escort him to Bloemfontein and see him safely started.

Haggitt wrote last week saying he thought it was about time I took a couple of days off to run up and see the 7th Co: and do some shopping!

Much love to all from your ever loving son Eric E.B. Wilson

Springfontein   Sunday 2nd March 1902

My dearest Father

Yours of Feb 7th received today after its now customary extra journey to Bloemfontein and back. I have written to the Army Postmaster at Cape Town enclosing this last envelope legibly addressed Springfontein and protesting against a repetition.

I am glad to hear from your last that Frank leaves probably on the 21st – as I can then tell when about to expect to see him. I want to arrange to go from here to Bloemfontein with him if possible, as Haggitt has told me to come up for a periodical adjustment of accounts etc etc when I think I can get away. The mails that come with Frank will, all well, reach here on Thursday the 13th of this month, his arrival will depend on the number of days which he spends in Cape Town before coming up. Possibly you may be using him as a postman for the occasion!

My Kaffir Collie "Van Zyl" is just one year old today or thereabouts. He was picked up on the Veldt on March 13th '01 – and his eyes were just open – say he was 11 days old. He has turned out a beautiful dog to the eye with a wonderful golden coat – but like all semi-wild dogs could not be trained to the pitch of a setter or retriever. He is a universal and well known favourite everywhere now. He has just picked up and brought me an old envelope with much tail-wagging and arching of the back as I write.

Splendid captures of boers were made last week, over 600 taken in one drive. This with the heavy captures in the preceding weeks will reduce the republican forces to an army of comic opera proportions – as the various 'wards' always call their 'commando' by the same title i.e. the 'Winberg Commando' etc. whatever its strength – most of them from being 800 – 1500 strong are now 20 – 60 strong and still keep to themselves – rarely joining hands with other Commandos for more than a day or two – this being one of the greatest obstacles to catching them.

I am very glad to hear that Harry Methold is on the road to recovery.

Since I last wrote, the Great Paardeburg Day (February 27th) has passed for the 2nd Anniversary – the red letter day in the annals of His Majesty's Seventh Company of Royal Engineers!

Much love to all, from your ever loving son Eric E.B. Wilson

P.S. The Norfolk Militia are off home – if you meet Richard Bagge he will report on my welfare.

Excuse official envelope, I cannot find a plain one.

Springfontein, Orange River Colony   Sunday March 9th 1902

My dearest Father

Your last to hand (viâ Bloemfontein) bore the date of 14th February – the day after Amy reached 8 – and the day on which Valentine E. Bagot Phillimore reached 27.

By the same mail I hear from Frank (dated Oriel College, Oxon) that he expects to land about the 11th – which may bring him up here by the next Friday as ever is!

My next letter may be written from Bloemfontein – or if one does not arrive you may assume that I am trotting Frank round Bloemfontein and have missed the mail! If Frank turns up on Friday – we shall probably go on to Bloemfontein by Saturday's up mail due there about 4 p.m. – and I shall return at 10 a.m. on the Monday or Tuesday.

I was down at Norvals Pont last week paying the monthly wages to my labourers – Natives receive 1/4d per diem and food in military employment, but money, I'm glad to say, has no hold on them – their wants are few – and they rarely work or engage for more than 3 months at a time – then return with £5 or £6 to their homes. This lasts them the rest of the year – perhaps the following year they will do the same.

Skilled white labour on the contrary commands high wages. A good carpenter would rather starve than work for less than 16/- per diem – other trades even higher. But you must remember that there is no copper money used or taken – 3d practically = ½d or 1d at home, and £5 a month is about a minimum boarding price at a restaurant or hôtel, for the artizan class. I could easily get employment at 30/= to £2 a day, if I wanted money, and left the Service or even joined the Constabulary etc.

However, I am quite contented with the 15/= a day, or so, that I draw with the 3/= colonial allowance and 2/6d Field allowance which are given extra to the European pay of 10/10d.

I am very sorry to hear such a bad account of Basil – he has had a terrible exile from his land and home – I often think of him, and marvel in gratitude at the inexplicable distribution of the Divine Favour in this life. (St. Matthew XXV 29.)

Many thanks for the notes about Richmond House. I think I could find my way there even now:– I remember going to see it with you some years ago. I expect you have your hands full now, with all your Lenten duties. Have you replaced Bicknell yet – I see by the Magazine that he is leaving his Redgrave work. I always get the Magazine punctually – I cannot recall any instance of it failing to reach me.

Much love to all at home from your ever loving son Eric E.B. Wilson

P.S. I am writing by this mail to the P.C. for her 25th Birthday.

Springfontein, Orange River Colony   Sunday 16th March 1902

My dearest Father,

Your last letter was dated Feb: 21st. I am glad that you and Mother are none the worse for your very unpleasant drop through the ice on the Lake. It must have been a bad shock for you both, and I am very thankful that the consequences were no worse.
You appear to have fallen through exactly at the spot at which Harry Horsfall dropped his gold signet ring into the water in '96 – and left the Hall for some journey by rail thinking it lost for good; after pointing out the spot to Piers and I who were on the lake at the time. As you may remember we dredged it up at the second scoop, and I pursued him to Mellis Station by bicycle and overtook him just before the departure of the train and restored the ring:– for which he solemnly handed me 1d. reward! I have the coin amongst my curios somewhere still!
I do not expect to see Frank before Tuesday or Wednesday at the earliest. His boat should have arrived yesterday at Cape Town. He then had to get all his papers and passes etc etc to come up country – which he would not do that night or today (Sunday), so he may get away 9 p.m. mail on Monday which reaches here Wednesday 10 a.m, when I shall detain him till the same hour Thursday and proceed with him to Bloemfontein, all being well.
Yesterday was the 2nd anniversary of our entry into Bloemfontein after fighting our way 100 miles across the wilderness.
I am sorry to hear that Lord Methuen had been badly wounded again – in fact they say compound fracture of the thigh – which, if he survives, will certainly cripple him for life.

We have not heard details of the fight – but from all accounts it appears to have been some kind of surprise attack by Delarey and Kemp – and Methuen's men do not appear to have behaved with too much gallantry – but one cannot judge details at present – as long as the net result was a few more boers killed or put out of action, that is the clear profit of the fight.

It is very sad sometimes to hear of these mobs of children (sent straight out from the wilds of Shoreditch) being sent out to attack a body of the enemy, who now consist only of the most hardy, cunning and desperate bushrangers fighting for their skins and too crass and ignorant of the broad aspect of their situation to realize their ultimate fate – it is just like sending 2000 lambs to round up 100 wolves and thinking that their numbers will do it. I lay the death, aye, and every drop of blood spilt, of these youths at the door of W.T.Stead, Bannerman, Labouchere, and a few other knock kneed, self advertising London sewer bred traitors, but for whom an honourable peace would have long been established, and a fine race of hardy men saved from the destruction, which in their blindness they brought on their own heads but have long since realized was more than encouraged by the slimy vipers amongst our own people for their miserable political ends.

Ever your loving son Eric E.B. Wilson

Springfontein, Orange River Colony   Sunday 23rd March 1902

My dearest Father

Your last letter arrived up to time this week – posted at King's Lynn on Feb 28th when you and Mother were touring round a Lenten course of preaching. Frank arrived safely yesterday afternoon – and is now sitting in my office reading and smoking a cigar. He seems very fit and well – and brings me all the home news – also a very good photo of Cicely's wedding group which I am very pleased with. I managed to identify all the family portraits – except Marion, who I had never seen out of short frocks and had no idea how she had grown up in the interim! Evelyn looks particularly fit and well, which Frank endorses.

Frank has grown very like Cousin George both in appearance and walk and brings a strong Redgrave atmosphere with him which is almost like a home visit to me!

We both go up to Bloemfontein tomorrow – about 9 a.m. – and I shall probably return on the Wednesday.

I was twice down at Norvals Pont last week on various business. One visit brought me in for a St Patrick's day dinner at the Hospital – followed by an impromptu dance – which was well supported. There I met – Freddy Barclay – ! who has come out with the 6th Manchester Regiment, though he belongs I think to some Berkshire Militia. He seemed very well and considerably grown since I last saw him. He appeared very pleased to see me – and from him I also got news of our part of the world – so I have been having plenty of special messengers lately!

Frank brought the first touch of cold weather with him, and last night was very sharp indeed. From now till October we shall have much colder nights.

This afternoon I am going to drive F. around the outlying grounds of Springfontein. He tells me that Walter has killed the game down pretty close at Redgrave and thinks it will take some time to recover.

He also brings a variety of messages from various people of which he says he has forgotten the precise nature but they all meant the same!

I expect I shall spend Easter Day here this year: last year I was down at Cape Town for it. I hope the next after this will be at home, but I could not guarantee as much.

Best love to all at home from your ever loving son Eric E.B. Wilson

Springfontein, Orange River Colony   Easter Eve Saturday 29th March 1902

My dearest Father

I am very sorry indeed to hear by yours of the 7th inst of poor Basil's end in New Zealand. I have written to Cousin George. I do not suppose Frank has heard of it yet in Bloemfontein – I shall be seeing him, I hope, again, about the 4th April. It will be a great blow for them all at Broom Hills – Basil, the first to leave of the 10 who have grown up for nearly 20 years together.

The whole of South Africa is full of the death of Cecil Rhodes – you can hardly imagine in England to what extent this country relied on this man to cut out their future of progress and prosperity – they hardly knew themselves till his death. It seems very hard that he should be taken just when his immense power would have been so valuable in straightening out the country after its devastation by the long war. I can think of no name in modern history which had the same mighty hold on a people – unless it were Abraham Lincoln in the American war.

I took Frank up to Bloemfontein on Monday and handed him over to Major Purvis – who is looking after him while he is casting about for congenial employment. He was just off to see the manager of a big government Horse Farm when I came back on Wednesday. That would suit him very well – but I have not heard of his arrangements since.

We had a good look round Bloemfontein together and I showed him the lie of the land for 20 miles round from various points of vantage.

He found another friend in Haggitt and they had great discussions on the Bury side of our district – in which Frank seemed well posted.

I have received today the March magazine, also a book from Aunt Amy, and a newspaper from Muriel.

The 'base' Post Office have been very sharp on my correspondence since I wrote a third time to ask if letters addressed Springfontein could not be delivered there! They now arrive deeply scored and underlined in blue pencil – but on the proper day!!

Yes – all your letters have turned up duly for some long while now – though for some time viâ Bloemfontein.

I hope to be up there this week again to see the dentist – a long course of hard biscuit and tough beef in earlier war time played the mischief with some of my molars! However I have parted with none to date!

Poor McClintock of my company says he has only two working teeth left and they are not opposite each other!

I shall spend Easter here this year – last year I was at Cape Town. They are having some sports on Monday – got up by the A.S. Corps.

Much love from your ever loving son Eric E.B. Wilson

Springfontein, Orange River Colony　　　　　　　　　**Sunday 6th April 1902**

My dearest Father

Your letter of Mar 14th to hand in good time.
You must have had a terrific drive to Southwold and back: I fear the pony was a bit stiff afterwards. Thirty five miles is a very different thing in this country, where roads are absolutely unknown and would take a lot of doing in a pony trap.
I was up in Bloemfontein from Thurs – Sat and came down with Haggitt yesterday, having persuaded him to look up our end of the country for once in a way – so tomorrow we trolley down to Norvals Pont and back and next day to Bethulie.
I heard from Harry Horsfall last mail giving an epitomé of his first seasons shooting at his new place, Gatacre Hall. He tells me that his home "Belleamour" was almost destroyed by fire recently – though they recovered £2500 from the Insurance Company. I do not suppose this will replace losses which have more than a monetary value.
He accounts in detail for about 1300 head of game shot on his 1500 acres: which he describes as good land but a bad shape.
I rode out to Fischers Farm from Bloemfontein, with Haggitt, and saw Frank, he seemed very contented and quite settled down, there is one thing about his job – he has the choice of about 2000 horses to ride around on! He had heard of poor Basil's death by letter. I am glad to hear that Harry Methold is better – I presume he may be considered out of danger if he can travel again.
Everyone is waiting to hear what punishment Lord Kitchener will award to the 500 cowards who bolted from Delarey the other day and let in poor Methuen and his devoted Infantry and gunners – (5th Fusiliers).

It is the most shameful thing which has occurred during the war – but what can you expect when you see the class of (?) man they send out for the Yeomanry now – though I believe the Diamond Fields Horse (Kimberley volunteers) behaved pretty badly too.

One in ten should drawn by lot and publicly shot, to stiffen the rest.

However as regards nett result – every boer killed and injured in the fight – such as it was – represents clear profit – our losses even if they amounted to 50,000 men in one skirmish wouldn't make the slightest difference to the hunting down of the few hundred bandits and marauders still uncaught.

Ever your loving son Eric E.B. Wilson

Yes: I should like the Baronetage copy: I regret not replying before.

Springfontein   **Sunday 13th April 1902**

My dearest Father

I got quite a big mail this week – yours of March 21st – and letters from Muriel (6 pages) Bertie (8 pages) and Lady Jenner 8 pages of Curragh news etc! Jenner is leaving the Curragh at last – after six years of very hard staff work there. His regiment – 9th Lancers – has gone from here to India – viâ England. I think he does not intend to rejoin them – but will retire now.

I don't know what to advise for Dick Partridge – as he has been in the country and knows pretty well how the land lies – under the circumstances the best thing he could do would be to write to the "Secretary to the Deputy Administrator Bloemfontein O.R.C."- if he wants to work in this colony – stating the sort of work he would like information about – adding his experience of the country and services – and stating whether he wants to take up land for farming etc.

I do not know of course what line he proposes to strike out in – Frank, as you know, did not take the work, which Major Purvis kindly offered him as an inducement to come out – but quickly toured round and asked for and accepted work to his taste on one of the government horse farms – which was really what I hoped he would do – but I could hardly use Major Purvis's good will to repeat the manoeuvre – as it was something of a speculation.

Dick can make sure of his ground in the way I have quoted above, and select the line he would like best. I should think Land Agency would be a good business – Dick might also write to J.G. Fraser Esq., Attorney and Land Agent, Bloemfontein who is the head of the fraternity in Bloemfontein and ask him if he wants an assistant or could put him in the way of employment.

I was very glad to hear that Cambridge won the Boat Race – Piers & Co's college at Oxford must be quite notorious pro: tem: on the strength of Rhodes wonderful bequests.

Everyone is lost in admiration at the insight of the man in founding the German and American Scholarships – especially the former – as £250 is a princely income to a German – and the Emperor will nominate a good class of man on the strength of it.

I have had a busy week touring with Haggitt. We trollied to Norvals Pont one day and following day drove to Bethulie by road (25 miles) and on to the Orange River (Bethulie Bridge) next day 3 miles and back to Springfontein, $3 + 3 + 25 = 31$ miles that day – inspecting defence works etc etc.

We had heavy rain last evening – the weather is keeping warm however longer than last year, when we had frost at night by now.

No news yet from the Peace Conference at Klerksdorp.

Much love to all from your ever loving son Eric E.B. Wilson

Bloemfontein Club   Saturday 19th April 1902

My dearest Father

Up here for two days – combining inspection duty on the Railway and a visit to the dentist, who has fixed me up now – at least for a time.

I managed to get your letter of 26th off the mail train at Springfontein – which waited half an hour – and on which I afterwards travelled.

I was under the impression that I had told you that Haggitt met Bertie and Muriel in Corsica in '99 – I meant to have done so – as it was one of the first items of mutual knowledge that Haggitt and I discovered when he came to our company in Dec '01.

Everyone is talking of and waiting for the results of the Boers overtures for Peace – we have no reliable news at time of writing – some rumours say that 'peace is assured' others that the Boers are asking for concessions which cannot possibly be granted – as they are too evidently with a view to promoting subsequent trouble and unrest.

From a purely 'Greatest Good' point of view – the longer the struggle takes to die – the heavier will the Dutch feel the miseries accompanying their insensate resistance and the more enduring will the subsequent peace of the country be – the pains and endurance borne by our generation will be forgotten in twenty years, and the glorious results will drown the pinch of the moment – even if the moment be ten years.

There is not the slightest doubt that the struggle would have been over once for all many months ago if, apart from open treason at home, we had not pursued such an unreal and false kindness sort of policy – pampering the women and children of the enemy – treating the half savage boer as a highly civilised and honourable foe, accepting his "Oath before God", which means no more than the cringing of a dog to avoid the lash – as though it was an English Gentleman's 'parole'- and so on.

In all of which the Boer sees : not – mercy – forbearance – and civilization – but conciliation, half-heartedness or even plain fear.

They will require an iron handed administration for many years after peace supervenes to bandit hunting or "driving" as it is now done.

Records are being called for of all kinds of R.E. works done during the Campaign, for the instruction of the future, and I am assisting Haggitt in a compilation of some of our more recent works – and have taken up the camera strongly once more as the best witness of the results of labour than can be found.

I am returning to Springfontein, I expect, tomorrow.

Best love to all with you Ever your loving son Eric E.B. Wilson

Springfontein   Sunday 27th April 1902

My dearest Father

I came back from Bloemfontein last Sunday – and have had a busy week with office work – plans drawings and records etc – rather weary work indoors in this country.

No letters of any description by last English mail – the first for a long time – as I usually hear from some one or other if not always the same correspondent.

There is no war news pending the big meeting which is expected to take place about the 15th May.

The Boer chieftains who met recently, have been given permission to tour the country collecting Commandants – Field Cornets and other smaller officers to a big war meeting somewhere between the two countries.

Everyone says that peace will ensue – perhaps gradually at first. The share market is however the strongest indication of peace, by its vitality.

Many of the officers serving out here will make a lot of money out of their investments in local stocks: at least if they sell out to the new settlers who will pour in later.

The civilian local officials (Doctors, Railway officials etc) are all crazy with the price of shares etc and their local knowledge carries them well through with their investments.

I fear I have given the subject no attention whatever up to date : and by now it is getting late to buy anything.

I have not heard from or seen Frank lately – but I expect by now he is fairly settled down.

All the little towns and 'dorps' are making great preparation for Coronation celebrations, towards which the Government has made them grants of various sums from £100.

I had one game of football last week – against the Hospital (staff) which we won by 1 – 0. Many thanks for the April magazine which arrived duly this week.

I have been fixing up a mule geared pump this week to one of our 'bore holes' – it works exactly like the ordinary horse chaff cutter one sees outside Romany barns etc.

Much love to all Ever your loving son Eric E.B. Wilson

Post Script

Just after posting to you: letters turned up. I do not know where they had been delayed.

One also from Helen and an invoice and receipt for proof of R.B.S. portrait. I am sorry to hear that Uncle Benjamin has passed away – I suppose that Henry Greene will live at Midgham now?
I hope you enjoyed your visit to Norwich.
I have another Norwich man here in my small party of sappers – W. Abel – his home is just out to West of Norwich but he knows Thorpe etc well. He is a 'balloonist' by (adopted) profession – but with me only in capacity of "labourer" as his balloon detachment have gone home. He talks good East Anglian- "enow" = enough, and "hooly" = "wholly" are in his repertoire!

I hope this will catch mail – Your loving son Eric E.B. Wilson

Springfontein
Ap: 27th 02.
11 p.m.

Springfontein, Orange River Colony   Sunday 4th May 1902

My dearest Father

First I must thank you for the volume of "Wide World Magazine" which arrived this mail, and is much appreciated and sought after by the Irish Fusiliers etc in our Mess. <u>They</u> study it to see if accounts Natal Army doings – in which they took no small part – for me it has interest in illustrating the doings of the Western army.

Of course many of Conan Doyle's <u>facts</u> are very inaccurate and cause much comment when studied by the actual 'factors' if I may use the expression. The general tone however of his account is generous and spirited, and very readable.

You ask me about poor Gordon McKenzie – well – I saw a lot of him at De Aar in old days, and knew him very well to speak to. He was a very charming man and we were all very sorry to hear afterwards that he had gone under. As far as I can recall, the last time I saw him was at Modder River. I fancy he managed to run up for a day or two about Dec. 8th or so. He (if I am not mistaken) came to see an old gunner friend called Forestier Walker – who persuaded him to stay on for the fight which we were all waiting for – the attack on Cronje's stronghold at Magersfontein, December 11th 1899.

On the morning of the 12th December, after it had been decided that the attack must be abandoned as we could get no 'forrarder', and were losing men too fast – I was riding back from the Artillery firing line, where I had been with a message, and fell in with Walker and, I think, McKenzie – I remember Walker saying: Well – , old man (some nickname) – to McKenzie – I'm sorry we could not show you a better days' sport – but you must come up and try again when we have our next turn at them! And we all three rode back to camp at Modder River together.

I fancy McK. went down soon after, to De Aar again – I did not see him afterwards.

I send you a snapshot I have had by me since De Aar days of the Remount Camp there of which he was in charge. It is too small to be distinct – but I expect McK. is one of the group by the tent to the left of the telegraph pole in the photo – examining a horse which is being led past there.

I was down at Bethulie this week building a new blockhouse – and have left a party in full swing there.

We are all anxiously waiting for the results of the big meeting on the 15th inst: Commandants and Field Cornets have been turning up out of the wilderness daily to be railed up North to the Vaal – it seems very strange to see them, men with well known names, that we have spent months and millions trying to catch – coming in and calmly asking for a free pass to proceed by our Railway for the meeting!

Ever your loving son Eric E.B. Wilson

Springfontein Sunday 11th May 1902

My dearest Father

Nearly missed this mail, as I have had so much running about to do this week, revising plans and making records etc. I have been to Norvals Pont – Bethulie and Edenburg this week. Just back from latter and am off again tomorrow early to Bloemfontein to go through works and plans with Haggitt. I may be detained there for some days.

I am very sorry to hear that Campbell (Jack Lake's brother in law) has been killed in an accident to an armoured train – which ran off the line just North of Pretoria. I think and fear it must be the same man as I know he was doing armoured train work: though it is just possible it may be another Campbell.

I travelled down from Edenburgh today with Kincaid – who is bound for Ireland on 3 months leave. That makes the third of the 7th Co: officers who have quitted the war, Boileau and Fraser having preceded him. I see Boileau has got a very high R.E. billet in the War Office – D.A.A.G. for R.E. – which will give him much influence over the destinies of individual R.E. Officers as regards employment, station etc.

Your letter of 18th April arrived duly on the 8th inst: – I am glad you are getting some assistance for Botesdale work.

I have not heard result of P.S. Racqets yet. I am glad Harrow have done well so far.

I met Col. Barter – of the King's Own Yorkshire Light Infantry this week – whom I have not seen since Modder River days – he was, you may remember, commanding at De Aar at the start and was my temporary chief at the time of building the early forts etc etc there.

I am glad to say that he also has not had a day sick or a day off duty since the first shot was fired. We compared notes and mutually congratulated each other – and hoped for a continuance of the same!

The Boers are all assembling for the big meeting at Vereeniging – on the Vaal, on the 15th: possibly by next letter we may have heard some result – one way or the other – not that it will make a scrap of difference for many months for the professional soldier, if they voted for peace – as all the I.Y.'S (5/= men) – volunteers – Militia – reserves and colonial men will get away before a soldier moves a foot.

Much love to all at home from your loving son Eric E.B. Wilson

7th Field Co R.E. Camp, Bloemfontein   **Whit Sunday May 18th 1902**

My dearest Father

I have been up here all this week, very busy assisting Haggitt to compile various reports and plans etc of works done by 7th Co during last year, and have spent a regular clerk's week in the R.E. offices in the town with pen and typewriter!

I shall probably return to Springfontein on Tuesday.

Your last letter was forwarded from S. and reached me yesterday. You were just taking Michael to school. I expect by now you are doing your tour in the Highlands – and will see the girls in their respective homes.

Yesterday Haggitt and I rode out to Fischer's Farm and saw Frank – who seemed in capital form. He gets on well with Captain Eassie – the Veterinary Officer in charge of the Depôt and finds plenty of congenial occupation in the horses and stock line. He tells me he is drawing 10/= a day – which is exceptionally good pay for his short acquaintance with the country – and his expenses are practically nil.

We all had tea in the evening with Eassie and his wife – who has joined him from Ireland with his two children. I knew Eassie well at the Curragh – I don't know if you ever heard me speak of him – he was in Veterinary charge of our troop horses and has doctored Fusilier ere now.

Today Haggitt is away with the C.R.E. – inspecting some farm within a drive – and Frank has ridden over to lunch and is sitting outside our hut as I write.

I heard from Cousin George this mail also – a very nice letter. He thinks the new tenants of the Hall are likely to prove more sociable than their predecessors. Frank heard from Rowland also – so we got plenty of home news this week.

The boer conference is still in full swing – we hear that they are being 'done well' unlimited free drinks and food etc! so possibly there may be a little extra deliberation in their movements on that account.

The general wish of the troops is that they should <u>not</u> be allowed now to surrender – but that we should dress them down to the last ounce, after all the insensate trouble they have given us.

It must be almost without parallel, the condition of affairs we have brought about by our childish policy of collecting and tending to their women and children etc so as to enable them to carry on brigandage with only their skins at stake. No other country in the world's history has done or would do such a suicidal thing.

However it is a fine proof of the power of the Empire, but I could have rather that my generation had not to bear the brunt of its execution!

Many of the women in the Dutch Refugee camps are better off in a hundred ways than they have ever been or will be again – and are among the the bitterest advocates of the prolongation of the struggle.

Does anyone suppose that if they had been left to the natural fate that their husbands and brothers brought on them; namely to take their chances of starvation and worse evils on lonely farms in the veldt – that they would not have long ago compelled their men to sue for peace in an honourable manner, when they saw that their hopes of a Dutch Empire in S.A. were hopelessly lost?

And worst of all the Boer himself laughs at us for pitiful fools for looking after their families in this manner – and considers it a sop to his majesty!

I hope some of the young men at home will add a few of our notorious traitors and scoundrelly unpatriotic politicians to the Coronation procession with a liberal adornmnent of tar and feathers!

The army out here would subscribe £100,000 pounds, on the nail, to see some half dozen of our vilest "Englishmen" dragged by the heels, by a jackass, in the coronation procession.

McClintock – who was here when I came up – has gone out to Ladybrand, on the Basuto Border, to take over the line of blockhouses from here to there.

Col Kincaid – I think I told you last week – has gone home on 3 months leave. Probably by next letter we shall know whether the war is to end in a few weeks or in a few more months – over 6,000 of the enemy have been caught since Jan 1st this year!

Think how we must have underestimated their numbers at the start. There must have been well over 100,000 of them in the field, with outside Europeans, at the start.

Cast your mind back to our little post of 500 men at De Aar and think what golden opportunities they lost!

Methuen might have had to land under the fire of Dutch guns at Cape Town, had they known their strength, or we been more tardy in grasping the situation.

And yet amateur writers in the papers pooh-pooh the elements of organisation and discipline, the two things which saved our Empire from going the way of Babylon and Rome in'99!

Much love to all at home from your ever loving son Eric E.B. Wilson

Springfontein   Sunday 25th May 1902

My dearest Father

Your last letter, of May 2nd, was very interesting and full of news – it is very nice to be a great-nephew, when it costs nothing and may receive fifty pounds. I am glad you were able to see Michael started off on his first plunge into the world of men and letters. It seems more than 18 years ago that I first made my début at Dummer House – I wonder who live there now.

I'm sorry to hear that Muriel's boy Raymond is causing anxiety – I hope you have had better reports since.

Jack Sawbridge should be appearing for ordination today – Trinity Sunday. As long as the Church can obtain recruits of Jack's kindliness of hereditary disposition, I think we need not fear for the proper interpretation of the Word of Life, with its principles exemplified in every day life for the enlightenment of those still in darkness. (St Mark xiii-31).

I received the account of the Racquet Matches and portrait of the Harrow pair safely – also the Magazine – many thanks for both.

I came down from Bloemfontein on Wednesday, and have been very busy with back numbers here, owing to my ten days in the C.R.E.'s office making up plans and reports etc at Bloemfontein.

On Friday I went down with Col. Carleton to Bethulie Bridge – and tomorrow I go with him to Bethulie Town – (3 miles this side of the bridge) to see about reserving a piece of Town Land for Military purposes in the future (peace time) – for camping on etc. I think we are to select about 100 acres – but have not seen the correspondence from Head Quarters yet. One has to take time in advance in these things – as once the country is settled down into individual ownership, the Government would have to pay through the nose for land forcibly reserved – (like our Railway Companies have to for new lines etc) but '<u>now</u> it is only a question of "I think this piece will suit us well for our purpose" and there you are!

We hear persistent rumours of 'peace' of some kind but get no official news to date – you are far more likely to know over the cable – before we hear by official announcement.

Much love to all from your ever loving son Eric E.B. Wilson

Springfontein   Monday 2nd June 1902

My dearest Father

You will enter your 60th year on Wednesday. I overlooked the calculation which should have prompted me to write two mails ago to reach you about the right day – however you have my very best love and wishes now.

We understand that a treaty of surrender was signed by the Burghers on the 31st – and that peace has been proclaimed. The tangible results have not begun to affect us yet so there is not the wild enthusiasm that one might expect. Then again one has so got to disregard any [of] the most sacred compacts entered into by the Boers – oaths or what not – as being of less binding value than the breath that speaks them, on the Dutch themselves – who have considered the entering into and swearing of an oath – followed by its opportune neglect when suitable, as one of the finest tricks by which you can take your enemy's life.

So altogether the edge of the joy of the announcement of any peace compact is somewhat blunted – until it proves itself by the test of time.

Very many thanks for the Debrett – it is most interesting to look up people in it. I see by the "tables of precedence" that a Companion of the D.S.O. takes precedence over all sorts of people – a fact which I am sure would be of more interest to the wife of a D.S.O., who takes precedence over other wives "pari-passu" with her husband – including wife of eldest son of a baronet and daughter of a baronet – things which I know appeal to the fair sex very acutely.

I am glad Piers did so well in his trial match – I hope he will secure a place at least in the Oriel team.

I have had a lot of running about this week – to Bethulie and Norvals Pont etc. The cessation of hostilities (if so) will of course make a vast difference to my area of charge for works and defences – but it is too soon yet to know what will be done.

I have a good deal of work in hand here for a few weeks – not of a defensive nature – so I do not expect to move suddenly.

We had a great Coronation meeting this week for Springfontein festivities – in which I can see I shall have some work to do!

I sincerely hope that when the reduction of troops commences the 7th R.E. will be among the first to return.

Much love to all at home from your ever loving son Eric E.B. Wilson

Springfontein   Sunday 8th June 1902

My dearest Father

Many thanks for three letter packets received from you this week – containing matters of interest.

By the time this reaches you, you will probably be at full steam with coronation holiday making. I could have hoped we might have been spared it here; as we are tired, and not very enthusiastic about coronations or anything else, all we want is rest and peace.

However the local and civil element are combining with the military in sports etc – and I have already been cast into many committees, as well as detailed for Clerk of the Course on the day. I sincerely hope I may be ordered away before it comes off.

I hope you enjoyed your trip north, and found everyone in good estate.

Now as regards the Reeves' house. I am quite prepared to buy the house and grounds if the cost will not exceed £150 or so – and if you and Uncle Rowland will do the business part of the transaction for me. However I do not propose to lay out a lot of additional money on <u>repairs</u> etc immediately; on the strength of becoming the landlord.

The first payment must be made by the sale of £100.00 of Greene King & Co. stock which Uncle R. holds. The next payment will be from £50.0.0 or so – likely to accrue from Uncle Benjamin's bequest: any further money required and I will draw by cheque on my war savings at Cox & Co. I do not want to reduce my ready money savings at Cox's as I shall have great expenses to meet when I get home, in the provision of new uniform etc. etc.

Moreover it costs me £100.0.0. a year besides my English pay to associate with my fellow men – and I am not due for an increase of pay till August '05 when I shall get a rise of £18 on 10 years' service, and again in August '06 when I shall get a further rise of £90 per annum as <u>Captain</u>. That is to say I have to tide over some four years as best I can.

Hitherto of course G.K.& Co have provided me with the £100 a year – but by reducing the capital amount from £1200 to £700 – including original outfit etc. Another £100 will leave me £600 G.K.& Co which I should be unwilling to reduce.

However I presume the Reeves' house would yield a few pounds a year in rent. If I find I am likely to run short of money I shall have to apply for Indian service – where our <u>pay</u> of about £1 a day is, I understand, ample to live on in the country. But I am not anxious at present to serve in India after 3 years hardship and discomfort here, if I can avoid it.

I have had no statement from Cox for some time – but am writing this mail. He should have at least £150 for me – and on return home a further war gratuity of £37.10. (Lieut's share)

A lot of troops have passed through here in special trains to get home in time for coronation.

An officer and 10 men from every battalion I understand. I had to send my clerk and right hand man with an R.E. detachment – as he was a Reservist, and am sorry to lose him.

No special news. The boers seem to be thoroughly delighted at the prospect of peace and I do not anticipate any outbreak of hostilities.

Much love from your ever loving son Eric E.B. Wilson

Have just received circular from Commandant to say that today and tomorrow have been proclaimed days of public thanks-giving – all public offices to close etc.

Springfontein   Sunday 15th June 1902

My dearest Father

Your last letter was from Aberdeenshire – May 22nd – I do not suppose your next will contain news of reception of Peace – possibly the one after that – about June 6th.

I hope you enjoyed your northern tour and found all well.

Our great event of the week has been a heavy fall of snow – about six to eight inches – falling continuously for 48 hours.

The astonishment of the natives and Dutch was very marked – as it is almost unknown in this latitude – except perhaps a little sleet once or twice in the cold weather (May:Aug:). An old Cape Colony man who works with me says that he can recall nothing like it since the early '70's! A good deal of it is still lying about though a powerful sun is rapidly melting it. Snowballing and snow men have both been in vogue this week!

On Thursday my sponge was a solid block of ice – and the ink in my inkpot also solid – I jabbed the pen on to it in vain! This is sunny South Africa with a vengeance!

All through the week also surrendered burghers have been passing up and down by rail to their homes or districts – some 12,000 have surrendered to date – since peace was signed! They all seem delighted that it is over – like children in their talk – it was evidently only their leaders who were keeping them in the field. They cannot understand our phlegmatic reception of peace and openly express surprise that we do not demonstrate more.

They also cannot understand the friendly manner – almost indifference with which they are treated – they seemed to expect that we should deal harshly with them. In fact it is evident that they have not the familiarity and confidence which an Englishman – born of the ruling caste of the world – has in dealing with a subject race. I have not the slightest doubt that they will make excellent British subjects – as they show all the indications of taking freely to their new position.

I hear that the 7th Co: have been turned on to Coronation decorations at Bloemfontein! The spade for the sword with a vengeance! Our late chaplain Bellamy has rejoined his cure at Johannesburg – and we have a Rev. Ashburner in his stead – an exceedingly good man – with a forceful delivery. All is interregnum at present and no-one knows who is moving where or what will be done about units going home etc.

I do not suppose much movement will occur until after the coronation.

Much love to all Ever your loving son Eric E.B. Wilson

Springfontein   **Sunday 22nd June 1902**

My dearest Father

We are all busy with preparations for Coronation Sports etc. for the 26th, I will try and send you a programme later.

I may possibly run up to Bloemfontein on the 27th to look them up at headquarters, and see the town decorations and so on.

Your last letter was from Lincoln – with a most interesting account of your visit to Muriel and Bertie. I hope to write to M. this week. I am glad your grand and my god-son is growing so favourably. I am looking forward very much to seeing him.

Last Wednesday I went to Norvals Pont to see my detachment of Royal Monmouth R.E. Militia (Lieut. Kenelm Digby and 19 men) off to Cape Town and home. They used to look after the big pontoon bridge over the Orange River there – this I have to now provide for from the remainder of my own small detachment – and I have installed 6 R.E. and 5 Natives in charge. The work is comparatively light in the present (dry) season – but when rains begin in Basutoland or the upper Orange River we sometimes get 15 and 20 feet of water down in a few hours – and have to be pretty sharp in opening our boat bridge in the centre and swinging the two halves to the banks – or the whole thing would be swept away like a nutshell.

I send you a small photo which I took showing most of the pontoon bridge, a portion of the railway bridge and one of the big masonry blockhouses – at Norvals Pont. You will notice that the floating bridge is supported partly on pontoons and partly on rafts of casks. It has been built and maintained now for over two years.

By the way I travelled in the same train to Norvals Pont with the famous ex-general Christian DeWet – aged 48 – who was visiting the burghers in the Norvals Pont Refugee Camp to address them on Peace.

I recognised him at once from his unmistakeable resemblance to his photographs. He looked a fine determined man, with a not unpleasant face, very much the cut and build of the late "Lucky Watling" – only more ferretty. Lord Kitchener of K. and A. passed through here last night about 1 a.m. – en route for Cape Town, and home, I believe. He ought to get a fine reception. We are busy pulling down and collecting hundreds of miles of barbed wire fencing etc, from blockhouse lines – and selling the same to the local farmers etc. The blockhouses are all sold to the Civil Government – and will be moved for temporary huts on farms etc., while the repatriation of the burghers is going on.

The numbers – almost incredible – of boers who have surrendered since peace was concluded, are astonishing. They could have kept us busy for another seven years!

Much love to all at home from your ever loving son – Eric.

Bloemfontein Club   Saturday 28th June 1902

My dearest Father

I have just run up here to see the Company and hear any news there may be – Coronation being put off enabled me to get away from Springfontein – where we had taken much trouble to prepare for all sorts of festivities and sports – as I expect was the case everywhere – and all for nothing. Bloemfontein when I arrived yesterday was in full warpaint for coronation – and I was fortunate to see it all just as it would have been. They had done a lot with bunting and electric lights etc.

Well, my news will please you though it is not very definite. There nineteen companies of R.E. serving in S.A. and nine are remaining = the 7th Company is for home. When, we do not yet know, but hope to get away within three months at the outside – possibly before. Should there be any change in this programme there is another loophole for home in a new order authorizing leave to England, not exceeding four months, to half the establishment of each grade in a unit (Captains, Lieutenants etc). That would not be so good, as in the first place 3 weeks leave is lost in going home, and a chance of losing 3 more in coming out again, besides the expense of paying for a private passage – some £50 one way and another – so we welcome our being cast for return to England as a happy solution.

Many thanks for you nice letter of 6th inst: Please convey my very kindest regards to Mr Stokes, and all good friends, whose friendly interest and appreciation are a very acceptable solace to our weary soldiery, and go far to make one forget the heavy work of the past three years – and the bitter venom of traitors, calling themselves Englishmen and eating bread earned with British money, which made many a dying soldier on the veldt curse them more bitterly than the honest enemy which caused his death.

We have little work at Springfontein at present beyond pulling down defences, collecting barbed wire and old material generally – for eventual sale.

The 38th Field Co are going to relieve us at Bloemfontein – probably a detachment of them will take over from me at Springfontein and will be glad of the huts and workshops I have run up from time to time there.

Frank is in the Club with me and lunched with us today – he is very well and happy and watched a game of football in which I assisted the company this afternoon to defeat the 17th Battery R.F.A. by 2 goals to none.

Much love to all at home from your ever loving son Eric

Springfontein   Sunday 6th July 1902

My dearest Father

I have just returned from Norvals Pont where I have been very busy seeing about the collection and disposal of old material etc – and paying my detachment there.

I was afraid I should miss the mail and so give you an impression that we had started for the coast – which is not so yet. Of course we are full of calculation as to the arrival of our turn for departure.

There are I believe, some 70,000 'occasional' soldiers to get off first – and <u>then</u> we cannot say how near the first lot of regulars we shall come. It is quite certain however that it will not be with the <u>first journey</u> of the 39 troop-ships who are taking the first 40,000 or so home. That gives us at least six weeks from about June 20th say – i.e. about 2nd week in August at the <u>very</u> earliest. It may not be till much later – as we cannot gauge the pace of movement yet.

Johnson of our company passed through this week for Cape Town to bring up all our heavy baggage – so that we may be compact and ready to proceed to any coast port. I hope to detain him for 24 hours on his return – as we have been parted for over <u>two years</u> – though in the same company He has been with a detachment at Potchefstroom and district, in Transvaal.

I will try and write to Stokes as you suggest – though I fear it will not be this mail now.

If Uncle George leaves Rickinghall I hope Leonard will be appointed – as he knows the local pulse so well.

I saw Freddy Barclay at N.P. yesterday – looking very well and cheerful – the 6th Manchesters – to whom he is attached will of course be off early (militia) – so Freddy will have had a nice little jaunt – though like many a hundred others he will never have seen a live boer armed and in action.

This deficiency I am sorry to say can be ascribed to many of the older soldiery – even to those in receipt of rewards for 'exceptional' services. Too often alas merely political tokens and to encourage the amateur military movement.

The railway is one long string of trucks of troops going south – with flags flying and smiling faces! Very different to the long train of terrified women and children that used to pass through De Aar in Sept: '99. The civil Government have taken over the railways and the Constabulary are taking over the country districts. The soldier's work is done for the present and I hope for good – in S. Africa.

Much love to all at home from your ever loving son Eric

We are all delighted to hear such good accounts of the old king. We all feared the strain of a <u>severe</u> operation – for his time of life and softly nurtured constitution.

Springfontein　　　　　　　　　　　　　　　　　　　　Sunday 13th July 1902

My dearest Father

Very cold here again and looks as if it were blowing up for more snow.
No letter from Redgrave to hand this week – but they often get delayed in Bloemfontein now. I got a note from Miss Margaret Bagge – from Hunstanton – asking me if I had come across a certain Bugler Jelly – but as his regiment is not specified – it would be rather hard for me to trace him! She hoped I would soon be home and mentioned that Richard <u>liked</u> S. Africa – which is surprising considering how little he saw of it.
We hope that the first drafts of regulars will soon be going to the coast now, but have nothing to go upon for certain yet.
I wrote to Mr Stokes this week, as you said he might like to hear from me.
Johnson passed up from Cape Town with our heavy baggage on Friday – midnight so I did not see him passing through.
We have nearly finished collecting the tons of barbed wire and fencing etc from outlying districts and my yard here is fairly choked with it.
I had to serve on a Court Martial last week, a very long day of it, from 10 a.m. to 6 p.m. – four prisoners to try, but interminable strings of witnesses – I hope we dispensed justice eventually!
The country is all apportioned into Military Districts now – on a peace footing – we are in the Bloemfontein Command – under Maj-Gen T. Stephenson – who was last commanding the area I was in when I was at Komati Poort and he was at Barberton.

Col. Carleton, the Commandant here (I think I told you he was a Capt. in Bertie's old regiment – 68th when B. retired) is trying to arrange for Haggitt and I to do about ten days in Natal, just to have a look round over what is to us 'terra incognita'.

Carleton was there at the beginning with his regiment – Royal Irish Fusiliers – at Talana etc, until they came to grief at Nicholson's Nek, so knows the ground. It would be most interesting if we can manage it.

I have met several of my old R.M.A. friends – (now <u>all</u> captains) in the gunners, going south lately.

I have very little indeed to do now compared to the last few months – my men are off in driblets for drafts of men due for the 'Reserve' – and daily diminishing.

There will be very little of the British Army left when time expired men have all gone – I don't know how the country is to face the recruiting problem, without enforcing the Militia Ballot Act, or some form of conscription – the government will lose a great opportunity if they do not grasp this opportunity for securing a proper army adequate to the needs of the Empire now, by some such step.

Much love to all – Ever your loving son Eric

Springfontein   Sunday 20th July 1902

My dearest Father

Two letters to hand from you this week – dated 20 and 26 June – the former must have been delayed somewhere. They do not contain very cheerful news – I was very sorry to hear of the deaths of Willie Hoste and Bertie Gwilt. I fear Lady Hoste will feel the loss very much.

I am very glad that Cousin Kitty Greene is well provided for in Uncle Ben G.'s will.

Your second letter contained the postponement of the Coronation Festivities. We had the same disappointment here; where we had made heavy preparations for sports and all sorts of things. We hear that it is likely to come off early in August now.

I am very sorry indeed to hear that Mr Stokes is down with enteric fever – I only wrote to him a mail or two back. I hope by now he is well on the way to recovery.

I have applied for and been granted fourteen days leave, with permission to go to Natal. I start tomorrow by going up to Bloemfontein, to the Company – then on Tuesday I hope to take the mail train North – Col. Carleton the Commandant here is arranging the itinerary and we are going together. He knows Natal and will be able to select what to visit in the time. It will be a nice change and I shall enjoy seeing the only corner of the civilized country in S.A. that I have not seen. Moreover it will no longer be necessary to fight ones way over the ground! which is an important item.

Col. C.'s brother, in the Leicesters, is Commandant at Durban – and thither we repair first – doing all halts on the way back.

Col. C. has to see about erecting memorials etc. on battlefields where his men fell – so we shall probably have some tramping about hunting for graves in obscure corners of the veldt.

We go vià Bloemfontein, Kroonstad, Elandsfontein (old ground to me), then S.E. vià Heidelburg – Standerton – Volksrust – Charlestown – Newcastle – Glencoe – Ladysmith – Pietermaritzburg to Durban – all new ground.

You will probably get my next letter from Durban – and I hope to be able to give you my impressions of Natal to date. This will make a nice hole in the monotony of waiting to be shipped home and I hope that the time will soon pass on my return.

We dug out a jackal from an ant-bear hole last week!

On Friday I rode out seven miles to a tea party at a very nice farm (house of course in ruins) given by some of the Hospital Staff. Yesterday we had a small dance in the Dutch schoolroom – so have been quite gay.

Ever your loving son Eric

I sold the Bay gelding 'Laddie' – (Fusilier's official successor) this week for £41. – a huge price for this country, where the best animals can be bought for £25. So you may imagine he was a good beast, He was not however quite the class I should want at home – so I decided to sell while good horses were scarce in this country – i.e. the boers are re-stocking farms with whatever they can get.

Fusilier cost £63 – so it has only cost me £22 to possess a big horse for six years. Ponies have bought and sold pretty well at "par". The Remount Dept. have been holding sales of surplus horses all this week and have realized splendid average prices – they have only been selling animals classed 'C & D' keeping A & B for Army use.

They took over £4,000 in cash (in) one day's sale – average price £20 for animals with 3 or less legs! Chiefly bought by dealers but I think the dealers will have their work cut out to turn a profit on some of their purchases, and forage is very costly everywhere.

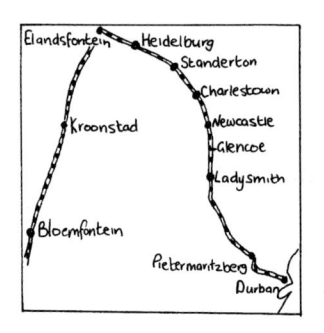

Ocean View Hotel, Berea, Durban, Natal.   **Thursday 24th July 1902**

My dearest Father

I think I warned you in my last letter that my next might be from Durban. I am not sure yet when the English mail boat leaves here – when I find out I will leave this open as long as possible.

Well, I got my fourteen days leave alright, and went up to Bloemfontein on Monday – there I went through all my heavy baggage – which had been lying packed for 2½ years and over, at Cape Town. I am glad to say that some of the clothing etc was alright –my tunic appears alright – but a good deal more was terribly motheaten, and many of the things will be quite useless – which means a lot of expense in replacing them.

On Tuesday I got on to the northbound mail train and joined Colonel Carleton who came straight up from Springfontein. We travelled all that day over ground I knew – and early Wednesday morning found us at Elandsfontein Junction once more.

Having an hour to wait for breakfast I took Col. Carleton round and showed him our old camping grounds and forts etc of 1900 – now of course all the mines are in full working order again and all is life and bustle on what I knew as the 'deserted Rand'

At 8 a.m. we got the Natal train for the S.E. line through the Transvaal – and passed down over new country – but very like other parts of the Transvaal that I knew well.

Heidelberg and Standerton were new towns to me – and the former very pretty and well watered to all appearances. Both full of troops concentrated from out districts waiting to go home or to their various peace garrison stations.

At 5 p.m. we reached Volksrust – the last town on the Transvaal side – there I hoped to see Charles Otley Place R.E. an old Curragh friend – but he was not at the station – and I hope to arrange to meet him on the way back.

A few miles – perhaps 3 – brought us to Charlestown – the first Natal town – which looked none the worse, or at least well recovered from its temporary occupation by the Boers in '99 and '00.

Daylight just carried us through the tunnel under the historic Laing's Nek (pass) through the Drakensburg Mountains and round the foot of the Majuba Mountain so deeply graven in our national history. I stared and stared at it. It is a most majestic hill and no everyday 'kopje'.

What Colley meant to do after he had occupied the top or how the boers ever turned him off it are both profound mysteries to me in the light of all the fighting I have seen since.

Private military history says that all his men were sound asleep after the toil of the night climb up it. But I hope to tell you more about Majuba as we are arranging to stop a day at Charleston on the way back and ride out to and climb it!

Darkness carried us right on through Ladysmith – Colenso – and Pietermaritzburg – all of which we are visiting in detail on our way back – my first glimpse of Natal proper by daylight this morning was of a wonderfully beautiful country.

Not only after the dreary monotony of the barren treeless veldt – but beautiful by any standard. One mass of tumbled hills and deep ravines – well covered with grass and abundant trees and water – it was like a glimpse of paradise after the wilderness of the veldt – dull trees and barren rock – no trees or water. Natal is well called the "garden colony" and I am enchanted with it. We reached Durban at 10. a.m. today. This afternoon we explored the town and docks. The harbour is a wonderful freak of nature – a large inland lake with only a passage some 400 yards wide leading in from the ocean. But it is shallow and requires constant dredging. We saw <u>nine</u> large liners at the quays – most of them waiting to load up with troops for home.

Durban is a far more English place than Cape Town – more progressive – better found with municipal extras like electric trams, fire alarms, clean streets, well kept public gardens etc etc, and better than all, the <u>people</u> are English to the backbone – look you in the face with honest English eyes – not the slinking-foxy-leaden countenances of the Anglo-Cape-Dutch that one meets elsewhere – and hears speaking English with a Dutch accent.

I am altogether enchanted with Natal and would never have forgiven myself if I had gone home without seeing it. Wonderfully fertile everywhere – we passed hundreds of acres of pine apple, banana, orange, quince etc, and plantations of semi-tropical bamboos and big ferns.

The magnificence of scenery the Drakensburg Mountains about Laings Nek and Majuba would be hard to beat. The sight of so much green lands and trees has quite taken the edge off the surprise I expected to feel on seeing closely cultivated country again.

We expect to go up to Pietermaritzburg on Sunday or Monday so I hope to be able to give you a further account of the country in my next letter.

Major and Mrs Harrison-Topham R.E. are in this Hotel waiting to sail in the S.S. Bulawayo in a day or two. I forget if you ever met him at Chatham – he is supposed to be my 'double' in appearance – and is also a D.S.O.

I expect to find mails from you of July 2nd and 9th on return to Springfontein. This hotel – a very comfortable and quiet one – is up on a bluff overlooking the town and bay, a magnificent view. The hill is known as the 'Berea' – you have probably seen it mentioned in books.

I find that some of my old uniform which I have been giving an airing – is somewhat <u>tight</u> at the <u>neck</u> and <u>waist</u> – which is not surprising when one remembers that I was measured for it at <u>19</u> by Messrs Daniel of Woolwich, and am now wearing it at 27!

I must close this now to make sure of the mail boat – and shall post it when we go down to the town this morning. (Friday).

Best love to all at home from your ever loving son Eric

P.O. Box 12, Royal Hotel, Ladysmith, Natal   Friday 1st August 1902

My dearest Father

My last to you was from Durban. Mail leaves here tomorrow, but as I shall be 'on tour' all day I am making sure tonight. We have done a lot of Natal since I wrote, so I think I had better adjust it in chronological order:

Fri 25th July   Durban – Visited Museum and Public Swimming Baths amongst other places. Former very interesting and has the usual collection of S. African fauna and mineral specimens. Also visited the Cemetery and Docks – saw many big liners awaiting troop cargoes for home – a Naval Captain in charge of embarkation affairs told us that 6,000 troops sailed this week. In the evening we patronized the theatre and saw a play "Gentleman Joe" very well and amusingly acted.

Sat 26th July   Very strong and dusty wind blowing, drove about some unexplored outskirts – and the esplanade fronting the bay. Also visited Messrs Cook's local office to get a sword for an officer at Springfontein which he had left in Cook's care. In the afternoon we explored inland along the 'Berea', the wooded bluff on which the Ocean View Hotel stands, and saw all the wealthy residents' villas and gardens; many most attractive.
In the evening we went to a concert in the Town Hall – a very fine building indeed – there we heard a good organist and a very fine professional tenor – the other performers were rather of the domestic order of merit.

Sun 27th July   Was a fine, calm sunny and beautiful day. I went to the Berea church – St Thomas' – at 11 a.m. – the vicar was rather a melancholy man and seemed to lack fire in his discourse – which was chiefly on the point of where licenced recreation and amusement ended and unlicensed began.
He gave me the impression that a little of both would cheer him up considerably.
In the p.m. the Col. and I had to shift camp to Pietermaritzburg – the inland capital. We arrived about 8 p.m. and put up at the Imperial Hotel – a very comfortable and quiet place. There to my great joy I found my old friend Geoff. Howell and his wife (nee Hickson)

staying, en route for home shortly. Geoff was in great good health and spirits – his wife in the latter but very nervous and worn out in health – I believe from the tension of Geoff's absence on the war path – so I hope it will soon wear off. We had a lot to talk about – Geoff asked after you all and was surprised to hear that Muriel had two sons and Helen a daughter. He knew of M's marriage but not of Helen's.

He tells me that his sister Madeleine has married one Palmer – his brother is about to marry and that Ozzy DuPort contemplates matrimony with a Dover young lady. But then he has plenty of money now.

Geoff has not changed an atom – he has seen a lot of the war but not much heavy fighting – plenty of marching in out of the way corners like Swaziland etc and has been well all through.

Mon 28th July We explored the town, a fair place in squares and right angle streets, more compact but not so interesting as Durban. The town hall is particularly fine, the shops not so high class as Durban, though Pietermaritzburg is the capital. Lots of trees and water and a fine public park.

In the afternoon the Howells and I went down to the latter and walked about and I saw a cricket match on the town ground – I think some actors versus military but not very high class! We drove round in 'rickshas' – the universal conveyance – a light two wheeled chair drawn by a Zulu – usually a very fine man. The Zulus are big fine cheery light hearted men and more 'taking' than the Basutos which I have always had with me.

Col. Carleton had a brother in the military camp, in the King's Own Royal Lancasters – with whom he spent most of his time. In the evening Geoff and I had a great billiard match of 300 up – of course I had not touched a cue for ages – I won the first 100 to his 35! But he won the 300 to my 271 at the end!! A great match – he used to be much better than me at Woolwich I remember.

Tues 29th July I went up to the barracks, "Fort Napier," with the Col. and lunched with the King's Own and met his brother – Major C. We saw Sir H. Mac Callum the Governor addressing the 'Scottish Horse' – homeward bound for disbandment. It rained hard most of the day which kept us more or less under cover.

On Wed 30th July we left early for here – coming by a day train specially to see the country. We passed all the most thrilling country of the war, Estcourt – Chievely – Colenso, and Pieters – every inch dyed with British blood – and saw all the boer positions and the famous Tugela river etc. Tomorrow (2nd) we go down by rail to ride over the more vital portions, the Col. knows it all as he has been over it before.

Well, we railed past the great Umbulwhana Mountain into the once beleaguered Ladysmith – so full of historic interest that I should have to quote all the books on the subject to commence any military description.

That evening we just had time to go round some of the nearer defences – most of them still standing more or less – and the Col. pointed out all the main boer and British positions in great detail so that I had a complete grasp of the situation.

The shell damage to some of the buildings – though repaired is easily traceable – the poor old town hall suffered from five 90lb Long Tom shells! The boers fired over 18,000 shells into the place – town and defences – and every 53rd shell averaged a human casualty of some sort – 336 in all from shell fire. The British reply totalled only 6,000 shells and 213,400 rifle shots. The garrison had 5,678,716 rounds at the beginning – so were in no danger of running out of small arm ammunition! They also had some 8,000 shell of various guns left in hand at the end – though some of the guns had nearly run out – viz: the 4.7" heavy naval guns (2) started with 556 rounds and fired no less than 514 during the siege! And the old 6" howitzers, antique old muzzle loaders – fired 776 rounds out of 887 shells on hand at start. The total deaths to the garrison – killed – died of wounds and disease were some 1180. To which the R.E. contributed, 2 officers and 9 men killed and 17 men died of disease and privation = 28 – also 9 wounded and recovered.

To resume the touring. Yesterday 31st we drove out 18 miles to Spion Kop – the famous scene of Bullers 2nd attempt to relieve the town. We got there about 11 a.m. and explored till 2.30 p.m. – all over the hill – taking photos of the monuments etc and examining the country round all of which though not known by name so much, formed part of the battlefield.

We actually had the luck to pick up a few cartridge cases etc on Spion Kop – after hundreds of people – and natives paid for the search – had been over the hills for the last two years!

It is a fine bit of the world – this stretch of hills and river – and it is very clear that could we have held on to the hill the boers must have fallen away all round as it dominates everything. The predominant feeling left on one after seeing it is what plucky men the boers must have been who stuck to it so well – without being soldiers by training or even choice for the most part. It is true that had we lasted the night after they would have run – as they say themselves but the cost was very heavy and I must say I think the right course was taken when we withdrew, and the wrong course was taken in not attacking more points of the boer defence <u>simultaneously</u>.

We got back to Ladysmith about 6 p.m. very tired. Today in the morning we drove out to Wagon Hill and Caesars Camp – and saw the famous battlefield of Jan. 6th and the spot where Digby Jones fell, and Deuniss after him, also all the graves and monuments which now freely mark the course of the fight – it was a terrible day I believe and a magnificent victory in repelling the boers at the end – remembering that our men were but wasted shadows then and too weak to do more than crawl about.

I cannot describe all I have seen at fuller length now – I have taken a good few photos and hope to be able to tell you more about these places when I get back to you presently!

This afternoon we drove out N.E. to Nicholson's Nek – so called – it is really a big hill over a farm owned by a Mr. Hyde, and 3 miles from the Nek.

That was a terrible affair – leaving 900 men to be surrounded and shot down by some 7 or 8000 boers – but then Sir George White – whose <u>plans</u> <u>would</u> have brought his forces round to them that day, got such a terrible thrashing with his main body that it was all he could do to withdraw safely to Ladysmith – vaguely hoping the odd 900 might escape.

After seeing the ground I think that Carleton's disposition and plans were the only practicable solution – he had his men well disposed to keep the boers off till dark when he might easily have slipped off the hill and withdrawn the 7 miles to Ladysmith – but as you probably know his hand was forced by some irresponsible officer of the Gloucesters putting up the white flag of surrender on his own account and thus involving the whole party in a premature and uncalled for surrender – a bitter day for the troops thus betrayed into captivity.

Well, its getting late so I must close for tonight – I may be able to add some Colenso and Pieters account tomorrow. Sunday we make for Dundee and

Talana if possible – trains awkward – then fly on to Bloemfontein where I am due Tuesday midnight!

We cannot do more detailed visit to Majuba now – but I have seen enough to remember it by!

<u>Sat: even: 2nd Aug</u> just back from Colenso battlefield and Pieters Hill etc – very pressed to catch English mail so cannot go into details this letter.

I do not think Sunday trains will get us to Talana Hill so we shall probably have a quiet day here and off back to Bloemfontein by the through mail train at <u>2.30 a.m.</u> on Monday – arrive Bloemfontein Tuesday midday.

Best love to all at home – I may hear news of movement at Bloemfontein.

Ever your loving son Eric

Springfontein   Sunday 10th August 1902

My dearest Father

Since my last letter to you from Ladysmith I have gradually found my way back here.

We left Ladysmith at <u>2.45 a.m.</u> on Monday – reaching Elandsfontein Junction at 5 p.m. Tuesday. We then went on by a local train into Johannesburg – partly because Col. Carleton had never set foot therein – and partly to ensure two good berths in the Cape Mail which is made up there and passes through Elandsfontein on its way South.

We just had time for a comfortable dinner at Heath's Hotel – which you may remember was were I was 'lunched' on the day we entered the town as invaders June 1st 1900.

We then walked through a few of the main streets to the Station and found the whole train of corridor carriages empty to choose from! so we got very comfortably settled down and left for South at 9.30 p.m, picking up our baggage and the Colonel's soldier servant at Elandsfontein again.

We reached Bloemfontein 3 p.m. Tuesday, after being delayed over two hours by a smash to another train which involved the removal of overturned trucks from the line, and the death of six oxen in a cattle truck.

The Col. went straight on to Springfontein – I up to the 7th Coy to report my return and see if there was any news of our departure or otherwise.

I found Haggitt and Johnson with the Co. – no further news – spent the Wednesday with them seeing the progress of the new barracks etc we are building there – and all the English papers in the Club – and returned here on Thursday.

The last two days have been pretty fully occupied with 'Coronation'. I found little had been done prior to my return – on which they had cheerfully reckoned – with the result that I had to get about 200 people to work on as many different jobs all Friday!

However all went off beautifully – a magnificently calm still day (though preceded by violent dust storms all Friday and followed by ditto today!)

We got through a service – some athletic events, (plus heats etc) and fireworks and bonfire and band playing in the evening. I think everyone enjoyed themselves – and I got many kind words of thanks for my humble assistances in various departments – and am very tired today! The tug-of-war in the Sports was the finest athletic contest I have ever witnessed in my life. The final tie resolved itself into a pull between the Royal Irish Fusiliers and the picked team of the local Boers. You may imagine the feeling was strong.

The burghers smallest man stood about 6ft 2in and over 13 stone – and the team ran up to about 6ft 7in and 16 or 17 stone – no unusual team for them, as they are a race of giants physically though not intellectually or in 'spirit'!

The Fusiliers team was a very average British working man team of about an average of 12 stone 7.

The conditions were "all over the centre line" which made it a great test of endurance. The first pull the Boers just pulled the Fusiliers straight over the mark in about two minutes steady drag – sheer weight and freshness. The second pull the Boers pulled them all over except the last two men and everyone thought it was all up. However the Fusiliers steadied up and anchored on for a minute and then solidly worked back, and in two more minutes had the whole burgher team over the mark! – one all.

The final pull both teams showed signs of distress and lay on the rope inert for a few moments – then the Fusiliers got to work and just marched away with the giants straight off the ground in one good pull. It was a grand sight.

Many of them had to be shaken up and rubbed down and given spirits to get them on their legs again!

One of the Boers was heard to say – My God – these English – I understand why they beat us now – they never know when to give in!! Which was very apposite – as in the third pull the Boers <u>hearts</u> gave way just like a pack of cards.

Anyone looking at the two teams on the rope would have laughed and walked away to see something less ridiculous.

I found two letters from you awaiting my return – and have since received a third – including the cheque for £50 which I am duly receipting and returning to Cox & Co.

I was very glad to see Cambridge and Harrow each pull off their match so well. I am sure it must have been a great source of pleasure to you.

I am glad to hear that Teddie Garnier is getting on well towards recovery – I hope by now he is on the road to convalescence.

I must break off to take the men to church now and will continue later and enclose programme.

You seem to have been doing long distances by road lately – I expect Mother enjoyed seeing all the Country you passed through, and which is practically only accessible by road.

I received a Rickinghall magazine this week containing a farewell notice by Uncle George – I hope he is keeping well – and has not suffered from inevitable strain in connection with Coronation business.

I am very glad to hear that you also figured as a hundred pounder in Uncle Benjamin's legacies.

The army officer will revert to a very poorly remunerated public servant again presently – the move from South Africa to England means a loss of 5/6d per diem; i.e. 3/- Colonial Allowance and 2/6 "Field Allowance" – which means a lot to those without other means to fall back on.

I make out that Messrs Cox have saved £250 approximately for me since I have been out here, but when a complete new outfit of uniform and a practical renovation of almost every item of "civilian" costume and requirement with the possibility of requirements like guns, bicycles or horses thrown in – there will not be much left to play with!

Had I been anxious to remain in this country I think I should have had no difficulty in getting employment either in the Public Works or Constabulary at about £7–800 per annum – (means about £350 at home) – but I think the normal routine and occupations of the Corps suit me best, and as long as I can keep afloat without difficulty I am quite happy without the extra money.

I was altogether charmed with my trip to Natal and should have been very sorry not to have been there – and in spite of heavy pony and trap hire and S.A. Hotel prices the whole thing only ran a little over £20 – (which came from sale of my horse just before) – so I got good value one way and another.

I am sending photos to M. and H. this week so you need not forward your copy for inspection.

Much love to all with you Ever your loving son Eric

I see that Uncle Ben's executors style me "de Boketon"! which shows good heraldic research!

Springfontein   Sunday 17th August 1902

My dearest Father

I received yours of 25th July this week: you had just heard that the 7th Co were under orders for home.

Do not stop writing, as at most only two letters would arrive after our departure, as I can warn you by cable from any coast port – we have no definite information as to probable date as yet. As far as I can make out they appear to be just coming to the end of shipping the Reserves – but this is not much to go on as we do not know how many that leaves between them and the first lot of regulars.

We now have a sort of hope that we may make a start ere September is out – but this is only conjecture.

I posted the B.B.G. cheque to Cox last week duly signed – so it should have reached them by now.

I am very interested to hear the progress of the purchase of the Reeves' house – and your proposal for its tenure – I fear it would be some years before I could afford to build a new house there, unless they do something to raise the officer's pay, or accelerate promotion in the R.E. – which is very stagnant in spite of war losses and retirements.

You mention Billy French as being at Bloemfontein in which case I have seen him some three or four times – in each case I stared at him but could not put a name to him – I think he showed a glimmer of recognition too – but we only passed in the street and never came to conversation!

We are having a truly dusty time here – this is the interregnum between cold weather and the rains due next month – all the grass burnt or eaten off the veldt and the most terrifying and persistent sandstorms all day long – covering everything and making locomotion almost unendurable.

I am having a very easy time – very few men and less work – I went down to Norvals Pont on Tuesday – to visit my detachment at the pontoon bridge – which we are about to remove, or sell in situ, after over two years of very expensive usefulness in spanning the Orange River.

I met Freddy Barclay in the best of spirits and hoping to get home shortly.

We had a great dinner party at the Hospital – followed by dancing and music. On the Wednesday I was taken down the River to a picnic to a very beautiful part – and in the evening, 3 of us temporarily staying at the Hospital and who had been their free guests at all hours for the past year entertained the whole Hospital Staff – Doctors (12) and nurses (8) to dinner at the Railway Rooms – and had a great evening. It fell to my lot to propose the toast of the 'Ladies' rather a trying ordeal.

I returned here on Thursday and on Friday attended another dance given by local people, lasting till 3.15 a.m. Sat. so you see we manage to keep ourselves alive although our community is limited in extent and far from civilization.

Best love to all from your ever loving son Eric

Springfontein Orange River Colony   Sunday 24th August 1902

My dearest Father

Your last two letters were dated August 1st – one a postscript of birthday good wishes.

We think they must have nearly come to the end of the Reserves etc now – though I have not heard of any move of regulars yet.

I was not far off coming home this last week – they sent down from Pretoria to tell the 7th Co to provide a Lieut. to take a draft of R.E. men home. The message only gave Haggitt a few hours notice. He wired out to McClintock at Ladybrand, on the Basuto border, as the senior subaltern to give him the first refusal – McC. apparently thought it would be too much of a rush to get in 80 miles in time and said 'no'. This took such a slice of the available time before the draft left Bloemfontein that Haggitt had not time to send to me and get a reply – so perforce sent Johnson – the only other subaltern – who was at Bloemfontein.

I saw them going through – many of our oldest men – all thoroughly seasoned hands – they no doubt were glad to be away – though many will have hard work in civil life to keep themselves going.

I was sorry to think of the loss to the 7th Co – but as we shall practically cease to exist by the time we get home – it will not matter if we have to train 50 or 150 new men – only there is a certain feeling of regret that so many magnificent men – trained to anything and in the prime of life, should be lost to the service, and scattered into the workshops of our big towns etc, and be replaced by the young and untrustworthy.

I had a very nice little expedition after 'buck' last week – our party consisted of Guthrie A.S.C. – 3 Boers named Rensburg, a colonial named Jellicoe and myself.

We drove out to a farm about 17 miles West of here, owned and occupied by Stephanus Rensburg (the middle in age of the 3) – wife and four children – there we spent two nights, and during the day scoured the country round after the 'springbok' which abounded in great numbers. We had great sport though the game was so wild that one could not get a shot nearer than 200 yards.

We shot and recovered 9 altogether – and I had to leave two more that we could not run down, I fear badly wounded – one shot through the shoulder rump and loins, the other through the near shoulder low down by the elbow. Our actual bag was made up by: Old Rensburg 3 – Guthrie 2 – S. Rensburg 2, Young Rensburg 1 and Self 1, = 9, Jellicoe did not secure one.

The buck season closes August 31 – so I was lucky to come in for such a good day. I suppose we covered some 60 – 70 miles in the search and pursuit during the day. The country lies about 10 miles North of Phillipolis on the map.

I am glad you have completed the purchase of the Reeves home.

I shall have to sell more G. K. & Co to pay the two £50 – next two years – as I shall be very hard up for cash after I have provided a complete new outfit etc etc.

I sent Uncle Walter a cheque for £50 in return for a loan in '98 – last mail.

Much love to all from your ever loving son Eric

Springfontein   **Sunday 31st August 1902**

My dearest Father

I got your note of the 8th inst: yesterday – also a very nice letter from Mr Stokes. I am so glad to think that he is recovering alright.

We have had quite a gay week here one way and another.

On Tuesday 26th I gave a small dance in honour of my birthday – and I think everyone enjoyed themselves – they say so anyhow. I think we had about 25 couples – the dance was in the Refugee Camp School – a fine new iron building with a good board floor – in splendid order from various dances already held there.

On Wednesday the hospital had a good Variety entertainment – and Concert.

On Thursday we had a dinner party given by the rest of the garrison to the Royal Irish Fusiliers Officers, who have done a lot for our recreation since they came.

On Friday I dined with the Fusiliers at their Camp – so I may say that entertainment has been the order of the day.

I believe there is to be a Fancy Dress dance next Friday – but that I expect I shall miss, as I believe the 7th Co starts for home (from Bloemfontein) that day – 5th September.

I got a wire this morning to rejoin with my detachment as soon as a party of the 38th Co R.E. arrived to relieve me and take over – so perhaps Wednesday will see us back with the Company and Friday off to Cape Town.

From Cape Town I will cable you the name of the ship, if possible, and date of sailing if we are not rushed on board in a hurry and far from the Cable office.

I shall be the junior of the four officers returning with the 7th Co. – Major Haggitt, Captain MacDonald, Lieut McClintock D.S.O. and myself – so it may be some time after arrival before I can get away on "Leave" – as it will be seniors first – and someone must stay with the Company!

All the troop moves seem to have been brought forward a good deal – as early this week we were officially notified to be ready for home about the middle of October – two days afterwards we were notified to be ready any time after second week of September – now, unless it is changed we appear to be starting on the 5th.

This letter ought to reach you just nicely by a mail ahead of us – if we really do get off – it seems too good to be likely! There are only the Col. and myself in the Head Quarter Mess here now, Stack the Staff officer being unfortunately laid up with bronchitis.

I have been doing his work lately in addition to my own – viz: Staff Officer to Officer Commanding Southern Section Lines of Communication O.R.C., a good mouthful!

If I get any more definite wires for Bloemfontein before mail bag closes I will add a P.S.

Much love to all at home from your ever loving son Eric

POST OFFICE TELEGRAPHS

Handed in at Cape Town 9/9 3.30 p.m. at 4.55 p received here at 1.45 p.m. Botesdale SP 10 02

To   Wilson   Botesdale

Canada sailing 9th   Eric

The Corps of Royal Engineers to their comrades who lost their lives in the South African War 1899-1902.
(South Side)

R.E. South Africa Memorial.—(West Side)